Nathaniel Holmes Bishop

Four Months in a Sneak-Box

A Boat Voyage of 2600 Miles Down the Ohio and Mississippi Rivers

Nathaniel Holmes Bishop

Four Months in a Sneak-Box

A Boat Voyage of 2600 Miles Down the Ohio and Mississippi Rivers

ISBN/EAN: 9783337413231

Printed in Europe, USA, Canada, Australia, Japan

Cover: Foto ©Andreas Hilbeck / pixelio.de

More available books at **www.hansebooks.com**

Four Months in a Sneak-Box.

A BOAT VOYAGE OF 2600 MILES DOWN THE OHIO
AND MISSISSIPPI RIVERS, AND ALONG
THE GULF OF MEXICO.

BY

NATHANIEL H. BISHOP,

AUTHOR OF "A THOUSAND MILES' WALK ACROSS SOUTH AMERICA,"
AND "VOYAGE OF THE PAPER CANOE."

BOSTON:
LEE AND SHEPARD, PUBLISHERS.
NEW YORK: CHARLES T. DILLINGHAM.
1879.

TO THE

OFFICERS AND EMPLOYEES

OF THE

LIGHT HOUSE ESTABLISHMENT OF THE UNITED STATES

This Book is Dedicated

BY ONE WHO HAS LEARNED TO RESPECT THEIR
HONEST, INTELLIGENT AND EFFICIENT LABORS
IN SERVING THEIR GOVERNMENT, THEIR
COUNTRYMEN, AND MANKIND
GENERALLY.

INTRODUCTION.

EIGHTEEN months ago the author gave to the public his "VOYAGE OF THE PAPER CANOE : — A GEOGRAPHICAL JOURNEY OF 2500 MILES FROM QUEBEC TO THE GULF OF MEXICO, DURING THE YEARS 1874-5."

The kind reception by the American press of the author's first journey to the great southern sea, and its republication in Great Britain and in France within so short a time of its appearance in the United States, have encouraged him to give the public a companion volume, — "FOUR MONTHS IN A SNEAK-BOX," — which is a relation of the experiences of a second cruise to the Gulf of Mexico, but by a different route from that followed in the "VOYAGE OF THE PAPER CANOE." This time the author procured one of the smallest and most comfortable of boats — a purely American model, developed by the bay-men of the New Jersey coast of the United States, and recently introduced to the gunning fraternity as the BARNEGAT SNEAK-BOX. This curious and stanch little craft, though only twelve feet in length, proved a most comfortable and serviceable home while the author rowed in it more than 2600 miles down the Ohio and Mississippi rivers, and along the coast of the Gulf of Mexico, until he reached the goal of his voyage — the mouth of the wild Suwanee River — which was the terminus of his "VOYAGE OF THE PAPER CANOE."

The maps which illustrate the contours of the coast of the Gulf of Mexico, like those in the other volume, are the most reliable ever given to the public, having been drawn and engraved, by contract for the work, by the United States Coast and Geodetic Survey Bureau.

LAKE GEORGE, WARREN CO.,
NEW YORK STATE,
SEPTEMBER 1st, 1879.

CONTENTS.

CHAPTER I.
THE BOAT FOR THE VOYAGE.

CANOES FOR SHALLOW STREAMS AND FREQUENT PORTAGES. — SNEAK-BOXES FOR DEEP WATERCOURSES. — HISTORY AND DESCRIPTION OF THE BARNEGAT SNEAK-BOX. — A WALK DOWN EEL STREET TO MANAHAWKEN MARSHES. — HONEST GEORGE THE BOAT-BUILDER. — THE BUILDING OF THE SNEAK-BOX "CENTENNIAL REPUBLIC." — ITS TRANSPORTATION TO THE OHIO RIVER 1

CHAPTER II.
SOURCES OF THE OHIO RIVER.

DESCRIPTION OF THE MONONGAHELA AND ALLEGHANY RIVERS. — THE OHIO RIVER. — EXPLORATIONS OF CAVELIER DE LA SALLE. — NAMES GIVEN BY ANCIENT CARTOGRAPHERS TO THE OHIO. — ROUTES OF THE ABORIGINES FROM THE GREAT LAKES TO THE OHIO RIVER 19

CHAPTER III.
FROM PITTSBURGH TO BLENNERHASSET'S ISLAND.

THE START FOR THE GULF. — CAUGHT IN THE ICE RAFT. — CAMPING ON THE OHIO. — THE GRAVE CREEK MOUND. — AN INDIAN SEPULCHRE. — BLENNERHASSET'S ISLAND. — AARON BURR'S CONSPIRACY. — A RUINED FAMILY 29

CHAPTER IV.

FROM BLENNERHASSET'S ISLAND TO CINCINNATI.

RIVER CAMPS. — THE SHANTY-BOATS AND RIVER MIGRANTS. — VARIOUS EXPERIENCES. — ARRIVAL AT CINCINNATI. — THE SNEAK-BOX FROZEN UP IN PLEASANT RUN. — A TAILOR'S FAMILY. — A NIGHT UNDER A GERMAN COVERLET 55

CHAPTER V.

FROM CINCINNATI TO THE MISSISSIPPI RIVER.

CINCINNATI. — MUSIC AND PORK IN PORKOPOLIS. — THE BIG BONE LICK OF FOSSIL ELEPHANTS. — COLONEL CROGHAN'S VISIT TO THE LICK. — PORTAGE AROUND THE "FALLS" AT LOUISVILLE, KENTUCKY. — STUCK IN THE MUD. — THE FIRST STEAMBOAT OF THE WEST. — VICTOR HUGO ON THE SITUATION. — A FREEBOOTER'S DEN. — WHOOPING AND SAND-HILL CRANES. — THE SNEAK-BOX ENTERS THE MISSISSIPPI . . . 79

CHAPTER VI.

DESCENT OF THE MISSISSIPPI RIVER.

LEAVE CAIRO, ILLINOIS. — THE LONGEST RIVER IN THE WORLD. — BOOK GEOGRAPHY AND BOAT GEOGRAPHY. — CHICKASAW BLUFF. — MEETING WITH THE PARAKEETS. — FORT DONALDSON. — EARTHQUAKES AND LAKES. — WEIRD BEAUTY OF REELFOOT LAKE. — JOE ECKEL'S BAR. — SHANTY-BOAT COOKING. — FORT PILLOW. — MEMPHIS. — A NEGRO JUSTICE. — "DE COMMON LAW OB MISSISSIPPI" 115

CHAPTER VII.

DESCENT OF THE MISSISSIPPI TO NEW ORLEANS.

A FLATBOAT BOUND FOR TEXAS. — A FLAT-MAN ON RIVER PHYSICS. — ADRIFT AND ASLEEP. — SEEING THE EARTH'S LITTLE MOON. — VICKSBURGH. — JEFFERSON DAVIS'S COT-

CONTENTS. ix

TON PLANTATION, AND ITS NEGRO OWNER. — DYING IN HIS
BOAT. — HOW TO CIVILIZE CHINESE. — A SWIM OF ONE HUN-
DRED AND TWENTY MILES ON THE MISSISSIPPI. — TWENTY-
FOUR HOURS IN THE WATER. — ARRIVAL IN THE CRESCENT
CITY 150

CHAPTER VIII.

NEW ORLEANS.

BIENVILLE AND THE CITY OF THE PAST. — FRENCH AND SPAN-
ISH RULE IN THE NEW WORLD. — LOUISIANA CEDED TO THE
UNITED STATES. — CAPTAIN EADS AND HIS JETTIES. —
TRANSPORTATIONS OF CEREALS TO EUROPE. — CHARLES
MORGAN. — CREOLE TYPES OF CITIZENS. — LEVEES AND
CRAWFISH. — DRAINAGE OF THE CITY INTO LAKE PONT-
CHARTRAIN 195

CHAPTER IX.

ON THE GULF OF MEXICO.

LEAVE NEW ORLEANS. — THE ROUGHS AT WORK. — DE-
TAINED AT NEW BASIN. — SADDLES INTRODUCES HIMSELF. —
CAMPING ON LAKE PONTCHARTRAIN. — THE LIGHT-HOUSE
OF POINT AUX HERBES. — THE RIGOLETS. — MARSHES AND
MOSQUITOES. — IMPORTANT USE OF THE MOSQUITO AND
BLOW-FLY. — ST. JOSEPH'S LIGHT. — AN EXCITING PULL
TO BAY ST. LOUIS. — A LIGHT-KEEPER LOST IN THE SEA. —
BATTLE OF THE SHARKS. — BILOXI. — THE WATER-CRESS
GARDEN. — LITTLE JENNIE 209

CHAPTER X.

FROM BILOXI TO CAPE SAN BLAS.

POINTS ON THE GULF COAST. — MOBILE BAY. — THE HERMIT
OF DAUPHINE ISLAND. — BON SECOURS BAY. — A CRACKER'S
DAUGHTERS. — THE PORTAGE TO THE PERDIDO. — THE PORT-
AGE FROM THE PERDIDO TO BIG LAGOON. — PENSACOLA

BAY. — SANTA ROSA SOUND. — A NEW LONDON FISHER-
MAN. — CATCHING THE POMPANO. — A NEGRO PREACHER
AND WHITE SINNERS. — A DAY AND A NIGHT WITH A MUR-
DERER. — ST. ANDREW'S SOUND. — ARRIVAL AT CAPE SAN
BLAS 240

CHAPTER XI.

FROM CAPE SAN BLAS TO ST. MARKS.

A PORTAGE ACROSS CAPE SAN BLAS. — THE COW-HUNTERS. —
A VISIT TO THE LIGHT-HOUSE. — ONCE MORE ON THE SEA. —
PORTAGE INTO ST. VINCENT SOUND. — APALACHICOLA. —
ST. GEORGE'S SOUND AND OCKLOCKONY RIVER. — ARRIVAL
AT ST. MARKS. — THE NEGRO POSTMASTER. — A PHILAN-
THROPIST AND HIS NEIGHBORS. — A CONTINUOUS AND PRO-
TECTED WATER-WAY FROM THE MISSISSIPPI RIVER TO THE
ATLANTIC COAST 273

CHAPTER XII.

FROM ST. MARKS TO THE SUWANEE RIVER.

ALONG THE COAST. — SADDLES BREAKS DOWN. — A REFUGE
WITH THE FISHERMEN. — CAMP IN THE PALM FOREST. —
PARTING WITH SADDLES. — OUR NEIGHBOR THE ALLIGA-
TOR. — DISCOVERY OF THE TRUE CROCODILE IN FLORIDA. —
THE DEVIL'S WOOD-PILE. — DEADMAN'S BAY. — BOWLEGS
POINT. — THE COAST SURVEY CAMP. — A DAY ABOARD THE
"READY." — THE SUWANEE RIVER. — THE END 288

ILLUSTRATIONS.

DRAWN BY F. T. MERRILL.   ENGRAVED BY JOHN ANDREW & SON.

	PAGE
SHANTY-BOATS. — THE CHAMPION FLOATERS OF THE WEST, ... *Frontispiece.*	
DIAGRAM OF PARTS OF BOAT, ...	14
INDIAN IN CANOE, ...	28
THE START. — HEAD OF THE OHIO RIVER, ...	31
INDIAN MOUND AT MOUNDSVILLE, WEST VIRGINIA, . . .	54
A NIGHT UNDER A GERMAN COVERLET, ...	78
POPULAR IDEA OF THE NESTING OF CRANES, ...	111
STERN-WHEEL WESTERN TOW-BOAT PUSHING FLATBOATS,	114
MEETING WITH THE PARAKEETS, ...	125
DYING IN HIS BOAT, ...	177
BOYTON DESCENDING THE MISSISSIPPI, ...	187
NEW ORLEANS ROUGHS AMUSING THEMSELVES, ...	214
ARRIVAL AT THE GULF OF MEXICO. — CAMP MOSQUITO,	239
THE PORTAGE ACROSS CROOKED ISLAND, ...	269
SADDLES BREAKS DOWN, ...	292
PARTING WITH SADDLES, ...	302
LAST NIGHT ON THE GULF OF MEXICO, ...	322

LIST OF MAPS

DRAWN AND ENGRAVED AT THE

UNITED STATES COAST AND GEODETIC SURVEY BUREAU,

TO ILLUSTRATE N. H. BISHOP'S BOAT VOYAGES.

PAGE

1. GENERAL MAP OF ROUTES FOLLOWED BY THE AUTHOR DURING TWO VOYAGES MADE TO THE GULF OF MEXICO, IN THE YEARS 1874-6. . . . Opposite 1

GUIDE MAPS OF ROUTE FOLLOWED

IN DUCK-BOAT "CENTENNIAL REPUBLIC," ALONG THE GULF OF MEXICO, IN 1876.

2. FROM NEW ORLEANS, LOUISIANA, TO MOBILE BAY, ALABAMA, ... Opposite 209
3. FROM MOBILE BAY, ALABAMA, TO CAPE SAN BLAS, FLORIDA, ... Opposite 247
4. FROM CAPE SAN BLAS, FLORIDA, TO CEDAR KEYS, FLORIDA, ... Opposite 273

MAP SHOWING RIVER AND PORTAGE ROUTES

ACROSS FLORIDA FROM THE GULF OF MEXICO TO THE ATLANTIC OCEAN.

5. ROUTE FOLLOWED BY THE AUTHOR IN PAPER CANOE "MARIA THERESA," IN 1875, ... Opposite 319

FOUR MONTHS IN A SNEAK-BOX.

CHAPTER I.

THE BOAT FOR THE VOYAGE.

CANOES FOR SHALLOW STREAMS AND FREQUENT PORTAGES. — SNEAK-BOXES FOR DEEP WATERCOURSES. — HISTORY AND DESCRIPTION OF THE BARNEGAT SNEAK-BOX. — A WALK DOWN EEL STREET TO MANAHAWKEN MARSHES. — HONEST GEORGE, THE BOAT-BUILDER. — THE BUILDING OF THE SNEAK-BOX "CENTENNIAL REPUBLIC." — ITS TRANSPORTATION TO THE OHIO RIVER.

THE reader who patiently followed the author in his long "VOYAGE OF THE PAPER CANOE," from the high latitude of the Gulf of St. Lawrence to the warmer regions of the Gulf of Mexico, may desire to know the reasons which impelled the canoeist to exchange his light, graceful, and swift paper craft for the comical-looking but more commodious and comfortable Barnegat sneak-box, or duck-boat.

Having navigated more than eight thousand miles in sail-boats, row-boats, and canoes, upon the fresh and salt watercourses of the North American continent (usually without a companion), a hard-earned experience has taught me that while the light, frail canoe is indispensable for exploring shallow streams, for shooting rapids, and for making long portages from one watercourse to another, the deeper and more continuous water-ways may be more comfortably traversed in a stronger and heavier boat, which offers many of the advantages of a portable home.

To find such a boat—one that possessed many desirable points in a small hull — had been with me a study of years. I commenced to search for it in my boyhood — twenty-five years ago ; and though I have carefully examined numerous small boats while travelling in seven foreign countries, and have studied the models of miniature craft in museums, and at exhibitions of marine architecture, I failed to discover the object of my desire, until, on the sea-shore of New Jersey, I saw for the first time what is known among gunners as the Barnegat sneak-box.

Having owned, and thoroughly tested in the waters of Barnegat and Little Egg Harbor bays, five of these boats, I became convinced that their claims for the good-will of the boating fraternity had not been over-estimated; so when I planned my second voyage from northern America to the Gulf of Mexico, and selected the great water-courses of the west and south (the Ohio and Mississippi rivers) as the route to be explored and studied, I chose the Barnegat sneak-box as the most comfortable model combined with other advantages for a voyager's use. The sneak-box offered ample stowage capacity, while canoes built to hold one person were not large enough to carry the amount of baggage necessary for the voyage; for I was to avoid hotels and towns, to live in my boat day and night, to carry an ample stock of provisions, and to travel in as comfortable a manner as possible. In fact, I adopted a very home-like boat, which, though only twelve feet long, four feet wide, and thirteen inches deep, was strong, stiff, dry, and safe; a craft that could be sailed or rowed, as wind, weather, or inclination might dictate, — the weight of which hardly exceeded two hundred pounds, — and could be conveniently transported from one stream to another in an ordinary wagon.

A Nautilus, or any improved type of canoe, would have been lighter and more easily transported, and could have been paddled at a higher speed with the same effort expended in rowing the heavier sneak-box; but the canoe did not offer the peculiar advantages of comfort and freedom of bodily motion possessed by its unique fellow-craft. Experienced canoeists agree that a canoe of fourteen feet in length, which weighs only seventy pounds, if built of wood, bark, canvas, or paper, when out of the water and resting upon the ground, or even when bedded on some soft material, like grass or rushes, cannot support the sleeping weight of the canoeist for many successive nights without becoming strained.

Light indeed must be the weight and slender and elastic the form of the man who can sleep many nights comfortably in a seventy-pound canoe without injuring it. Cedar canoes, after being subjected to such use for some time, generally become leaky; so, to avoid this disaster, the canoeist, when threatened with wet weather, is forced to the disagreeable task of troubling some private householder for a shelter, or run the risk of injuring his boat by packing himself away in its narrow, coffin-like quarters and dreaming that he is a sardine, while his restless weight is every moment straining his delicate canoe, and visions of future leaks arise to disturb his tranquillity.

The one great advantage possessed by a canoe is its lightness. Canoeists dwell upon the importance of the LIGHT WEIGHT of their canoes, and the ease with which they can be carried. If the canoeist is to sleep in his delicate craft while making a long journey, she must be made much heavier than the perfected models now in use in this country, many of which are under seventy-five pounds' weight. This additional weight is at once fatal to speed, and becomes burdensome when the canoeist is forced to carry his canoe upon his own shoulders over a portage. A sneak-box built to carry one person weighs about three times as much as a well-built cedar canoe.

This remarkable little boat has a history which does not reach very far back into the present century. With the assistance of Mr. William Errickson of Barnegat, and Dr. William P. Haywood of West Creek, Ocean County, New Jersey, I have been able to rescue from oblivion and bring to the light of day a correct history of the Barnegat sneak-box.

Captain Hazelton Seaman, of West Creek village, New Jersey, a boat-builder and an expert shooter of wild-fowl, about the year 1836, conceived the idea of constructing for his own use a low-decked boat, or gunning-punt, in which, when its deck was covered with sedge, he could secrete himself from the wild-fowl while gunning in Barnegat and Little Egg Harbor bays.

It was important that the boat should be sufficiently light to enable a single sportsman to pull her from the water on to the low points of the bay shores. During the winter months, when the great marshes were at times incrusted with snow, and the shallow creeks covered with ice,— obstacles which must be crossed to reach the open waters of the sound, — it would be necessary to use her as a sled, to effect which end a pair of light oaken strips were screwed to the bottom of the sneak-box, when she could be easily pushed by the gunner, and the transportation of the oars, sail, blankets, guns, ammunition, and provisions (all of which stowed under the hatch and locked up as snugly as if in a strong chest) became a very simple matter. While secreted in his boat, on the watch for fowl, with his craft hidden by a covering of grass or sedge, the gunner could approach within shooting-distance of a flock of unsuspicious ducks; and this being done in a sneaking manner (though Mr. Seaman named the result of his first effort the "Devil's Coffin"), the bay-men gave her the sobriquet of "SNEAK-BOX"; and this name she has retained to the present day.

Since Captain Seaman built his "Devil's Coffin," forty years ago, the model has been improved by various builders, until it is believed that it has almost attained perfection. The boat has no sheer, and sets low in the water. This lack of sheer is supplied by a light canvas apron which is tacked to the deck, and presents, when stretched upward by a stick two feet in length, a convex surface to a head sea. The water which breaks upon the deck, forward of the cockpit, is turned off at the sides of the boat in almost the same manner as a snow-plough clears a railroad track of snow. The apron also protects the head and shoulders of the rower from cold head winds.

The first sneak-box built by Captain Seaman had a piece of canvas stretched upon an oaken hoop, so fastened to the deck that when a head sea struck the bow, the hoop and canvas were forced upward so as to throw the water off its sides, thus effectually preventing its ingress into the hold of the craft. The improved apron originated with Mr. John Crammer, Jr., a short time after Captain Seaman built the first sneak-box. The second sneak-box was constructed by Mr. Crammer; and afterwards Mr. Samuel Perine, an old and much respected bay-man, of Barnegat, built the third one. The last two men have finished their voyage of life, but "Uncle Haze,"— as he is familiarly called by his many admirers,— the originator of the tiny craft which may well be called *multum in parvo*, and which carried me, its single occupant, safely and comfortably twenty-six hundred miles, from Pittsburgh to Cedar Keys, still lives at West Creek, builds yachts as well as he does sneak-boxes, and puts to the blush younger gunners by the energy displayed and success attained in the vigorous pursuit of wild-fowl shooting in the bays which fringe the coast of Ocean County, New Jersey.

A few years since, this ingenious man invented an improvement on the marine life-saving car, which has been adopted by the United States government; and during the year 1875 he constructed a new ducking-punt with a low paddle-wheel at its stern, for the purpose of more easily and secretly approaching flocks of wild-fowl.

The peculiar advantages of the sneak-box were known to but few of the hunting and shooting fraternity, and, with the exception of an occasional visitor, were used only by the oystermen, fishermen, and wild-fowl shooters of Barnegat and Little Egg Harbor bays, until the New Jersey Southern Railroad and its connecting branches penetrated to the eastern shores of New Jersey, when educated amateur sportsmen from the cities quickly recognized in the little gunning-punt all they had long desired to combine in one small boat.

Mr. Charles Hallock, in his paper the "Forest and Stream," of April 23, 1874, gave drawings and a description of the sneak-box, and fairly presented its claims to public favor.

The sneak-box is not a monopoly of any particular builder, but it requires peculiar talent to build one,—the kind of talent which enables one man to cut out a perfect axe-handle, while the master-carpenter finds it difficult to accomplish the same thing. The best yacht-builders in Ocean County generally fail in modelling a sneak-box, while many second-rate mechanics along the shore, who could not possibly construct a yacht that would sail well, can make a perfect sneak-box, or gunning-skiff. All this may be accounted for by recognizing the fact that the water-lines of the sneak-box are peculiar, and differ materially from those of row-boats, sail-boats, and yachts. Having a spoon-shaped bottom and bow, the sneak-box moves rather over the water than through it, and this peculiarity, together with its broad beam, gives the boat such stiffness that two persons may stand upright in her while she is moving through the water, and troll their lines while fishing, or discharge their guns, without careening the boat; a valuable advantage not possessed by our best cruising canoes.

The boat sails well on the wind, though hard to pull against a strong head sea. A fin-shaped centre-board takes the place of a keel. It can be quickly removed from the trunk, or centre-board well, and stored under the deck. The flatness of her floor permits the sneak-box to run in very shallow water while being rowed or when sailing before the wind without the centre-board. Some of these boats, carrying a weight of three hundred pounds, will float in four to six inches of water.

The favorite material for boat-building in the United States is white cedar (*Cupressus thyoides*), which grows in dense forests in the swamps along the coast of New Jersey, as well as in other parts of North America. The wood is both white and brown, soft, fine-grained, and very light and durable. No wood used in boat-building can compare with the white cedar in resisting the changes from a wet to a dry state, and *vice versa*. The tree grows tall and straight. The lower part of the trunk with the diverging roots furnish knee timbers and carlines for the sneak-box. The ribs or timbers, and the carlines, are usually $1\frac{1}{4} \times 1\frac{1}{4}$ inches in dimension, and are placed about ten inches apart. The frame above and below is covered with half-inch cedar sheathing, which is not less than six inches in width. The boat is strong enough to support a heavy man upon its deck, and when well built will rank next to the seamless paper boats of Mr. Waters of Troy, and the seamless wooden canoes of Messrs. Herald, Gordon & Stephenson, of the province of Ontario, Canada, in freedom from leakage.

During a cruise of twenty-six hundred miles not one drop of water leaked through the seams of the Centennial Republic. Her under planking was nicely joined, and the seams calked with cotton wicking, and afterwards filled with white-lead paint and putty. The deck planks, of seven inches width, were not joined, but were tongued and grooved, the tongues and grooves being well covered with a thick coat of white-lead paint.

The item of cost is another thing to be considered in regard to this boat. The usual cost of a first-class canoe of seventy pounds' weight, built after the model of the Rob Roy or Nautilus, with all its belongings, is about one hundred and twenty-five dollars; and these figures deter many a young man from enjoying the ennobling and healthful exercise of canoeing. A first-class sneak-box, with spars, sail, oars, anchor, &c., can be obtained for seventy-five dollars, and if several were ordered by a club they could probably be bought for sixty-five dollars each. The price of a sneak-box, as ordinarily built in Ocean County, New Jersey, is about forty dollars. The Centennial Republic cost about seventy-five dollars, and a city boat-builder would not duplicate her for less than one hundred and twenty-five dollars. The builders of the sneak-boxes have not yet acquired the art of overcharging their customers; they do not expect to receive more than one dollar and fifty cents or two dollars per day for their labor; and some of them are even so unwise as to risk their reputation by offering to furnish these boats for twenty-five dollars each. Such a craft, after a little hard usage, would leak as badly as most cedar canoes, and would be totally unfit for the trials of a long cruise.

The diagram given of the Centennial Republic will enable the reader of aquatic proclivities to understand the general principles upon which these boats are built. As they should be rated as third-class freight on railroads, it is more economical for the amateur to purchase a first-class boat at Barnegat, Manahawken, or West Creek, in Ocean County, New Jersey, along the Tuckerton Railroad, than to have a workman elsewhere, and one unacquainted with this peculiar model, experiment upon its construction at the purchaser's cost, and perhaps loss.

One bright morning, in the early part of the fall of 1875, I trudged on foot down one of the level roads which lead from the village of Manahawken through the swamps to the edge of the extensive salt marshes that fringe the shores of the bay. This road bore the euphonious name of *Eel Street*,— so named by the boys of the town. When about half-way from its end, I turned off to the right, and followed a wooded lane to the house of an honest surf-man, Captain George Bogart, who had recently left his old home on the beach, beside the restless waves of the Atlantic, and had resumed his avocation as a sneak-box builder.

The house and its small fields of low, arable land were environed on three sides by dense cedar and whortleberry swamps, but on the eastern boundary of the farm the broad salt marshes opened to the view, and beyond their limit were the salt waters of the bay, which were shut in from the ocean by a long, narrow, sandy island, known to the fishermen and wreckers as Long Beach,— the low, white sand-dunes of which were lifted above the horizon, and seemed suspended in the air as by a mirage. Across the wide, savanna-like plains came in gentle breezes the tonic breath of the sea, while hundreds, aye, thousands of mosquitoes settled quietly upon me, and quickly presented their bills.

In this sequestered nook, far from the bustle of the town, I found " Honest George," so much occupied in the construction of a sneak-box, under the shade of spreading willows, as to be wholly unconscious of the presence of the myriads of phlebotomists which covered every available inch of his person exposed to their attacks. The appropriate surroundings of a surf-man's house were here, scattered on every side in delightful confusion. There were piles of old rigging, iron bolts and rings, tarred parcelling, and cabin-doors, — in fact, all the spoils that a treacherous sea had thrown upon the beach; a sea so disastrous to many, but so friendly to the Barnegat wrecker, — who, by the way, is not so black a character as Mistress Rumor paints him. A tar-like odor everywhere prevailed, and I wondered, while breathing this wholesome air, why this surf-man of daring and renown had left his proper place upon the beach near the life-saving station, where his valuable experience, brave heart, and strong, brawny arms were needed to rescue from the ocean's grasp the poor victims of misfortune whose dead bodies are washed upon the hard strand of the Jersey shores every year from the wrecks of the many vessels which pound out their existence upon the dreaded coast of Barnegat? A question easily answered, — political preferment. His place had been filled by a man who had never pulled an oar in the surf, but had followed the occupation of a tradesman.

Thus Honest George, rejected by " the service," had left the beach, and crossing the wide bays to the main land, had taken up his abode under the willows by the marshes, but not too far from his natural element, for he could even now, while he hammered away on his sneak-boxes, hear the ceaseless moaning of the sea.

A verbal contract was soon made, and George agreed to build me for twenty-five dollars the best boat that had ever left his shop; he to do all the work upon the hull and spars, while the future owner was to supply all the materials at his own cost. The oars and sail were not included in the contract, but were made by other parties. In November, when I settled all the bills of construction, cost of materials, oar-locks, oars, spars, sail, anchor, &c., the sum-total did not exceed seventy-five dollars; and when the accounts of more than twenty boats and canoes built for me had been looked over, I concluded that the little craft, constructed by the surf-man, was, for the amount it cost and the advantages

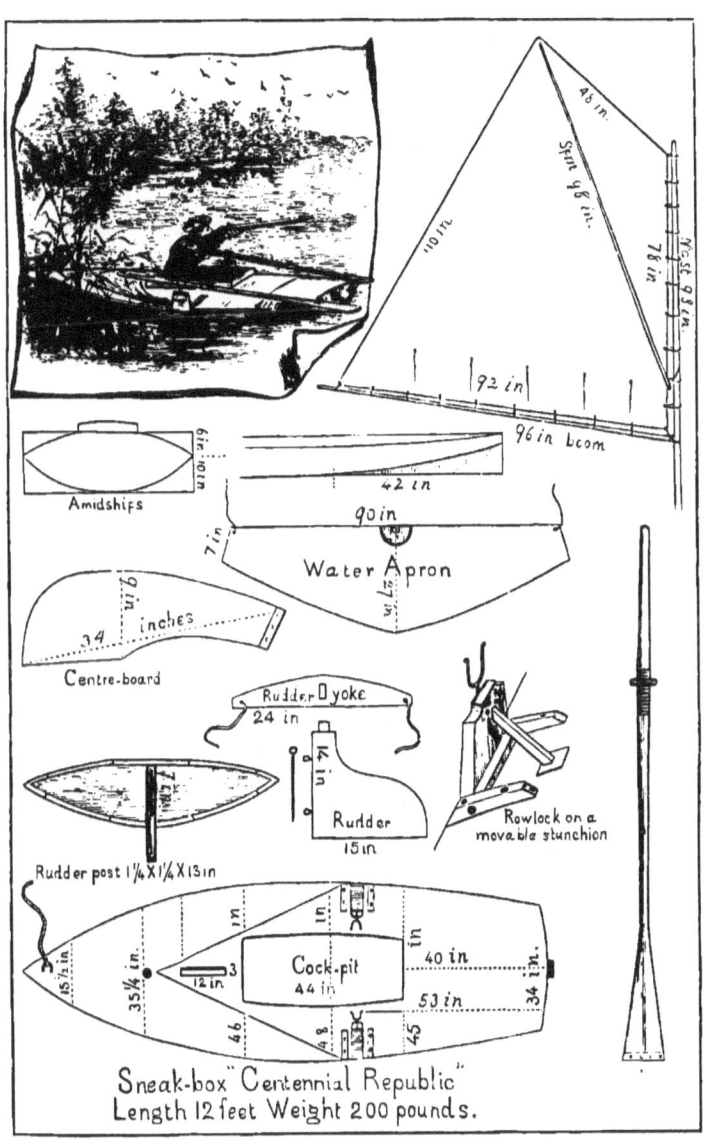

Sneak-box "Centennial Republic"
Length 12 feet Weight 200 pounds.

it gave me, the best investment I had ever made in things that float upon the water. Without a name painted upon her hull, and, like the "Maria Theresa" paper canoe, without a flag to decorate her, but with spars, sail, oars, rudder, anchor, cushions, blankets, cooking-kit, and double-barrelled gun, with ammunition securely locked under the hatch, the Centennial Republic, my future travelling companion, was ready by the middle of November for the descent of the western rivers to the Gulf of Mexico.

Captain George Bogart, attentive to the last to his pet craft, affectionately sewed her up in a covering of burlap, to protect her smooth surface from scratches during the transit over railroads. The two light oaken strips, which had been screwed to the bottom of the boat, kept the hull secure from injury by contact with nails, bolt-heads, &c., while she was being carried in the freight-cars of the Tuckerton, New Jersey, Southern and Pennsylvania railroads to Philadelphia, where she was delivered to the freight agent of the Pennsylvania Railroad, to be sent to Pittsburgh, at the head of the Ohio River.

Here I must speak of a subject full of interest to all owners of boats, hoping that when our large corporations have their attention drawn to the fact they will make some provision for it. There appears to be no fixed freighting tariff established for boats, and the aquatic tourist is placed at the mercy of agents who too frequently, in their zeal for the interests of their employers, heavily tax the owner of the craft. The agent of the Pennsylvania Railroad in Philadelphia was sorely puzzled to know what to charge for a BOAT. He had loaded thousands of cars for Pittsburgh, but could find only one precedent to guide him. "We took a boat once to Pittsburgh," he said, "for twenty-five dollars, and yours should be charged the same." The shipping-clerk of a mercantile house, who had overheard the conversation, interrupted the agent with a loud laugh. "A charge of twenty-five dollars freight on a little thing like that! WHY, MAN, THAT SUM IS NEARLY HALF HER VALUE! How LARGE was the boat you shipped last fall to Pittsburgh for twenty-five dollars?" "Oh, about twice the size of this one," answered the agent; "but, size or no size, a boat's a boat, and we handle so few of them that we have no special tariff on them." "But," said the clerk, "you can easily and honestly establish a tariff if you will treat a boat as you do all other freight of the same class. Now, for instance, how do common boats rank, as first or third class freight?" "Third class, I should think," slowly responded the agent. "Ease your conscience, my friend," continued the clerk, "by weighing the boat, and charging the usual tariff rate for third class freight."

The boat, with its cargo still locked up inside, was put upon the scales, and the total weight was three hundred and ten pounds, for which a charge of seventy-two cents per one hundred pounds was made, and the boat placed on some barrels in a car. Thus did the common-sense and business-like arrangement of the friendly clerk secure for me the freight charge of two dollars and twenty-three cents, instead of twenty-five dollars, on a little boat for its carriage three hundred and fifty-three miles to Pittsburgh, and saved me not only from a pecuniary loss, but also from the uncomfortable feeling of being imposed upon.

In these days of canoe and boat voyages, when portages by rail are a necessary evil, a fixed tariff for such freight would save dollars and tempers, and some action in the matter is anxiously looked for by all interested parties.

I gave a parting look at my little craft snugly ensconced upon the top of a pile of barrels, and smiled as I turned away, thinking how precious she had already become to me, and philosophizing upon the strange genus, man, who could so readily twine his affections about an inanimate object. Upon consideration, it did not seem so strange a thing, however, for did not this boat represent the work of brains and hands for a generation past? Was it not the result of the study and hard-earned experiences of many men for many years?

Men whose humble lives had been spent along the rough coast in daily struggles with the storms of ocean and of life? Many of them now slept in obscure graves, some in the deep sea, others under the tender, green turf; but here was the concentration of their ideas, the ultimatum of their labors, and I inwardly resolved, that, since to me was given the enjoyment, to them should be the honor, and that it should be through no fault of her captain if the Centennial Republic did not before many months reach her far-distant point of destination, twenty-six hundred miles away, on the white strands of the Gulf of Mexico.

CHAPTER II.

SOURCES OF THE OHIO RIVER.

DESCRIPTION OF THE MONONGAHELA AND ALLEGHANY RIVERS. — THE OHIO RIVER.—EXPLORATIONS OF CAVELIER DE LA SALLE.— NAMES GIVEN BY ANCIENT CARTOGRAPHERS TO THE OHIO. — ROUTES OF THE ABORIGINES FROM THE GREAT LAKES TO THE OHIO RIVER.

THE southerly branch of the Ohio River, and one of its chief affluents, is made by the union of the West Fork and Tygart Valley rivers, in the county of Marion, state of Virginia, the united waters of which flow north into Pennsylvania as the Monongahela River, and is there joined by the Cheat River, its principal tributary. The Monongahela unites with the Alleghany to form the Ohio, at Pittsburgh, Pennsylvania. The length of the Monongahela, without computing that of its tributaries, is about one hundred and fifty miles; but if we include its eastern fork, the Tygart Valley River, which flows from Randolph County, Virginia, the whole length of this tributary of the Ohio may exceed three hundred miles. It has a width at its union with the Alleghany of nearly one-fourth of a mile, and a depth of water sufficient for large steamboats to ascend sixty miles, to Brownsville, Pennsylvania, while light-draught vessels can reach its head, at Fairmont, Virginia.

The northern branch of the Ohio, known as the Alleghany River, has a length of four hundred miles, and its source is in the county of Potter, in northern Pennsylvania. It takes a very circuitous course through a portion of New York state, and re-enters Pennsylvania flowing through a hilly region, and at the flourishing city of Pittsburgh mingles its waters with its southern sister, the Monongahela.

The region traversed by the Alleghany is wild and mountainous, rich in pine forests, coal, and petroleum oil; and the extraction from its rocky beds of the last-named article is so enormous in quantity, that at the present time more than four million barrels of oil are awaiting shipment in the oil districts of Pennsylvania. The smaller steamboats can ascend the river to Olean, about two hundred and fifty miles above Pittsburgh. At Olean, the river has a breadth of twenty rods.

In consequence of its high latitude, the clear waters of the Alleghany usually freeze over by the 25th of December, after having transported upon its current the season's work, from the numerous saw-mills of the great wilderness through which it flows, in the form of rafts consisting of two hundred million feet of excellent lumber.

The Ohio River has a width of about half a mile below Pittsburgh, and this is its medial breadth along its winding course to its mouth at Cairo; but in places it narrows to less than twenty-five hundred feet, while it frequently widens to more than a mile. A geographical writer says, that, "In tracing the Ohio to its source, we must regard the Alleghany as its proper continuation. A *boat* may start with sufficient water within seven miles of Lake Erie, in sight sometimes of the sails which whiten the approach to the harbor of Buffalo, and float securely down the Conewango, or Cassadaga, to the Alleghany, down the Alleghany to the Ohio, and thence uninterruptedly to the Gulf of Mexico."

There are grave reasons for doubting that part of the statement which refers to a boat starting from a point within seven miles of Lake Erie. It is to be hoped that some member of the New York Canoe Club will explore the route mentioned, and give the results of his investigations to the public. He would need a canoe light enough to be easily carried upon the shoulders of one man, with the aid of the canoeist's indispensable assistant — the canoe-yoke.

It will be seen that the Ohio with its affluents drains an immense extent of country composed of portions of seven large states of the Union, rich in agricultural wealth, in timber, iron, coal, petroleum, salt, clays, and building-stone. The rainfall of the Ohio Valley is so great as to give the river a mean discharge at its mouth (according to the report of the United States government engineers) of one hundred and fifty-eight thousand cubic feet per second. This is the drainage of an area embracing two hundred and fourteen thousand square miles.

The head of the Ohio River, at Pittsburgh, has an elevation of eleven hundred and fifty feet above the sea, while in the long descent to its mouth there is a gradual fall of only four hundred feet; hence its current, excepting during the seasons of freshets, is more gentle and uniform than that of any other North American river of equal length. During half the year the depth of water is sufficient to float steamboats of the largest class along its entire length. Between the lowest stage of water, in the month of September, and the highest, in March, there is sometimes a range of fifty feet in depth. The spring freshets in the tributaries will cause the waters of the great river to rise twelve feet in twelve hours. During the season of low water the current of the Ohio is so slow, as flatboat-men have informed me, that their boats are carried by the flow of the stream only ten miles in a day. The most shallow portion of the river is between Troy and Evansville. Troy is twelve miles below the historic Blennerhasset's Island, which lies between the states of Ohio and Virginia. Here the water sometimes shoals to a depth of only two feet.

Robert Cavelier de la Salle is credited with having made the discovery of the Ohio River. From the St. Lawrence country he went to Onondaga, and reaching a tributary of the Ohio River, he descended the great stream to the "Falls," at Louisville, Kentucky. His men having deserted him, he returned alone to Lake Erie. This exploration of the Ohio was made in the winter of 1669-70, or in the following spring.

The director of the Dépôt des Cartes of the Marine and Colonies, at Paris, in 1872 possessed a rich mass of historical documents, the collection of which had covered thirty years of his life. This material related chiefly to the French rule in North America, and its owner had offered to dispose of it to the French government on condition that the entire collection should be published. The French government was, however, only willing to publish parts of the whole, and the director retained possession of his property. Through the efforts of Mr. Francis Parkman, the truthful American historian, supported by friends, an appropriation was made by Congress, in 1873, for the purchase and publication of this valuable collection of the French director; and it is now the property of the United States government. All that relates to the Sieur de la

Salle — his journals and letters — has been published in the original French, in three large volumes of six hundred pages each. La Salle discovered the Ohio, yet the possession of the rich historical matter referred to throws but little light upon the details of this important event. The discoverer of the great west, in an address to Frontenac, the governor of Canada, made in 1677, asserted that he had discovered the Ohio, and had descended it to a fall which obstructed it. This locality is now known as the "Falls of the Ohio," at Louisville, Kentucky.

The second manuscript map of Galinée, made about the year 1672, has upon it this inscription: "River Ohio, so called by the Iroquois on account of its beauty, which the Sieur de la Salle descended." It was probably the interpretation of the Iroquois word *Ohio* which caused the French frequently to designate this noble stream as "La belle rivière."

A little later the missionary Marquette designed a map, upon which he calls the Ohio the "Ouabouskiaou." Louis Joliet's first map gives the Ohio without a name, but supplies its place with an inscription stating that La Salle had descended it. In Joliet's second map he calls the Ohio "Ouboustikou."

After the missionaries and other explorers had given to the world the knowledge possessed at that early day of the great west, a young and talented engineer of the French government, living in Quebec, and named Jean Baptiste Louis Franquelin, completed, in 1684, the most elaborate map of the times, a carefully traced copy of which, through the courtesy of Mr. Francis Parkman, I have been allowed to examine. The original map of Franquelin has recently disappeared, and is supposed to have been destroyed. This map is described in the appendix to Mr. Parkman's "Discovery of the Great West," as being "six feet long and four and a half wide." On it, the Ohio is called "Fleuve St. Louis, ou Chucagoa, ou Casquinampogamou;" but the appellation of "River St. Louis" was dropped very soon after the appearance of Franquelin's map, and to the present time it justly retains the Iroquois name given it by its brave discoverer La Salle.

It would be interesting to know by which of the routes used by the Indians in those early days La Salle travelled to the Ohio. After the existence of the Ohio was made known, the first route made use of in reaching that river by the *coureurs de bois* and other French travellers from Canada, was that from the southern shore of Lake Erie, from a point near where the town of Westfield now stands, across the wilderness by portage southward about nine miles to Chautaugue Lake. These parties used light bark canoes, which were easily carried upon the shoulders of men whenever a "carry" between the two streams became necessary. The canoes were paddled on the lake to its southern end, out of which flowed a shallow brook, which afforded water enough in places to float the frail craft. The shoal water, and the obstructions made by fallen trees, necessitated frequent portages. This wild and tortuous stream led the voyagers to the Alleghany River, where an ample depth of water and a propitious current carried them into the Ohio.

The French, finding this a laborious and tedious route, abandoned it for a better one. Where the town of Erie now stands, on the southern shore of the lake of the same name, a small stream flows from the southward into that inland sea. Opposite its mouth is Presque Isle, which protects the locality from the north winds, and, acting as a barrier to the turbulent waves, offers to the mariner a safe port of refuge behind its shores. The French ascended the little stream, and from its banks made a short portage to the Rivière des bœuf, or some tributary of French Creek, and descended it to the Alleghany and the Ohio. This Erie and French River route finally became the military highway of the Canadians to the Ohio Valley, and may be called the second route from Lake Erie.

The third route to the Ohio from Lake Erie commenced at the extreme southwestern end of that inland sea. The voyagers entered Maumee Bay and ascended the Maumee River, hauling their birch canoes around the rapids between Maumee City and Perrysburgh, and between Providence and Grand Rapids. Surmounting these obstacles, they reached the site of Fort Wayne, where the St. Joseph and St. Mary rivers unite, and make, according to the author of the " History of the Maumee Valley," the "Maumee," or "Mother of Waters," as interpreted from the Indian tongue. At this point, when ninety-eight miles from Lake Erie, the travellers were forced to make a portage of a mile and a half to a branch called Little River, which they descended to the Wabash, which stream, in the early days of French exploration, was thought to be the main river of the Ohio system. The Wabash is now the boundary line for a distance of two hundred miles between the states of Indiana and Illinois. Following the Wabash, the voyager would enter the Ohio River about one hundred and forty miles above its junction with the Mississippi.

The great Indian diplomatist, "Little Turtle," in making a treaty speech in 1795, when confronting Anthony Wayne, insisted that the Fort Wayne portage was the "key or gateway" of the tribes ʻhaving communication with the inland chain of lakes and the gulf coast. It is now claimed by many persons that this was the principal and favorite route of communication between the high and low latitudes followed by the savages hundreds of years before Europeans commenced the exploration of the great west.

There was a fourth route from the north to the tributaries of the Ohio, which was used by the Seneca Indians frequently, though rarely by the whites. It was further east than the three already described. The Genesee River flows into Lake Ontario about midway between its eastern shores and the longitude of the eastern end of Lake Erie. In using this fourth route, the savages followed the Genesee, and made a portage to some one of the affluents of the Alleghany to reach the Ohio River.

CHAPTER III.

FROM PITTSBURGH TO BLENNERHASSET'S ISLAND.

THE START FOR THE GULF. — CAUGHT IN THE ICE-RAFT. — CAMPING ON THE OHIO. — THE GRAVE CREEK MOUND. — AN INDIAN SEPULCHRE. — BLENNERHASSET'S ISLAND. — AARON BURR'S CONSPIRACY. — A RUINED FAMILY.

UPON arriving at Pittsburgh, on the morning of December 2d, 1875, after a dreary night's ride by rail from the Atlantic coast, I found my boat — it having preceded me — safely perched upon a pile of barrels in the freight-house of the railroad company, which was conveniently situated within a few rods of the muddy waters of the Monongahela.

The sneak-box, with the necessary stores for the cruise, was transported to the river's side, and as it was already a little past noon, and only a few hours of daylight left me, prudence demanded an instant departure in search of a more retired camping-ground than that afforded by the great city and its neighboring towns, with the united population of one hundred and eighty thousand souls. There was not one friend to give me a cheering word, the happy remembrance of which might encourage me all through my lonely voyage to the Gulf of Mexico.

The little street Arabs fought among themselves for the empty provision-boxes left upon the bank as I pushed my well-freighted boat out upon the whirling current that caught it in its strong embrace, and, like a true friend, never deserted or lured it into danger while I trusted to its vigorous help for more than two thousand miles, until the land of the orange and sugar-cane was reached, and its fresh, sweet waters were exchanged for the restless and treacherous waves of the briny sea. Ah, great river, you were indeed, of all material things, my truest friend for many a day!

The rains in the south had filled the gulches of the Virginia mountains, the sources of the Monongahela, and it now exhibited a great degree of turbulence. I was not then aware of the tumultuous state of the sister tributary, the Alleghany, on the other side of the city. I supposed that its upper affluents, congealed during the late cold weather, were quietly enjoying a winter's nap under the heavy coat in which Jack Frost had robed them. I expected to have an easy and uninterrupted passage down the river in advance of floating ice; and, so congratulating myself, I drew near to the confluence of the Monongahela and Alleghany, from the union of which the great Ohio has its birth, and rolls

FOUR MONTHS IN A SNEAK-BOX. 31

steadily across the country a thousand miles to the mightier Mississippi.

The current of the Monongahela, as it flowed from the south, covered with mists rising into the wintry air, — for the temperature was but a few degrees above zero, — had not a particle of ice upon its turbid bosom.

I rowed gayly on, pleased with the auspicious

THE START — HEAD OF THE OHIO RIVER

beginning of the voyage, hoping at the close of the month to be at the mouth of the river, and far enough south to escape any inconvenience from a sudden freezing of its surface, for along its course between its source at Pittsburgh and its debouchure at Cairo the Ohio makes only two hundred and twelve miles of southing, or a difference of about two and a half degrees of latitude. It is not surprising, therefore, that this river during exceedingly cold winters sometimes freezes over for a few days, from the state of Pennsylvania to its junction with the Mississippi.

In a few minutes my boat had passed nearly the whole length of the Pittsburgh shore, when suddenly, upon looking over my shoulder, I beheld the river covered with an ice-raft, which was passing out of the Alleghany, and which completely blocked the Ohio from shore to shore. French Creek, Oil Creek, and all the other tributaries of the Alleghany, had burst from their icy barriers, thrown off the wintry coat of mail, and were pouring their combined wrath into the Ohio.

This unforeseen trouble had to be met without much time for calculating the results of entering the ice-pack. A light canoe would have been ground to pieces in the multitude of icy cakes, but the half-inch skin of soft but elastic white swamp-cedar of the decked sneak-box, with its light oaken runner-strips firmly screwed to its bottom, was fully able to cope with the difficulty; so I pressed the boat into the floating ice, and by dint of hard work forced her several rods beyond the eddies, and fairly into the steady flow of the strong current of the river.

There was nothing more to be done to expedite the journey, so I sat down in the little hold, and, wrapped comfortably in blankets, watched the progress made by the receding points of interest upon the high banks of the stream. Towards night some channel-ways opened in the pack, and, seizing upon the opportunity, I rowed along the ice-bound lanes until dusk, when happily a chance was offered for leaving the frosty surroundings, and the duck-boat was soon resting on a shelving, pebbly strand on the left bank of the river, two miles above the little village of Freedom.

The rapid current had carried me twenty-two miles in four hours and a half.

Not having slept for thirty-six hours, or eaten since morning, I was well prepared physically to retire at an early hour. A few minutes sufficed to securely stake my boat, to prevent her being carried off by a sudden rise in the river during my slumbers; a few moments more were occupied in arranging the thin hair cushions and a thick cotton coverlet upon the floor of the boat. The bag which contained my wardrobe, consisting of a blue flannel suit, &c., served for a pillow. A heavy shawl and two thin blankets furnished sufficient covering for the bed. Bread and butter, with Shakers' peach-sauce, and a generous slice of Wilson's compressed beef, a tin of water from the icy reservoir that flowed past my boat and within reach of my arm, all contributed to furnish a most satisfactory meal, and a half hour afterwards, when a soft, damp fog settled down upon the land, the atmosphere became so quiet that the rubbing of every ice-cake against the shore could be distinctly heard as I sank into a sweeter slumber than I had ever experienced in the most luxurious bed of the daintiest of guest-chambers, for my apartment, though small, was comfortable, and with the hatch securely closed, I was safe from invasion by man or beast, and enjoyed the well-earned repose with a full feeling of security. The owl softly winnowed the air with his feathery pinions as he searched for his prey along the beach, sending forth an occasional to-hoot! as he rested for a moment on the leafless branches of an old tree, reminding me to take a peep at the night, and to inquire " what its signs of promise " were.

All was silence and security; but even while I thought that here at least Nature ruled supreme, Art sent to my listening ear, upon the dense night air, the shrill whistle of the steam-freighter, trying to enter the ice-pack several miles down the river.

So the peaceful night wore away, and in the early dawn, enveloped in a thick fog. I hastily dispatched a cold breakfast, and at half-past eight o'clock pushed off into the floating ice, which became more and more disintegrated and less troublesome as the day advanced. The use of the soft bituminous coal in the towns along the river, and also by the steamboats navigating it, filled the valley with clouds of smoke. These clouds rested upon everything. Your five senses were fully aware of the presence of the disagreeable, impalpable *something* surrounding you. Eyes, ears, taste, touch, and smell, each felt the presence. Smoky towns along the banks gave smoky views. Smoky chimneys rose high above the smoky foundries and forges, where smoke-begrimed men toiled day and night in the smoky atmosphere. Ah, how I sighed for a glimpse of God's blessed sunlight! and even while I gazed saw in memory the bright pure valleys of the north-east; the sparkling waters of lakes George and Champlain, and the majestic scenery, with the life-giving atmosphere, of the Adirondacks. The contrast seemed to increase the smoke, and no cheerfulness was added to the scene by the dismal-looking holes in the mountain-sides I now passed. They were the entrances to mines from which the bituminous coal was taken. Some of them were being actively worked, and long, trough-like shoots were used to send the coal by its own gravity from the entrance of the mine to the hold of the barge or coal-ark at the steamboat landing. Some of these mines were worked by three men and a horse. The horse drew the coal on a little car along the horizontal gallery from the heart of the mountain to the light of day.

During the second day the current of the Ohio became less violent. I fought a passage among the ice-cakes, and whenever openings appeared rowed briskly along the sides of the chilly raft, with the intent of getting below the frosty zone as soon as possible.

About half-past eight o'clock in the evening, when some distance above King's Creek, the struggling starlight enabled me to push my boat on to a muddy flat, destined soon to be overflowed, but offering me a secure resting-place for a few hours. Upon peeping out of my warm nest under the hatch the next day, it was a cause of great satisfaction to note that a rise in the temperature had taken place, and that the ice was disappearing by degrees.

An open-air toilet, and a breakfast of about the temperature of a family refrigerator, with sundry other inconveniences, made me wish for just enough hot water to remove a little of the begriming results of the smoky atmosphere through which I had rowed.

At eleven o'clock, A. M., the first bridge that

spans the Ohio River was passed. It was at Steubenville, and the property of the Pan-Handle Railroad.

Soon after four o'clock in the afternoon the busy manufacturing city of Wheeling, West Virginia, with its great suspension bridge crossing the river to the state of Ohio, loomed into sight.

This city of Wheeling, on the left bank of the river, some eighty miles from Pittsburgh, was the most impressive sight of that dreary day's row. Above its masses of brick walls hung a dense cloud of smoke, into which shot the flames emitted from the numerous chimneys of forges, glass-works, and factories, which made it the busy place it was. Ever and anon came the deafening sound of the trip-hammer, the rap-a-tap-tap of the rivet-headers' tools striking upon the heavy boiler-plates; the screeching of steam-whistles; the babel of men's voices; the clanging of deep-toned bells. Each in turn striking upon my ear, seemed as a whole to furnish sufficient *noise-tonic* for even the most ardent upholder of that remedy, and to serve as a type for a second Inferno, promising to vie with Dante's own. Yet with all this din and dirt, this ever-present cloud of blackness settling down each hour upon clean and unclean in a sooty coating, I was told that hundreds of families of wealth and refinement, whose circumstances enabled them to select a home where they pleased, lingered here, apparently well satisfied with their surroundings. We are, indeed, the children of habit, and singularly adaptable. It is, perhaps, best that it should be so, but I thought, as I brushed off the thin layer of soot with which the Wheeling cloud of enterprise had discolored the pure white deck of my little craft, that if this was civilization and enterprise, I should rather take a little less of those two commodities and a little more of cleanliness and quiet.

At Wheeling I left the last of the ice-drifts, but now observed a new feature on the river's surface. It was a floating coat of oil from the petroleum regions, and it followed me many a mile down the stream.

The river being now free from ice, numerous crafts passed me, and among them many steamboats with their immense stern-wheels beating the water, being so constructed for shallow streams. They were ascending the current, and pushing their "tows" of two, four, and six long, wide coal-barges fastened in pairs in front of them. How the pilots of these stern-wheel freighters managed to guide these heavily loaded barges against the treacherous current was a mystery to me.

It suddenly grew dark, and wishing to be secure from molestation by steamboats, I ran into a narrow creek, with high, muddy banks, which were so steep and so slippery that my boat slid into the water as fast as I could haul her on to the shore. This difficulty was overcome by digging with my oar a bed for her to rest in, and she soon settled into the damp ooze, where she quietly remained until morning.

During this part of my journey particularly, the need of a small coal-oil stove was felt, as the usual custom of making a camp-fire could not be followed for many days on the upper Ohio River. The rains had wet the fire-wood, which in a settled and cultivated country is found only in small quantities on the banks of the stream. The drift-wood thrown up by the river was almost saturated with water, and the damp, wild trees of the swamp afforded only green wood.

Coal-Oil Stove.

In a less settled country, or where there is an old forest growth, as along the lower Ohio and upon the banks of the Mississippi, fallen trees, with resinous, dry hearts, can be found; and even during a heavy fall of rain a skilful use of the axe will bring out these ancient interiors to cheer the voyager's heart by affording him excellent fuel for his camp-fire.

The recently perfected coal-oil stove does not give out disagreeable odors when the petroleum used is refined, like that known in the market as *Pratt's Astral Oil*. This brand of oil does not contain naphtha, the existence of which in the partially refined oils is the cause of so many dangerous explosions of kerosene lamps.

Recent experiences with coal-oil burners lead me to adopt, for camp use, the No. 0 single-wick stove of the "Florence Machine Co.," whose excellent wares attracted so much attention at the Centennial Exhibition in Philadelphia. The No. 0 Florence stove will sustain the weight of one hundred and fifty pounds, and is one of the few absolutely safe oil stoves, with perfect combustion, and no unpleasant odor or gas. This statement presupposes that the wicks are wiped along the burnt edges after being used, and that a certain degree of cleanliness is observed in the care of the oil cistern. I do not stand alone in my appreciation of this faithful little stove, for the company sold forty thousand of them in one year. In Johnson's Universal Cyclopædia, Dr. L. P. Brockett, of Brooklyn, N. Y., expresses himself in the most enthusiastic terms in regard to this stove. He says: "For summer use it will be a great boon to the thousands of women whose lives have been made bitter and wretched by confinement in close and intensely heated kitchens; in many cases it will give health for disease, strength for weakness, cheerfulness for depression, and profound thankfulness in place of gloom and despair."

Boatmen and canoeists should never travel without one of these indispensable comforts.

Alcohol stoves are small, and the fuel used too expensive, as well as difficult to obtain, while good coal-oil can now be had even on the borders of the remote wilderness. The economy of its use is wonderful. A heat sufficient to boil a gallon of water in thirty minutes can be sustained for ten hours at the cost of three cents.

For lack of one of these little blessings — which the prejudice of friends had influenced me to leave behind — my daily meals for the first two or three weeks generally consisted of cold, cooked canned beef, bread and butter, canned fruits, and cold river water. The absence of hot coffee and other stimulants did not affect my appetite, nor the enjoyment of the morning and evening repasts, cold and untempting as they were. The vigorous day's row in the open air, the sweet slumbers that followed it at night in a well-ventilated apartment, a simple, unexciting life, the mental rest from vexatious business cares, all proved superior to any tonic a physician could prescribe, and I became more rugged as I grew accustomed to the duties of an oarsman, and gained several pounds avoirdupois by the time I ended the row of twenty-six hundred miles and landed on the sunny shores of the Gulf of Mexico.

Sunday broke upon me a sunless day. The water of the creek was too muddy to drink, and the rain began to fall in torrents. I had anticipated a season of rest and quiet in camp, with a bright fire to cheer the lonely hours of my frosty sojourn on the Ohio, but there was not a piece of dry wood to be found, and it became necessary to change my position for a more propitious locality; so I rowed down the stream twelve miles, to Big Grave Creek, below which, and on the left bank of the Ohio, is the town of Moundsville. One of the interesting features of this place is its frontage on a channel possessing a depth of fifteen feet of water even in the dryest seasons. Wheeling, at the same time of the year, can claim but seven feet. Here, also, is the great Indian mound from which it derives its name.

The resting-place of my craft was upon a muddy slope in the rear of a citizen's yard which faced the river; but when the storm ended, on Monday morning, my personal effects were hidden from the gaze of idlers by securely locking the hatch, which was done with the same facility with which one locks his trunk — and the former occupant was at liberty to visit the "Big Grave."

I walked through the muddy streets of the uninteresting village to the conspicuous monument of the aboriginal inhabitant of the river's margin. It was a conical hill, situated within the limits of the town, and known to students of American pre-historic races as the "Grave Creek Mound." This particular creation of a lost race is the most important of the numerous works of the Mound Builders which are found throughout the Ohio Valley. Its circumference at the base is nine hundred feet, and its height seventy feet. In 1838 the location was owned by Mr. Tomlinson, who penetrated to the centre of the mound by excavating a passage on a level with the foundation of the structure. He then sank a shaft from the apex to intercept the ground passage. Mr. Tomlinson's statement is as follows:

"At the distance of one hundred and eleven feet we came to a vault which had been excavated before the mound was commenced, eight by twelve feet, and seven in depth. Along each side, and across the ends, upright timbers had been placed, which supported timbers thrown across the vault as a ceiling. These timbers were covered with loose unhewn stone common to the neighborhood. The timbers had rotted, and had tumbled into the vault. In this vault were two human skeletons, one of which had no ornaments; the other was surrounded by six hundred and fifty ivory (shell) beads, and an ivory (bone) ornament six inches long. In sinking the shaft, at thirty-four feet above the first, or bottom vault, a similar one was found, enclosing a skeleton which had been decorated with a profusion of shell beads, copper rings, and plates of mica."

Dr. Clemmens, who was much interested in the work of exploration here, says: "At a distance of twelve or fifteen feet were found numerous layers composed of charcoal and burnt bones. On reaching the lower vault from the top, it was determined to enlarge it for the accommodation of visitors, when ten more skeletons were discovered. This mound was supposed to be the tomb of a royal personage."

At the time of my visit, the ground was covered with a grassy sod, and large trees arose from its sloping sides. The horizontal passage was kept in a safe state by a lining of bricks, and I walked through it into the heart of the Indian sepulchre. It was a damp, dark, weird interior; but the perpendicular shaft, which ascended to the apex, kept up an uninterrupted current of air. I found it anything but a pleasant place in which to linger, and soon retraced my steps to the boat, where I once more embarked upon the ceaseless current, and kept upon my winding course, praying for even one glimpse of the sun, whose face had been veiled from my sight during the entire voyage, save for one brief moment when the brightness burst from the surrounding gloom only to be instantly eclipsed, and making all seem, by contrast, more dismal than ever.

It would not interest the general reader to give a description of the few cities and many small villages that were passed during the descent of the Ohio. Few of these places possess even a local interest, and the eye soon wearies of the air of monotony found in them all. Even the guide-books dispose of these villages with a little dry detail, and rarely recommend the tourist to visit one of them.

One feature may be, however, remarked in descending the Ohio, and that is the ambition displayed by the pioneers of civilization in the west in naming hamlets and towns — which, with few exceptions, are still of little importance — after the great cities of the older parts of the United States, and also of foreign lands. These names, which occupy such important positions on the maps, excite the imagination of the traveller, and when the reality comes into view, and he enters their narrow limits, the commonplace architecture and generally unattractive surroundings have a most depressing effect, and he sighs, "What's in a name?" We find upon the map the name and appearance of a city, but it proves to be the most uninteresting of villages, though known as Amsterdam. We also find many towns of the Hudson duplicated in name on the Ohio, and pass Troy, Albany, Newburg, and New York. The cities of Great Britain are in many instances perpetuated by the names of Aberdeen, Manchester, Dover, Portsmouth, Liverpool, and London; while other nations are represented by Rome, Carthage, Ghent, Warsaw, Moscow, Gallipolis, Bethlehem, and Cairo. Strangely sandwiched with these old names we find the southern states represented, as in Augusta, Charleston, &c.; while the Indian names Miami, Guyandot, Paducah, Wabash, and Kanawha are thrown in for variety.

In the evening I sought the shelter of an island on the left side of the river, about three miles above Sisterville, which proved to be a restful camping-place during the dark night that settled down upon the surrounding country.

Tuesday being a rainy day, I was forced by the inclemency of the weather to seek for better quarters in a retired creek about three miles above the thriving town of Marietta, so named in honor of Maria Antoinette of Austria.

The country was now becoming more pleasing in character, and many of the islands, as I floated past them on the current, gave evidence of great fertility where cultivation had been bestowed upon them. Some of these islands were connected to one shore of the river by low dams, carelessly constructed of stones, their purpose being to deepen the channel upon the opposite side by diverting a considerable volume of water into it. When the water is very low, the tops of these dams can be seen, and must, of course, be avoided by boatmen; but when the Ohio increases its depth of water, these artificial aids to navigation are submerged, and even steamboats float securely over them.

On Wednesday the river began to rise, in consequence of the heavy rains; so, with an increased current, the duck-boat left her quarters about eleven o'clock in the forenoon. Early in the afternoon, Parkersburgh, situated at the mouth of the Little Kanawha River, in Virginia, came into view. This is the outlet of the petroleum region of West Virginia, and is opposite the little village of Belpré, which is in the state of Ohio. These towns are connected by a massive iron bridge, built by the Baltimore and Ohio Railroad Company.

Two miles below Belpré lay the beautiful island, formerly the home of Blennerhasset, an English gentleman of Irish descent, of whom a most interesting account was given in a late number of Harper's Magazine. Mr. Blennerhasset came to New York in 1797, with his wife and one child, hoping to find in America freedom of opinion and action denied him at home, as his relations and friends were all royalists, and opposed to the republican principles he had imbibed. Here, on this sunny island, under the grand old trees, he built a stately mansion, where wealth and culture, combined with all things rich and rare from the old world, made an Eden for all who entered it.

Ten negro servants were bought to minister to the daily needs of the household. Over forty thousand dollars in gold were spent upon the buildings and grounds. A telescope of high power to assist in his researches, books of every description, musical instruments, chemical and philosophical apparatus, everything, in fact, that could add to the progress and comfort of an intellectual man, was here collected. Docks were built, and a miniature fleet moored in the soft waters of the ever-flowing Ohio. Nature had begun, Blennerhasset finished; and we cannot wonder when we read of the best families in the neighboring country going often thirty and forty miles to partake of the generous hospitality here offered them. Mrs. Blennerhasset, endowed by nature with beauty and winsome manners, was always a charming and attractive hostess, as well as a true wife and mother.

For eight years Blennerhasset lived upon his island, enjoying more than is accorded to the lot of most mortals; but the story of his position, his intelligence, his wealth, his wonderful social influence upon those around him, reached at length the ear of one who marked him for his prey.

Aaron Burr had been chosen vice-president of the United States in 1800, with Thomas Jefferson as president; but in 1804, when Jefferson was re-elected, Burr was not. The brain of this brilliant but ill-balanced and unprincipled man was ever rife with ambitious schemes, and the taste of political power in his position as vice-president of the United States seemed to have driven him towards the accomplishment of one of the boldest and most extravagant dreams he ever imagined. Mexico he thought could be wrested from Spain, and the then almost unpeopled valleys of the Ohio and Mississippi taken from the United States. This fair region, with its fertile soil and varied climate, should be blended into one empire. On the north, the Great Lakes should be his boundary line, while the Gulf of Mexico should lave with its salt waters his southern shores. The high cliffs of the Rocky Mountains should protect the western boundary, and on the east the towering Alleghanies form a barrier to invading foe.

Such was the dream, and a fair one it was. Of this new empire, Aaron Burr would of course be Imperator; and the ways and means for its establishment must be found. The distant Blennerhasset seemed to point to the happy termination of at least some of the difficulties. His wealth, if not his personal influence, must be gained, and no man was better suited to win his point than the fascinating Aaron Burr. We will not enter into the plans of the artful insinuator made to enlist the sympathies of the unsuspecting Englishman, but we must ever feel sure that the cloven foot was well concealed until the last, for Blennerhasset loved the land of his adoption, and would not have listened to any plan for its impoverishment. His means were given lavishly for the aid of the new colony, as Burr called it, and his personal influence made use of in enlisting recruits. Arms were furnished, and the Indian foe given as an excuse for this measure.

Burr during this time resided at Marietta, on the right bank of the river, fifteen miles above Blennerhasset's Island. He occupied himself in overseeing the building of fifteen large bateaux in which to transport his colony. Ten of these flat-bottomed boats were forty feet long, ten feet wide, and two and a half feet deep. The ends of the boats were similar, so that they could be pushed up or down stream. One boat was luxuriously fitted up, and intended to transport Mr. Blennerhasset and family, proving most conclusively that he knew nothing of any treasonable scheme against the United States.

The boats were intended to carry five hundred men, and the energy of Colonel Burr had engaged nearly the whole number. The El Dorado held out to these young men was painted in the most brilliant hues of Burr's eloquence. He told them that Jefferson, who was popular with them all, approved the plan. That they were to take possession of the immense grant purchased of Baron Bastrop, but that in case of a war between the United States and Spain, which might at any time occur, as the Mexicans were very weary of the Spanish yoke, Congress would send an army to protect the settlers and help Mexico, so that a new empire would be founded of a democratic type, and the settlers finding all on an equality, would be enabled to enrich themselves beyond all former precedent.

About this time rumors were circulated that Aaron Burr was plotting some mischief against the United States. Jefferson himself became alarmed, knowing as he so well did the ambition of Burr and his unprincipled character. A secret agent was sent to make inquiries in regard to the doings at Blennerhasset's Island and Marietta. This agent, Mr. John Graham, was assured by Mr. Blennerhasset that nothing was intended save the peaceful establishment of a colony on the banks of the Washita.

Various reports still continued to greet the public ear, and of such a nature as to make Blennerhasset's name disliked. Some said treason was lurking, and blamed him for it. He was openly spoken of as the accomplice of Burr. The legislature of Ohio even made a law to suppress all expeditions found armed, and to seize all boats and provisions belonging to such expeditions. The governor was ready at a moment's notice to call out the state militia. A cannon was placed on the river-bank at Marietta, and strict orders given to examine every boat that descended the stream.

Mr. Blennerhasset had no idea of resisting the authorities, and gave up the whole scheme, determined to meet his heavy losses as best he might.

Four boats, with about thirty men, had been landed upon Blennerhasset's Island a short time before these rigorous measures had been taken. They were under the care of Mr. Tyler, one of Burr's agents from New York, and he did all in his power to urge Blennerhasset not to retire at so critical a moment. It was, however, too late to avert calamity, and the unfortunate family was doomed to misfortune.

The alarming intelligence now reached the island that the Wood County militia was *en route* for that place, that the boats would be seized, the men taken prisoners, and probably the mansion burned, as the most desperate characters in the surrounding country had volunteered for the attack. Urged by his friends, Blennerhasset and the few men with him escaped by the boats. His flight was not a moment too soon, for having been branded as a traitor, no one knows what might have befallen him had the lawless men who arrived immediately after his departure found him in their power. Colonel Phelps, the commander of the militia, started in pursuit, and the remainder of his men, with no one to restrain them, gave full play to their savage feelings. Seven days of riot followed. They took possession of the house, broke into the cellars, and drank the choice wines, until, more like beasts than men, they made havoc of the rich accumulation of years. Everything was destroyed. The paintings, the ornaments, rare glass and china, family silver, furniture, and, worst vandalism of all, the flames were fed with the choicest volumes, many of which never could be duplicated, for the value of Blennerhasset's library was known through all the country.

Mrs. Blennerhasset had remained upon the island during this week of terror, hoping by her presence to restrain the lawless band, but the brave woman was at last obliged to fly with her two little sons, taking refuge on one of the flat river boats sent by a friend to afford her a way of escape.

Mr. Blennerhasset was afterwards arrested for treason, but no evidence could be found against him, and he was never brought to trial. He invested the little means left him in a cotton plantation near Natchez, where, with his devoted wife, he tried to retrieve his fallen fortunes. The second war with England rendered his plantation worthless, and returning by way of Montreal to his native land, he died a broken-hearted man, leaving his wife in destitute circumstances. An attempt was made by her friends to obtain some return for the destruction of their property from the United States government, but all proved of no avail, and she who had always been surrounded by wealth and luxury, was, during her last hours, dependent upon the charity of a society of Irish ladies in New York city, who with tenderness nursed her unto the end, and then took upon themselves the expenses of her interment.

Such is the sad story of Blennerhasset and his wife; and I thought, as I quietly moored my boat in a little creek that mingled its current with the great river, near the lower end of the island which was once such a happy home, of the uncertainty of all earthly prosperity, and the necessity there was for making the most of the present, — which last idea sent a sleepy sailor hastily under his hatch.

Indian Mound, at Moundsville, West Virginia.

CHAPTER IV.

FROM BLENNERHASSET'S ISLAND TO CINCINNATI.

RIVER CAMPS.—THE SHANTY-BOATS AND RIVER MIGRANTS.— VARIOUS EXPERIENCES. — ARRIVAL AT CINCINNATI. — THE SNEAK-BOX FROZEN UP IN PLEASANT RUN. — A TAILOR'S FAMILY.—A NIGHT UNDER A GERMAN COVERLET.

ABOUT this time the selection of resting-places for the night became an important feature of the voyage. It was easy to draw the little craft out of the water on to a smooth, shelving beach, but such places did not always appear at the proper time for ending the day's rowing. The banks were frequently precipitous, and, destitute of beaches, frowned down upon the lonely voyager in anything but a hospitable manner. There were also present two elements antagonistic to my peace of mind. One was the night steamer, which, as it struggled up stream, coursing along shore to avoid the strong current, sent swashy waves to disturb my dreams by pitching my little craft about in the roughest manner. A light canoe could easily have been carried further inland, out of reach of the unwelcome waves, and would, so far as that went, have made a more quiet resting-place than the heavy duck-boat; but then, on the other hand, a sleeping-apartment in a canoe would have lacked the roominess and security of the sneak-box.

After the first few nights' camping on the Ohio, I naturally took to the channelless side of one of the numerous islands which dot the river's surface, or, what was still better, penetrated into the wild-looking creeks and rivers, more than one hundred of which enter the parent stream along the thousand miles of its course. Here, in these secluded nooks, I found security from the steamer's swash.

The second objectionable element on the Ohio was the presence of tramps, rough boatmen, and scoundrels of all kinds. In fact, the Ohio and Mississippi rivers are the grand highway of the West for a large class of vagabonds. One of these fellows will steal something of value from a farm near the river, seize the first bateau, or skiff, he can find, cross the stream, and descend it for fifty or a hundred miles. He will then abandon the stolen boat if he cannot sell it, ship as working-hand upon the first steamer or coal-ark he happens to meet, descend the river still further, and so escape detection.

To avoid these rough characters, as well as the drunken crews of shanty-boats, it was necessary always to enter the night's camping-ground unobserved; but when once secreted on the wooded shore of some friendly creek, covered by the dusky shades of night, I felt perfectly safe, and had no fear of a night attack from any one. Securely shut in my strong box, with a hatchet and a Colt's revolver by my side, and a double-barrelled gun, carefully charged, snugly stowed under the deck, the intruder would have been in danger, and not the occupant of the sneak-box.

The hatch, or cover, which rested upon the stern of the boat during rowing-hours, was at night dropped over the hold, or well, in such a way as to give plenty of ventilation, and still, at the same time, to be easily and instantly removed in case of need.

I must not fail here to mention one characteristic feature possessed by the sneak-box which gives it an advantage over every other boat I have examined. Its deck is nowhere level, and if a person attempts to step upon it while it is afloat, his foot touches the periphery of a circle, and the spoon-shaped, keelless, little craft flies out as if by magic from under the pressure of the foot, and without further warning the luckless intruder falls into the water.

At the summer watering-places in Barnegat Bay it used to be a great source of amusement to the boatmen to tie a sneak-box to a landing, and wait quietly near by to see the city boys attempt to get into her. Instead of stepping safely and easily into the hold, they would invariably step upon the rounded deck, when away would shoot the slippery craft, and the unsuccessful boarder would fall into two feet of water, to the great amusement of his comrades. When once inside of the sneak-box, it becomes the stiffest and steadiest of crafts. Two men can stand upright upon the flooring of the hold and paddle her along rapidly, with very little careening to right or left.

By far the most interesting and peculiar features of a winter's row down the Ohio are the life-studies offered by the occupants of the numerous shanty-boats daily encountered. They are sometimes called, and justly too, family-boats, and serve as the winter homes of a singular class of people, carrying their passengers and cargoes from the icy region of the Ohio to New Orleans. Their annual descent of the river resembles the migration of birds, and we invariably find those of a feather flocking together. It would be hard to trace these creatures to their lair; but the Alleghany and Monongahela region, with the towns of the upper Ohio, may be said to furnish most of them. Let them come from where they may (and we feel sure none will quarrel for the honor of calling them citizens), the fall of the leaf seems to be the signal for looking up winter-quarters, and the river with its swift current the inviting path to warmer suns and an easy life.

The shanty-boatman looks to the river not only for his life, but also for the means of making that life pleasant; so he fishes in the stream for floating lumber in the form of boards, planks, and scantling for framing to build his home. It is soon ready. A scow, or flatboat, about twenty feet long by ten or twelve wide, is roughly constructed. It is made of two-inch planks spiked together. These scows are calked with oakum and rags, and the seams are made water-tight with pitch or tar. A small, low house is built upon the boat, and covers about two-thirds of it, leaving a cockpit at each end, in which the crews work the sweeps, or oars, which govern the motions of the shanty-boat. If the proprietor of the boat has a family, he puts its members on board, — not forgetting the pet dogs and cats, — with a small stock of salt pork, bacon, flour, potatoes, molasses, salt, and coffee. An old cooking-stove is set up in the shanty, and its sheet-iron pipe, projecting through the roof, makes a chimney a superfluity. Rough bunks, or berths, are constructed for sleeping-quarters; but if the family are the happy possessors of any furniture, it is put on board, and adds greatly to their respectability. A number of steel traps, with the usual double-barrelled gun, or rifle, and a good supply of ammunition, constitute the most important supplies of the shanty-boat, and are never forgotten. Of these family-boats alone I passed over two hundred on the Ohio.

This rude, unpainted structure, with its door at each end of the shanty, and a few windows relieving the barrenness of its sides, makes a very comfortable home for its rough occupants.

If the shanty-man be a widower or a bachelor, or even if he be a married man laboring under the belief that his wife and he are not true affinities, and that there is more war in the house than is good for the peace of the household, he looks about for a housekeeper. She must be some congenial spirit, who will fry his bacon and wash his shirts without murmuring. Having found one whom he fondly thinks will "fill the bill," he next proceeds to picture to her vivid imagination the delights of "*drifting.*" "Nothing to do," he says, "but to float with the current, and eat *fresh* pork, and take a hand at euchre." The woods, he tells her, are full of hogs. They shall fall an easy prey to his unfailing gun, and after them, when further south, the golden orange shall delight her thirsty soul, while all the sugar-cane she can chew shall be gathered for her. Add to these the luxury of plenty of snuff with which to rub her dainty gums, with the promise of tobacco enough to keep her pipe always full, and it will be hard to find among this class a fair one with sufficient strength of mind to resist such an offer; so she promises to keep house for him as long as the shanty-boat holds together.

Her embarkation is characteristic. Whatever her attire, the bonnet is there, gay with flowers; a pack of cards is tightly grasped in her hand; while a worn, old trunk, tied with a cord and fondly called a "saratoga," is hoisted on board; and so, for better or for worse, she goes forth to meet her fate, or, as she expresses it, "to find luck."

More than one quarrel usually occurs during the descent of the Mississippi, and by the time New Orleans is reached the shanty-boatman sets his quondam housekeeper adrift, where, in the swift current of life, she is caught by kindred spirits, and being introduced to city society as the Northern Lily, or Pittsburgh Rose, is soon lost to sight, and never returns to the far distant up-river country.

Another shanty-boat is built by a party of young men suffering from impecuniosity. They are "out of a job," and to them the charms of an independent life on the river is irresistible. Having pooled their few dollars to build their floating home, they descend to New Orleans as negro minstrels, trappers, or thieves, as necessity may demand.

Cobblers set afloat their establishments, calling attention to the fact by the creaking sign of a boot; and here on the rushing river a man can have his heel tapped as easily as on shore.

Tin-smiths, agents and repairers of sewing-machines, grocers, saloon-keepers, barbers, and every trade indeed is here represented on these floating dens. I saw one circus-boat with a ring twenty-five feet in diameter upon it, in which a troop of horsemen, acrobats, and flying trapeze artists performed while their boat was tied to a landing.

The occupants of the shanty-boats float upon the stream with the current, rarely doing any rowing with their heavy sweeps. They keep steadily on their course till a milder climate is reached, when they work their clumsy craft into some little creek or river, and securely fasten it to the bank. The men set their well-baited steel traps along the wooded watercourse for mink, coons, and foxes. They give their whole attention to these traps, and in the course of a winter secure many skins. While in the Mississippi country, however, they find other game, and feast upon the hogs of the woods' people. To prevent detection, the skin, with the swine-herd's peculiar mark upon it, is stripped off and buried.

When engaged in the precarious occupation of hog-stealing, the shanty-man is careful to keep a goodly number of the skins of wild animals stretched upon the outside walls of his cabin, so that visitors to his boat may be led to imagine that he is an industrious and legitimate trapper, of high-toned feelings, and one "who wouldn't stick a man's hog for no money." If there be a religious meeting in the vicinity of the shanty-boat, the whole family attend it with alacrity, and prove that their BELIEF in honest doctrines is a very different thing from their daily PRACTICE of the same. They join with vigor in the shoutings, and their "amens" drown all others, while their excitable natures, worked upon by the wild eloquence of the backwoods' preacher, seem to give evidence of a firm desire to lead Christian lives, and the spectator is often deceived by their apparent earnestness and sincerity. Such ideas are, however, quickly dispelled by a visit to a shanty-boat, and a glimpse of these people "*at home.*"

The great fleet of shanty-boats does not begin to reach New Orleans until the approach of spring. Once there, they find a market for the skins of the animals trapped during the winter, and these being sold for cash, the trapper disposes of his boat for a nominal sum to some one in need of cheap firewood, and purchasing lower-deck tickets for Cairo, or Pittsburgh, at from four to six dollars per head, places his family upon an up-river steamer, and returns with the spring birds to the Ohio River, to rent a small piece of ground for the season, where he can "make a crop of corn," and raise some cabbage and potatoes, upon which to subsist until it be time to repeat his southern migration.

In this descent of the river, many persons, who have clubbed together to meet the expenses of a shanty-boat life for the first time, and who are of a sentimental turn of mind, look upon the voyage as a romantic era in their lives. Visions of basking in the sunlight, feasting, and sleeping, dance before their benighted eyes; for they are not all of the low, ignorant class I have described. Professors, teachers, musicians, all drift at times down the river; and one is often startled at finding in the apparently rough crew men who seem worthy of a better fate. To these the river experiences are generally new, and the ribald jokes and low river slang, with the ever-accompanying cheap corn-whiskey and the nightly riots over cutthroat euchre, must be at first a revelation. Hundreds of these low fellows will swear to you that the world owes them a living, and that they mean to have it; that they are gentlemen, and therefore cannot work. They pay a good price for their indolence, as the neglect of their craft and their loose ideas of navigation seldom fail to bring them to grief before they even reach the Mississippi at Cairo. Their heavy, flat-bottomed boat gets impaled upon a snag or the sharp top of a sawyer; and as the luckless craft spins round with the current, a hole is punched through the bottom, the water rushes in and takes possession, driving the inexperienced crew to the little boat usually carried in tow for any emergency.

Into this boat the shanty-men hastily store their guns, whiskey, and such property as they can save from the wreck, and making for the shore, hold a council of war.

There, in the swift current, lies the centre of their hopes, quickly settling in the deep water, soon to be seen no more. The fact now seems to dawn upon them for the first time that a little seamanship is needed even in descending a river, that with a little care their Noah's Ark might have been kept afloat, and the treacherous "bob sawyer" avoided. This trap for careless sailors is a tree, with its roots held in the river's bottom, and its broken top bobbing up and down with the undulations of the current. Boatmen give it the euphonious title of "bob sawyer" because of the bobbing and sawing motions imparted to it by the pulsations of the water.

Destitute of means, these children of circumstance resolve never to say die. Their ship has gone down, but their pride is left, and they will not go home till they have "*done*" the river; and so, repairing to the first landing, they ship in pairs upon freighters descending the stream. Some months later they return to their homes with seedy habiliments but an enlarged experience, sadder but wiser men.

And so the great flood of river life goes on, and out of this annual custom of shanty-boat migration a peculiar phase of American character is developed, a curious set of educated and illiterate nomads, as restless and unprofitable a class of inhabitants as can be found in all the great West.

After leaving my camp near Blennerhasset's Island, on December 9, the features of the landscape changed. The hills lost their altitude, and seemed farther back from the water, while the river itself appeared to widen. Snow squalls filled the air, and the thought of a comfortable camping-ground for the night was a welcome one. About dusk I retired into the first creek above Letart's Landing, on the left bank of the Ohio, where I spent the night. The next forenoon I entered a region of salt wells, with a number of flourishing little towns scattered here and there upon the borders of the stream. One of these, called Hartford City, had a well eleven hundred and seventy feet in depth. From another well in the vicinity both oil and salt-water were raised by means of a steam-pump. These oil-wells were half a mile back of the river. Coal-mines were frequently passed in this neighborhood on both sides of the Ohio.

After dark I was fortunate enough to find a

camping-place in a low swamp on the right bank of the stream, in the vicinity of which was a gloomy-looking, deserted house. I climbed the slippery bank with my cooking kit upon my back, and finding some refuse wood in what had once been a kitchen, made a fire, and enjoyed the first meal I had been able to cook in camp since the voyage was commenced.

Cold winds whistled round me all night, but the snug nest in my boat was warm and cheerful, for I lighted my candle, and by its clear flame made up my daily " log." There were, of course, some inconveniences in regard to lighting so low-studded a chamber. It was important to have a candle of not more than two inches in length, so that the flame should not go too near the roof of my domicile. Then the space being small, my literary labors were of necessity performed in a reclining position; while lying upon my side, my shoulder almost touched the carlines of the hatch above.

Saturday was as raw and blustering as the previous day, so hastily breakfasting upon the remains of my supper, — COLD chocolate, COLD corned beef, and COLD crackers, — I determined to get into a milder region as soon as possible.

As I rowed down the stream, the peculiar appearance of the Barnegat sneak-box attracted the attention of the men on board the coal-barges, shanty-boats, &c., and they invariably crowded to the side I passed, besieging me with questions of every description, such as, "Say, stranger, where did you steal that pumpkin-seed looking boat from?" "How much did she cost, any way?" "Ain't ye afeard some steamboat will swash the life out of her?" On several occasions I raised the water-apron, and explained how the little sneak-box shed the water that washed over her bows, when these rough fellows seemed much impressed with the excellent qualities of the boat, and frankly acknowledged that "it might pay a fellow to steal one if there was a good show for such a trick."

At three o'clock P. M. I passed the town of Guyandot, which is situated on the left bank of the Ohio, at its junction with the Big Guyandot. Three miles below Guyandot is the growing city of Huntington, the Ohio River terminus of the Chesapeake and Ohio Railroad, which has a total length of four hundred and sixty-five miles, exclusive of six private branches. The Atlantic coast terminus is on the James River, Chesapeake Bay.

The snow squalls now became so frequent, and the atmosphere was so chilly and penetrating, that I was driven from the swashy waves of the troubled Ohio, and eagerly sought refuge in Fourfold Creek, about a league below Huntington, where the high, wooded banks of the little tributary offered me protection and rest.

At an early hour the next morning I was conscious of a change of temperature. It was growing colder. A keen wind whistled through the tree-tops. I was alarmed at the prospect of having my boat fastened in the creek by the congealing of its waters, so I pushed out upon the Ohio and hastened towards a warmer climate as fast as oars, muscles, and a friendly current would carry me. The shanty-boatmen had informed me that the Ohio might freeze up in a single night, *in places*, even as near its mouth as Cairo. I did not, however, feel so much alarmed in regard to the river as I did about its tributaries. The Ohio was not likely to remain sealed up for more than a few days at a time, but the creeks, my harbors of refuge, my lodging-places, might remain frozen up for a long time, and put me to serious inconvenience.

About ten o'clock A.M. the duck-boat crossed the mouth of the Big Sandy River, the limit of Virginia, and I floated along the shores of the grand old state of Kentucky on the left, while the immense state of Ohio still skirted the right bank of the river.

The agricultural features of the Ohio valley had been increasing in attractiveness with the descent of the stream. The high bottom-lands of the valley exhibited signs of careful cultivation, while substantial brick houses here and there dotted the landscape. Interspersed with these were the inevitable log-cabins and dingy hovels, speaking plainly of the poverty and shiftlessness of some of the inhabitants.

At four P. M. I could endure the cold no longer, and when a beautiful creek with wooded shores, which divided fine farms, opened invitingly before me on the Kentucky side, I quickly entered it, and moored the sneak-box to an ancient sycamore whose trunk rose out of the water twelve feet from shore. I was not a moment too soon in leaving the wide river, for as I quietly supped on my cold bread and meat, which needed no better sauce than my daily increasing appetite to make it tempting, the wind increased to a tempest, and screeched and howled through the forest with such wintry blasts that I was glad to creep under my hatch before dark.

On Monday, December 13, the violent wind storm continuing, I remained all day in my box, writing letters and watching the scuds flying over the tops of high trees. At noon a party of hunters, with a small pack of hounds, came abruptly upon my camp. Though boys only, they carried shot-guns, and expectorated enough tobacco-juice to pass for the type of western manhood. They chatted pleasantly round my boat, though each sentence that fell from their lips was emphasized by its accompanying oath. I asked them the name of the creek, when one replied, "Why, boss, you don't call this a CREEK, do you? Why, there is twenty foot of water in it. It's the Tiger River, and comes a heap of a long way off." Another said, " Look here, cap'n, I wouldn't travel alone in that 'ere little skiff, for when you're in camp any feller might put a ball into you from a high bank." "Yes," added another, "there is plenty o' folks along the river that would do it, too."

As my camp had become known, I acted upon the friendly hint of the boy-hunters, and took my departure the next day at an early hour, following the left bank of the river, which afforded me a lee shore. As I dashed through the swashy waves, with the apron of the boat securely set to keep the water from wetting my back, the sun in all its grandeur parted the clouds and lighted up the landscape until everything partook of its brightness. This was the second time in two weeks that the God of Day had asserted his supremacy, and his advent was fully appreciated.

Two miles below Portsmouth, Ohio, I encountered a solitary voyager in a skiff, shooting mallards about the mouths of the creeks, and having discovered that he was a gentleman, I intrusted my mail to his keeping, and pushed on to a little creek beyond Rome, where, thanks to good fortune, some dry wood was discovered. A bright blaze was soon lighting up the darkness of the thicket into which I had drawn my boat, and the hot supper, now cooked in camp, and served without ceremony, was duly relished.

The deck of the boat was covered with a thin coating of ice, and as the wind went down the temperature continued to fall until six o'clock in the morning, when I considered it unsafe to linger a moment longer in the creek, the surface of which was already frozen over, and the ice becoming thicker every hour. An oar served to break a passage-way from the creek to the Ohio, which I descended in a blustering wind, being frequently driven to seek shelter under the lee afforded by points of land.

At sunset I reached Maysville, where the celebrated Daniel Boone, the pioneer of Kentucky backwoods life, once lived; and as the wind began to fall, I pulled into a fine creek about four miles below the village, having made twenty-nine miles under most discouraging circumstances. The river was here, as elsewhere, lighted by small hand-lanterns hung upon posts. The lights were, however, so dull, and, where the channel was not devious, at such long intervals, that they only added to the gloom.

As the wind generally rose and fell with the sun, it became necessary to adopt a new plan to expedite my voyage, and the river being usually smooth at dawn of day, an early start was an imperative duty. At four o'clock in the morning the duck-boat was under way, her captain cheered by the hope of arriving in Cincinnati, the great city of the Ohio valley, by sunset. I plied my oars vigorously all day, and when darkness settled upon the land, was rewarded for my exertions by having my little craft shoot under the first bridge that connects Cincinnati with Kentucky. Here steamers, coal-barges, and river craft of every description lined the Ohio as well as the Kentucky shore. Iron cages filled with burning coals were suspended from cranes erected upon flatboats for the purpose of lighting the river, which was most effectually done, the unwonted brilliancy giving to the busy scene a strange weirdness, and making a picture never to be forgotten.

The swift current now carried me under the suspension-bridge which connects Cincinnati and Covington, and my boat entered the dark area below, when suddenly the river was clouded in snow, as fierce squalls came up the stream, and I eagerly scanned the high, dark banks to find some inlet to serve as harbor for the night. It was very dark, and I hugged the Kentucky shore as closely as I dared. Suddenly a gleam of light, like a break in a fog-bank, opened upon my craft, and the dim outlines of the sides of a gorge in the high coast caught my eye. It was not necessary to row into the cleft in the hillside, for a fierce blast of the tempest blew me into the little creek; nor was my progress stayed until the sneak-box was driven several rods into its dark interior, and entangled in the branches of a fallen tree.

In the blinding snowfall it was impossible to discern anything upon the steep banks of the little creek which had fairly forced its hospitality upon me; so, carefully fastening my painter to the fallen tree, I hastily disappeared below my hatch. During the night the mercury fell to six degrees above zero, but my quarters were so comfortable that little inconvenience from the cold was experienced until morning, when I attempted to make my toilet with an open hatch. Then I discovered the unpleasant fact that my boat was securely frozen up in the waters of the creek! Being without a stove, and finding that my canned provisions — not having been wrapped in several coverings like their owner, and having no power to convert oxygen into fuel for warmth — were solidifying, I locked my hatch, and scrambled up the high banks to seek the comforts of that civilization which I had so gladly left behind when I embarked at a point five hundred miles further up the river, thinking as I went what a contrary mortal man was, myself among the number, for I was as eager now to find my human brother as I had been to turn my back upon him a short time before. The poetry of solitude was frozen into prose, and the low temperature around me made life under a roof seem attractive for the time being, though, judging from the general aspect of things, there was not much to look forward to, in either a social or comfortable light, in my immediate vicinity. I was, however, too cold and too hungry to be dainty, and felt like Dickens's Mrs. Bloss, that I "must have nourishment."

A turnpike crossed the ravine a few rods from my boat, and the tollgate-keeper informed me that I was frozen up in Pleasant Run, near which were several small houses. Upon application for "*boarding*" accommodations I discovered that breakfast at Pleasant Run was a movable feast, that some had already taken it at seven A. M., and that others would not have it ready till three P. M. This was anything but encouraging to a cold and hungry man; but I at length obtained admission to the house of a German tailor, and, explaining my condition, offered to pay him liberally for the privilege of becoming his guest until the cold snap was over. He examined me closely, and having made, as it were, a mental inventory of my features, dress, &c., exclaimed, "Mine friend, in dese times nobody knows who's which. I say, sar, nobody knows who's what. Fellers land here and eats mine grub, and den shoves off dere poats, and nevar says 'tank you, sar,' for mine grub. Since de confederate war all men is skamps, I does fully pelieve. I fights twenty-doo pattles for de Union, nots for de monish, but because I likes de free government; but it is imbossible to feeds all de beebles what lands at Pleasant Run."

I assured this patriotic tailor and adopted citizen that I would pay him well for the trouble of boarding me, but he answered in a surly way:

"Dat's vat dey all says. It's to be all pay, but dey eats up de sour-crout and de fresh pork, and drinks de coffee, and ven I looks for de monish, de gentlemens has disappeared down de rivver. Now you don't looks as much rascal as some of dem does, and as it ish cold to-day, I vill make dish corntract mid you. You shall stay here till de cold goes away, and you shall hab de pest I've got for twenty-five cents a meal, but you shall pays me de twenty-five cents a meal *down in advance*, beforehand."

"Here is a character," I thought, "a new type to study, and perhaps, after all, being frozen up in Pleasant Run may not be a fact to regret."

My landlord's proposition was at once accepted, and I offered to pay him for *three* meals in advance, to which he replied, "Dat dree pays at one time was not in de corntract." "You have forgotten one point," I said, addressing him as he led me to the kitchen, where "mine frau" was up to her elbows in work. "And what ish dat?" he asked, rather suspiciously eying me. "You have not fixed a price for my lodgings." "De use of de pedclothes costs me notting, so I never charges for de lodgings wen de boarder WASHES himself every day," answered mine host. Having settled this point, and ordered his wife, in commanding terms, "to gib dish man his breakfast," he withdrew. The woman treated me very kindly, apologizing for her husband's exacting demands by assuring me that "Nobody knows who's *when nowadays*. Seems as if everybody had got 'moralized by de war." The coffee the good lady made me, though thoroughly boiled, was excellent, and I complimented her upon it. "Yes," she replied, "my coffee is coffee. De 'Merican beeble forgets de coffee wen dey makes it, and puts all water. Oh, wishy-washy is 'Merican coffee. It's like peas and beans ground up. De German beebles won't drink de stuff."

A generous repast of sausage, fresh pork, good bread, butter, and coffee, was placed before me, when the tailor returned with darkened brow, and rudely demanded the whereabouts of my boat. " I looks everywhere," he said, " and don't finds de poat. *Hab* you one poat, or hab you not?" I carefully described the exact location of the sneak-box in the rear of the tollgate-house, when he hastily disappeared. The old lady and I had fully discussed the wishy-washy coffee question, when mine host returned. This time he wore a pleasant countenance, and took me into his shop, where he introduced me to three of his apprentices. At night I was given a bed in an unfinished attic, under a shingled roof, which was not even ceiled, so the constant

78　FOUR MONTHS IN A SNEAK-BOX.

draughts of air whistling through the interstices overhead and at the sides of my apartment, kept up a ventilation more perfect than was desirable; and I should have suffered from the cold had it not been for my German coverlet, which was a feather-bed about twenty inches in thickness. It, of course, half smothered me, but there seemed no choice between that and freezing to death, so I patiently accepted my fate.

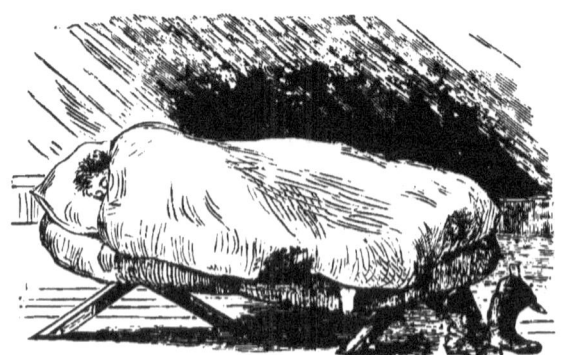

A Night under a German Coverlet.

CHAPTER V.

FROM CINCINNATI TO THE MISSISSIPPI RIVER.

CINCINNATI. — MUSIC AND PORK IN PORKOPOLIS. — THE BIG BONE LICK OF FOSSIL ELEPHANTS. — COLONEL CROGHAN'S VISIT TO THE LICK. — PORTAGE AROUND THE "FALLS," AT LOUISVILLE, KENTUCKY. — STUCK IN THE MUD. — THE FIRST STEAMBOAT OF THE WEST. — VICTOR HUGO ON THE SITUATION. — A FREEBOOTER'S DEN. — WHOOPING AND SAND-HILL CRANES. — THE SNEAK-BOX ENTERS THE MISSISSIPPI.

THE next day being Saturday, and the mercury still standing at seven degrees above zero, I walked to Covington, and crossed the suspension-bridge to Cincinnati. It was the season of the year when the vast pork-packing establishments were in full blast, and the amount of work done spoke well for western enterprise.

Pork-raising and pork-packing is one of the great industries of the Ohio valley, and the Cincinnati and Louisville merchants have control of the largest portion of the business growing out of it.

When a stranger visits the pork-packing establishments of Cincinnati he marvels at the immensity and celerity of the various manipulations, which commence with the killing of a squealing pig, and the transformation of his hogship, in a few minutes, into a well-cleaned animal, hanging up to cool in a store-room, from which he is taken a little later and immediately cut up and packed in barrels for market. The reader may have a distaste for statistics, but I cannot impress upon him the magnitude of this great industry without giving a few reliable figures.

The number of hogs packed in Cincinnati during the past twenty-one years, from 1853 to 1875, was 9,242,972. While Cincinnati was at work on one season's crop of pork of 632,302 pigs, her rival, Chicago, on the shore of Lake Michigan, killed and packed in the same time her crop of 2,501,285 animals.

The "Twenty-ninth Annual Report of the Cincinnati Price Current," published while the author has been writing this chapter, shows what our country can do in supplying meat for foreign as well as home markets. The states of Ohio, Indiana, Illinois, Iowa, Wisconsin, Michigan, Minnesota, Nebraska, Missouri, Kansas, Kentucky, and Tennessee, contributed to the packing establishments between November 1, 1877, and March 1, 1878, during the winter season of six months, 6,505,446 hogs; and during the summer season, from March 1 to November 1, 2,543,120 animals, — making a one year's total of 9,048,566 pigs, which averaged a net weight, when dressed, of two hundred and twenty-six pounds. Thus the weight of meat alone packed in one year was 2,044,975,916 pounds. Add to this the crop of California, Oregon, and Canada of the same year, and the total swells to 12,301,589 hogs, duly registered as having been killed by the pork-packers, and there still remain uncounted all the pigs killed in thirty-eight states by farmers for their own and neighbors' consumption.

This annual crop of pork a jocund professor once described as "a prodigious mass of heavy carburetted hydrogen gas and scrofula;" but the chemists of our day would more properly stigmatize it as a vast quantity of Luzic, Myristic, Palmitic, Margaric, and Stearic acids in combination with glycerine and fibre.

A western savant, having investigated the parasites existing in hogs, affirms that in western pork, eight animals out of every one hundred are affected by that muscle-boring pest so dangerous to those who have eaten the infected meat, and so well known to all students as the *Trichina spiralis*. The distinguished writer Letheby says of this parasite: "As found in the human subject (after death) it is usually in the encysted state, when it has passed beyond its dangerous condition, and has become harmless. In most cases, when thus discovered, there is no record of its action, and therefore it was once thought to be an innocent visitor; but we now know that while it was free, (that is, before nature had barricaded it up in the little cyst,) its presence was the cause of frightful disorders, killing about fifty per centum of its victims in terrible agony. The young worms having hatched in the body of man, migrate to the numerous muscles, causing the most excruciating pain, so that the patient, fearing to move his inflamed muscles, would lie motionless upon his back, and if he did not die in this state of the disorder, nature came to the rescue and imprisoned the creature by surrounding it with a fibrous cyst, where it lives for years, being ready at any moment to acquire activity when it is swallowed and released from its cell."

Another parasite found in the muscles of the pig is known as the *Cysticercus cellulosus*, and the animals afflicted by it are said to have the measles. This larva of the tapeworm exists in the pig in little sacs not larger than a pin's head, and can be seen by the naked eye. The strong brine of the packer does not kill them, and I have known them to be taken alive from a boiled ham. The great heat of frying alone renders them harmless. When partially-cooked, measly pork is eaten by man, the gastric juice of the stomach dissolves the membranous sac which contains the living larva, and the animal soon passes into the intestines, where, clinging by its hooks, it holds on with wonderful tenacity, rapidly sending out joint after joint, until the perfect tapeworm sometimes attains a length of thirty feet.

Let us hope, for the credit of humanity, that these facts are not generally known, for man has ills enough without incurring the risks of such a diet. If pork must form a staple, let the genealogical tree of his pigship be carefully sought after, and let the would-be consumer ask the question considered so important in a certain river-bounded city of Pennsylvania, " Who was his grandfather?"

In the year 1800 Cincinnati was a little pioneer settlement of seven hundred and fifty men, women, and children. Her census of 1880 will not fall far short of a quarter of a million. She contributes more than her share to feed the world, and is, strange to say, as celebrated for the terpsichorean art as for her pork. Even Boston must yield her the palm as a musical centre, and give to the inhabitants of the once rough western city the credit due them for their versatility of talent, and the ease with which they render Beethoven, or "take a turn in pork," as occasion may demand, many of the music-loving citizens being engaged at times in a commercial way with this staple.

Having obtained at a bookstore a copy of Lloyd's Map of the Mississippi River, I returned to the tailor's, where I was greeted in the most kindly manner, and informed that the young lady of the house, the only daughter of my host, had voluntarily left home to visit some city relations, that I might occupy her comfortably furnished room, with the open fireplace, which was now filled with blazing wood, and sending forth a genial glow into the heavily-curtained apartment. When I protested against this promotion in the social scale, and refused to deprive the young lady of her room, I was informed that she knew "WHO WAS WHO," and had insisted upon leaving her room that a *gentleman* might be·properly entertained in it. From this time my now agreeable host stoutly refused to accept payment in advance for my daily rations, while, with his family and apprentices, he took up his quarters each evening in my new room, relating his experiences during the war, and giving me many original ideas.

It grew warmer, but the ice of the creek in which my boat lay did not melt. The water was, however, falling, and it became necessary to cut out the sneak-box, and slide her over the ice into the unfrozen Ohio. My host had become alarmed, and kept an anxious eye upon the boat. "De peoples knows de poat is here, and some of dem hab told others about it. If you don't hide her down de rivver to-night, she will be stolen by de rivver thieves." I was thus forced to leave these kind people, who about noon escorted me to the duck-boat, and showered upon me their best wishes for a prosperous voyage. It was a glorious afternoon, and the sun poured all his wealth of light and cheerfulness upon the valley.

Late in the day I passed the mouth of the Big Miami River. Indiana was on the right, while Kentucky still skirted the left bank of the river. The state of Ohio had furnished the Ohio River with a margin for four hundred and seventy-five miles. The Little Miami River joins the Ohio six miles above Cincinnati; the Big Miami enters it twenty miles below the city. These streams flow through rich farming regions, but they are not navigable. After passing the town of Aurora, which is six miles below the Big Miami, I caught sight of the mouth of a creek, whose thickets of trees, in the gloom of the fast approaching night, almost hid from view the outlines of a forlorn-looking shanty-boat. Clouds of smoke, with the bright glare of the fire, shot out of the rusty stove-pipe in the roof, but I soon discovered that it was the abode of one who attended strictly to his own business, and expected the same behavior from his neighbors. So, saying good evening to this man of solitary habits, I quickly rowed past his floating hermitage into the darkness of the neighboring swamp. I soon put my own home in order, ate my supper, and retired, feeling happy in the thought that I should before long reach a climate where my out-door life would not be attended with so many inconveniences.

The next day a milder but damper atmosphere greeted me. By noon I had rowed twenty-two miles, and was off the mouth of Big Bone Lick Creek, in Kentucky. Two miles from the mouth of this creek are some springs, the waters of which are charged with sulphur and salt. The most interesting feature of this locality was the fact that here were buried in one vast bed the fossil bones of "The Mastodon and the Arctic Elephant." Formerly these prehistoric relics of a departed fauna were scattered over the surface of the earth. The first mention of this locality was made, I think, by a French explorer in 1649. It is again referred to by a British subject in 1765. A rare copy of a private journal kept by this early explorer of the Ohio, Colonel George Croghan, was published in G. W. Featherstonhaugh's "American Journal of Geology," of December, 1831. This monthly publication ended with its first year's existence. Only five copies of this number were known to be in print three years since, when Professor Thomas, of Mount Holly, New Jersey, encouraged the issue of a reprint of one hundred copies, from which some of our public libraries have been supplied.

This Colonel George Croghan, in company with deputies from the Seneca, Shawnesse, and Delaware nations, left Fort Pitt (Pittsburgh), in two bateaux, on the 15th of May, 1765, bound on a mission to the Indian tribes of the Ohio valley.

On the 29th of the month the expedition reached the Little Miami River. Colonel Croghan there commences his account of the Big Bone Lick region. He says: "May 30th we passed the Great Miami River, about thirty miles from the little river of that name, *and in the* EVENING *arrived at the place* WHERE THE ELEPHANTS' BONES ARE FOUND, when we encamped, intending to take a view of the place next morning. This day we came about seventy miles. The country on both sides level, and rich bottoms, well watered. May 31st. Early in the morning we went to the great Lick, where those bones are only found, about four miles from the river, on the south-east side. In our way we passed through a fine-timbered, clear wood: we passed into a large road, which the buffaloes have beaten, spacious enough for two wagons to go abreast, and leading straight into the Lick. It appears that there are vast quantities of these bones lying five or six feet under ground, which we discovered in the bank at the edge of the Lick. We found here two tusks above six feet long; we carried one, with some other bones, to our boat, and set off."

In relation to the aboriginal inhabitants of the country of the Ohio valley, it is interesting to note that the " Six Nations " held six of the gates to New York, and were strong because they were united, for Colonel Croghan's enumeration of them shows that they had only two thousand one hundred and twenty fighting-men, and were never supported by more than about two thousand warriors from tributary tribes, when at war with the whites.

That the Iroquois, with their adopted children, have not lost in numbers up to the present day, is a curious fact. About six thousand of the descendants of the "Six Nations" are at Forestville, Wisconsin, on government reservations; and the official agent reports that nearly two thousand of them can read and write; that they have twenty-nine day schools, and two manual-labor schools; that they cultivate their lands so diligently that they pay all the expenses of their living. They are reported as advancing in church discipline, growing in temperance; and are making rapid progress towards a complete civilization.

These six thousand, with other descendants of the Iroquois in Canada, will no doubt make up a total equal in number to the members of the old "Indian Confederacy," so graphically pictured in the glowing pages of Mr. Francis Parkman, the reliable historian, who has given us such vivid descriptions of the French rule in America as have called forth the unqualified praise of students of American history on both sides of the Atlantic.

Having rowed forty-three miles in twelve

hours, I reached the town of Vevay, Indiana, which was first settled by a Swiss colony, to whom Congress granted lands for the purpose of encouraging grape-culture. Keeping close under the banks of the river, I entered a little creek a mile below the village, where a night, restful as usual, was passed.

On Tuesday I rose with the moon, though it was as late as five o'clock in the morning; but, although fertile farms were stretched along the river's bank, and the land gave every sign of careful culture, it was anything but an enjoyable day, as the rain fell in almost uninterrupted showers from eight o'clock A. M. until dusk, when I was glad to find an inviting creek on the Kentucky shore, about one mile below Bethlehem, and had the great satisfaction of logging thirty-eight miles as the day's run.

It was necessary to make an early start the next day, as I must run the falls of the Ohio at Louisville, Kentucky, or make a portage round them. The river was enveloped in fog; but I followed the shore closely, hour after hour, until the sun dispelled the mists, and my little duck-boat ran in among the barges at the great Kentucky city. Here, at Louisville, is the only barrier to safe navigation on the Ohio River. These so-called *Falls* of the Ohio are in fact rapids which almost disappear when the river is at its full height. At such times, steamboats, with skilful pilots aboard, safely follow the channel, which avoids the rocks of the river. During the low stage of the water, navigation is entirely suspended. The fall of the current is twenty-three feet in two miles. To avoid this descent, in low water, and to allow vessels to ascend the river at all times, a canal was excavated along the left shore of the rapids from Louisville to Shippingsport, a distance of two miles and a half. It was a stupendous enterprise, as the passage was cut almost the entire distance through the solid rock, and in some places to the great depth of forty feet.

On the 25th of September, 1816, when Louisville had a population of three thousand inhabitants, her first steamboat, the *Washington*, left the young city for New Orleans. A second trip was commenced by the Washington on March 3, 1817. The whole time consumed by the voyage from Louisville to New Orleans, including the return trip, was forty-one days. The now confident Captain Shreve, of the Washington, predicted that steamboats would be built which could make the passage to New Orleans in *ten days*. I have been a passenger on a steamboat which ascended the strong currents of the river from New Orleans to Louisville in *five* days; while the once pioneer hamlet now boasts a population exceeding one hundred thousand souls.

As the bow of my little craft grounded upon the city levee, a crowd of good-natured men gathered round to examine her. From them I ascertained that the descent of the rapids could not be made without a pilot; and as the limited quarters of the sneak-box would not allow any addition to her passenger-list, a portage round the falls became a necessity. The canal was not to be thought of, as it would have been a troublesome matter, without special passes from some official, to have obtained the privilege of passing through with so small a boat. The crowd cheerfully lifted the sneak-box into an express-wagon, and fifteen minutes after reaching Louisville I was *en route* for Portland, mailing letters as I passed through the city. The portage was made in about an hour. At sunset the little boat was launched in the Ohio, and I felt that I had returned to an old friend. The expressman entered with entire sympathy into the voyage, and could not be prevailed upon to accept more than a dollar and a half for transporting the boat and her captain four miles.

When night came on, and no friendly creek offered me shelter, I pushed the boat into a soft, muddy flat of willows, which fringed a portion of the Kentucky shore, where there was just enough water to float the sneak-box. The passing steamers during the night sent swashy waves into my lair, which kept me in constant fear of a ducking, and gave me anything but a peaceful night. This was, however, all forgotten the next morning, when the startling discovery was made that the river had fallen during the night and left me in a quagmire, from which it seemed at first impossible to extricate myself.

The boat was imbedded in the mud, which was so soft and slimy that it would not support my weight when I attempted to step upon it for the purpose of pushing my little craft into the water, which had receded only a few feet from my camp. I tried pushing with my oak oar; but it sunk into the mire almost out of sight. Then a small watch-tackle was rigged, one block fastened to the boat, the other to the limb of a willow which projected over the water. The result of this was a successful downward movement of the willow, but the boat remained *in statu quo*, the soft mud holding it as though it possessed the sucking powers of a cuttlefish.

I could not reach the firm shore, for the willow brush would not support my weight. There was no assistance to be looked for from fellow-voyagers, as the river-craft seemed to follow the channel of the opposite shore; and my camp could not be seen from the river, as I had taken pains to hide myself in the thicket of young willows from all curious eyes. There was no hope that my voice would penetrate to the other side of the stream, neither could I reach the water beyond the soft ooze. Being well provisioned, however, it would be an easy matter to await the rise of the river; and if no friendly freshet sent me the required assistance, the winds would harden the ooze in a few days so that it would bear my weight, and enable me to escape from my bonds of mud.

While partaking of a light breakfast, an idea suddenly presented itself to my mind. I had frequently built crossways over treacherous swamps. Why not mattress the muddy flat? Standing upon the deck of my boat, I grasped every twig and bough of willow I could reach, and making a mattress of them, about two feet square and a few inches thick, on the surface of the mud at the stern of my craft, I placed upon it the hatch-cover of my boat. Standing upon this, the sneak-box was relieved of my weight, and by dint of persevering effort the after part was successfully lifted, and the heavy burden slowly worked out of its tenacious bed, and moved two or three feet nearer the water. By shifting the willow mattress nearer the boat, which was now ON the surface of the mud, and not IN it, my floating home was soon again upon the current, and its captain had a new experience, which, though dearly bought, would teach him to avoid in future a camp on a soft flat when a river was falling.

A foggy day followed my departure from the unfortunate camp of willows; but through the mist I caught glimpses of the fine lands of the Kentucky farmers, with the grand old trees shading their comfortable homes. In the drizzle I had passed French's Creek, and after dark ran upon a stony beach, where, high and dry upon the bank, was a shanty-boat, which had been converted into a landing-house, and was occupied by two men who received the freight left there by passing steamers. The locality was six miles below Brandenburg, Kentucky, and was known as "Richardson's Landing." Having rowed forty miles since morning, I "turned in" soon after drawing my boat upon the shelving strand, anticipating a quiet night.

At midnight a loud noise, accompanied with bright flashes of light, warned me of the approach of a steamboat. She soon after ran her bow hard on to the beach, within a few feet of my boat. Though the rain was falling in torrents, the passengers crowded upon the upper deck to examine the snow-white, peculiarly shaped craft, or "skiff" as they called it, which lay upon the bank, little suspecting that her owner was snugly stowed beneath her deck. I suddenly threw up the hatch and sat upright, while the strong glare of light from the steamer's furnaces brought out every detail of the boat's interior.

This sudden apparition struck the crowd with surprise, and, as is usual upon such an occasion in western America, the whole company showered a fire of raillery and "chaff" upon me, to which, on account of the heavy rain, I could not reply, but, dropping backward into my bed, drew the hatch into its place. The good-natured crowd would not permit me to escape so easily. Calling the entire ship's company from the staterooms and cabins to join them, they used every artifice in their power to induce me to show my head above the deck of my boat. One shouted, "Here, you deck-hand, don't cut that man's rope; it's mean to steal a fellow's painter!" Another cried, "Don't put that heavy plank against that little skiff!" Suspecting their game, however, I kept under cover during the fifteen minutes' stay of the boat, when, moving off, they all shouted a jolly farewell, which mingled in the darkness with the hoarse whistle of the steamer, while the night air echoed with cries of, "Snug as a bug in a rug;" "I never seed the like afore;" "He'll git used to livin' in a coffin afore he needs one," &c.

The reader who may have looked heretofore upon swamps and gloomy creeks as too lonely for camping-grounds, may now appreciate the necessity for selecting such places, and understand why a voyager prefers the security of the wilderness to the annoying curiosity of his fellow-man.

The rains of the past two days had swollen the Kentucky River, which enters the Ohio above Louisville, as well as the Salt River, which I had passed twenty miles below that city, besides many other branches, so that the main stream was now rapidly rising. After leaving Richardson's Landing, the rain continued to fall, and as each tributary, affected by the freshet, poured logs, fallen trees, fence-rails, stumps from clearings, and even occasionally a small frame shanty, into the Ohio, there was a floating raft of these materials miles in length. Sometimes an unlucky shanty-boat was caught in an eddy by the mass of floating timber, and at once becoming an integral portion of the whole, would float with the great raft for two or three days. The owners, being in the mean time unable to free themselves from their prison-like surroundings, made the best of the blockade, and their fires burned all the brighter, while the enlivening music of the fiddle, and the hilarity induced by frequent potions of corn whiskey, with the inevitable games of cards, made all "merry as a marriage bell," as they floated down the river.

In the evening, a little creek below Alton was reached, which sheltered me during the night. Soon the rain ceased, and the stars shone kindly upon my lonely camp. I left the creek at half-past four o'clock in the morning. The water had risen two feet and a half in ten hours, and the broad river was in places covered from shore to shore with drift stuff, which made my course a devious one, and the little duck-boat had many a narrow escape in my attempts to avoid the floating mass. The booming of guns along the shore reminded me that it was Christmas, and, in imagination, I pictured to myself the many happy families in the valley enjoying their Christmas cheer. The contrast between their condition and mine was great, for I could not even find enough dry wood to cook my simple camp-fare.

An hour before sunset, while skirting the Indiana shore, I passed a little village called Batesville, and soon after came to the mouth of a crooked creek, out of which, borne on the flood of a freshet, came a long, narrow line of drift stuff. Just within the mouth of the creek, in a deep indenture of the high bank, a shanty-boat was snugly lashed to the trees. A young man stood in the open doorway of the cabin, washing dishes, and as I passed he kindly wished me a "Merry Christmas," inviting me on board. He eagerly inspected the sneak-box, and pronounced it one of the prettiest "tricks" afloat. "How my father and brother would like to see you and your boat!" exclaimed he. "Can't you tie up here, just under yonder p'int on the bank? There's an eddy there, and the drift won't work in enough to trouble you."

The invitation so kindly given was accepted, and with the assistance of my new acquaintance my boat was worked against the strong current into a curve of the bank, and there securely fastened. I set to work about my house-keeping cares, and had my cabin comfortably arranged for the night, when I was hailed from the shanty-boat to "come aboard." Entering the rough cabin, a surprise greeted me, for a table stood in the centre of the room, covered with a clean white cloth, and groaning under the weight of such a variety of appetizing dishes as I had not seen for many a day.

"I thought," said the boy, "that you hadn't had much Christmas to-day, being as you're away from your folks; and we had a royal dinner, and there's lots left fur you — so help yourself." He then explained that his father and brother had gone to a shooting-match on the other side of the river; and when I expressed my astonishment at the excellent fare, which, upon closer acquaintance, proved to be of a dainty nature (game and delicate pastry making a *menu* rather peculiar for a shanty-boat), he informed me that his brother had been first cook on a big passenger steamer, and had received good wages; but their mother died, and their father married a second time, and — Here the young fellow paused, evidently considering how much of their private life he should show to a stranger. "Well," he continued, "our new mother liked cities better than flatboats, and father's a good quiet man, who likes to live in peace with every one, so he lets mother live in Arkansas, and he stays on the shanty-boat. We boys joined him, fur he's a good old fellow, and we have all that's going. We git plenty of cat-fish, buffalo-fish, yellow perch, and bass, and sell them at the little towns along the river. Then in summer we hire a high flat ashore, — not a flatboat, — I mean a bit of land along the river, and raise a crop of corn, 'taters, and cabbage. We have plenty of shooting, and don't git *much* fever 'n ager."

I had rowed fifty-three miles that day, and did ample justice to the Christmas dinner on the flatboat. The father and brother joined us in the evening, and gave me much good advice in regard to river navigation. The rain fell heavily before midnight, and they insisted that I should share one of their beds in the boat; but as small streams of water were trickling through the roof of the shanty, and my little craft was water-tight, I declined the kindly offer, and bade them good-night.

The next day being Sunday, I again visited my new acquaintances upon the shanty-boat, and gathered from their varied experiences much of the river's lore. The rain continued, accompanied with lightning and thunder, during the entire day, so that Monday's sun was indeed welcome; and with kind farewells on all sides I broke camp and descended the current with the now almost continuous raft of drift-wood. For several hours a sewing-machine repair-shop and a photographic gallery floated with me.

The creeks were now so swollen from the heavy rains, and so full of drift-wood, that my usual retreat into some creek seemed cut off; so I ran under the sheltered side of "Three Mile Island," below Newburg, Indiana. The climate was daily improving, and I no longer feared an ice blockade; but a new difficulty arose. The heavy rafts of timber threatened to shut me in my camp. At dusk, all might be open water; but at break of day "a change came o'er the spirit of my dream," and heavy blockades of timber rafts made it no easy matter to escape. There were times when, shut in behind these barriers, I looked out upon the river with envious eyes at the steamboats steadily plodding up stream against the current, keeping free of the rafts by the skill of their pilots; and thoughts of the genius and perseverance of the inventors of these peculiar craft crowded my mind.

In these days of successful application of mechanical inventions, but few persons can realize the amount of distrust and opposition against which a Watts or a Fulton had to contend while forcing upon an illiberal and unappreciative public the valuable results of their busy brains and fertile genius. It is well for us who now enjoy these blessings,— the utilized ideas of a lifetime of unrequited labors, — to look back upon the epoch of history so full of gloom for the men to whom we owe so much.

At the beginning of the present century the navigation of the Ohio was limited to canoes, bateaux, scows, rafts, arks, and the rudest models of sailing-boats. The ever downward course of the strong current must be stemmed in ascending the river. Against this powerful resistance upon tortuous streams, wind, as a motor, was found to be only partially successful, and for sure and rapid transit between settlements along the banks of great waterways a most discouraging failure. Down-river journeys were easily made, but the up-river or return trip was a very slow and unsatisfactory affair, excepting to those who travelled in light canoes.

The influx of population to the fertile Ohio valley, and the settling up of the rich bottoms of the Mississippi, demanded a more expeditious system of communication. The necessities of the people called loudly for this improvement, but at the same time their prejudices and ignorance prevented them from aiding or encouraging any such plans. The hour came at length for the delivery of the people of the great West, and with it the man. Fulton, aided by Watts, offered to solve the problem by unravelling rather than by cutting the "Gordian knot." It was whispered through the wilderness that a fire-ship, called the "Clermont," built by a crazy speculator named Fulton, had started from New York, and, steaming up the Hudson, had forced itself against the current one hundred and fifty miles to Albany, in thirty-six hours. This was in September, 1807.

The fool and the fool's fire-ship became the butt of all sensible people in Europe as well as in America. Victor Hugo remarks that, "In the year 1807, when the first steamboat of Fulton, commanded by Livingston, furnished with one of Watts's engines sent from England, and manœuvred, besides her ordinary crew, by two Frenchmen only, André Michaux and another, made her first voyage from New York to Albany, it happened that she set sail on the 17th of August. The ministers took up this important fact, and in numberless chapels preachers were heard calling down a malediction on the machine, and declaring that this number seventeen was no other than the total of the ten horns and seven heads of the beasts in the Apocalypse. In America they invoked against the steamboat the beast from the book of Revelation; in Europe, the reptile of the book of Genesis. The SAVANS had rejected steamboats as impossible; the PRIESTS had anathematized them as impious; SCIENCE had condemned, and RELIGION consigned them to perdition."

"In the archipelago of the British Channel islands," this learned author goes on to say, "the first steamboat which made its appearance receeived the name of the 'Devil Boat.' In the eyes of these worthy fishermen, once Catholics, now Calvinists, but always bigots, it seemed to be a portion of the infernal regions which had been somehow set afloat. A local preacher selected for his discourse the question of, 'Whether man has the right to make fire and water work together when God had divided them.' (Gen. ch. i. v. 4.) No; this beast composed of iron and fire did not resemble leviathan! Was it not an attempt to bring chaos again into the universe?"

So much for young America, and so much for old mother England! Now listen, men and women of to-day, to the wisdom of France — *scientific France*. "A mad notion, a gross delusion, an absurdity!" Such was the verdict of the Academy of Sciences when consulted by Napoleon on the subject of steamboats early in the present century.

It seems scarcely credible now that all this transpired in the days of our fathers, not so very long ago. Time is a great leveller. Education of the head as well as of the heart has liberalized the pulpit, and the man of theoretical science to-day would not dare to stake his reputation by denying any apparently well-established theory, while the inventors of telephones, perpetual-motion motors, &c., are gladly hailed as leaders in the march of progress so dear to every American heart. The pulpit is now on the side of honest science, and the savant teaches great truths, while the public mind is being educated to receive and utilize the heretofore concealed or undeveloped mysteries of a wise and generous Creator, who has taught his children that they must labor in order to possess.

The Clermont was the pioneer steamer of the Hudson River, and its trial trip was made in 1807. The first steamboat which descended the Ohio and Mississippi rivers was christened the "New Orleans." It was designed and built by Mr. N. J. Roosevelt, and commenced its voyage from Pittsburgh in September, 1811. The bold proprietor of this enterprise, with his wife, Mrs. Lydia M. Roosevelt, accompanied the captain, engineer, pilot, six hands, two female servants, a man waiter, a cook, and a large Newfoundland dog, to the end of the voyage. The friends of this lady — the first woman who descended the great rivers of the West in a steamboat — used every argument they could offer to dissuade her from undertaking what was considered a dangerous experiment, an absolute folly. The good wife, however, clung to her husband, and accepted the risks, preferring to be drowned or blown up, as her friends predicted, rather than to desert her better-half in his hour of trial. A few weeks would decide his success or failure, and she would be at his side to condole or rejoice with him, as the case might be.

The citizens of Pittsburgh gathered upon the banks of the Monongahela to witness the inception of the enterprise which was to change the whole destiny of the West. One can imagine the criticisms flung at the departing steamer as she left her moorings and boldly faced her fate. As the curious craft was borne along the current of the river, the Indians attempted to approach her, bent upon hostile attempts, and once a party of them pursued the boat in hot chase, but their endurance was not equal to that of steam. These children of the forest gazed upon the snorting, fire-breathing monster with undisguised awe, and called it "*Penelore*" — the fire-canoe. They imagined it to have close relationship with the comet that they believed had produced the earthquakes of that year. The voyage of the "New

Orleans" was a romantic reality in two ways. The wonderful experiment was proved a success, and its originator won his laurel wreath; while the bold captain of the fire-ship, falling in love with one of the chambermaids, won a wife.

The river's travel now became somewhat monotonous. I had reached a low country, heavily wooded in places, and was entering the great prairie region of Illinois. Having left my island camp by starlight on Tuesday morning, and having rowed steadily all day until dusk, I passed the wild-looking mouth of the Wabash River, and went into camp behind an island, logging with pleasure my day's run at sixty-seven miles. I was now only one hundred and forty-two miles from the mouth of the Ohio, and with the rising and rapidly increasing current there were only a few hours' travel between me and the Mississippi.

Wednesday morning, December 29th, I discovered that the river had risen two feet during the night, and the stump of the tree to which I had moored my boat was submerged. The river was wide and the banks covered with heavy forests, with clearings here and there, which afforded attractive vistas of prairies in the background. I passed a bold, stratified crag, covered with a little growth of cedars. These adventurous trees, growing out of the crevices of the rock, formed a picturesque covering for its rough surface. A cavern, about thirty feet in width, penetrated a short distance into the rock. This natural curiosity bore the name of "Cave-in-Rock," and was, in 1801, the rendezvous of a band of outlaws, who lived by plundering the boats going up and down the river, oftentimes adding the crime of murder to their other misdeeds. Just below the cliff nestled a little village also called "Cave-in-Rock."

Wild birds flew about me on all sides, and had I cared to linger I might have had a good bag of game. This was not, however, a gunning cruise, and the temptation was set aside as inconsistent with the systematic pulling which alone would take me to my goal. The birds were left for my quondam friends of the shanty-boat, they being the happy possessors of more TIME than they could well handle, and the killing of it the aim of their existence.

The soft shores of alluvium were constantly caving and falling into the river, bringing down tons of earth and tall forest-trees. The latter, after freeing their roots of the soil, would be swept out into the stream as contributions to the great floating raft of drift-wood, a large portion of which was destined to a long voyage, for much of this floating forest is carried into the Gulf of Mexico, and travels over many hundreds of miles of salt water, until it is washed up on to the strands of the isles of the sea or the beaches of the continent.

Having tied up for the night to a low bank, with no thought of danger, it was startling, to say the least, to have an avalanche of earth from the bank above deposit itself upon my boat, so effectually sealing down my hatch-cover that it seemed at first impossible to break from my prison. After repeated trials I succeeded in dislodging the mass, and, thankful to escape premature interment, at once pushed off in search of a better camp.

A creek soon appeared, but its entrance was barred by a large tree which had fallen across its mouth. My heavy hatchet now proved a friend in need, and putting my boat close to the tree, I went systematically to work, and soon cut out a section five feet in length. Entering through this gateway, my labors were rewarded by finding upon the bank some dry fence-rails, with which a rude kitchen was soon constructed to protect me from the wind while preparing my meal. The unusual luxury of a fire brightened the weird scene, and the flames shot upward, cheering the lone voyager and frightening the owls and coons from their accustomed lairs. The strong current had been of great assistance, for that night my log registered sixty-two miles for the day's row.

Leaving the creek the next morning by starlight, I passed large flocks of geese and ducks, while Whooping-cranes (*Grus Americanus*) and Sand-hill cranes (*Grus Canadensis*), in little flocks, dotted the grassy prairies, or flew from one swamp to another, filling the air with their startling cries. Both these species are found associated in flocks upon the cultivated prairie farms, where they pillage the grain and vegetable fields of the farmer. Their habits are somewhat similar, though the Whooping-crane is the most wary of the two. The adult Whooping-cranes are white, the younger birds of a brownish color. This species is larger than the Sand-hill Crane, the latter having a total length of from forty to forty-two inches. The Sand-hill species may be distinguished from the Whooping-crane by its slate-blue color. The cackling, whooping, and screaming voices of an assembled multitude of these birds cannot be described. They can be heard for miles upon the open plains. These birds are found in Florida and along the Gulf coast as well as over large areas of the northern states. They feed upon soft roots, which they excavate from the swamps, and upon bugs and reptiles of all kinds. It requires the most cautious stalking on the part of the hunter to get within gunshot of them, and when so approached the Whooping-crane is usually the first of the two species which takes to the wing. The social customs of these birds are most entertaining to the observer who may lie hidden in the grass and watch them through a glass. Their tall, angular figures, made up of so much wing, leg, neck, and bill, counterpoised by so little body, incline the spectator to look upon them as ornithological caricatures. After balancing himself upon one foot for an hour, with the other drawn up close to his scanty robe of feathers, and his head poised in a most contemplative attitude, one of these queer birds will suddenly turn a somersault, and, returning to his previous posture, continue his cogitations as though nothing had interrupted his reflections. With wings spread, they slowly winnow the air, rising or hopping from the ground a few feet at a time, then whirling in circles upon their toes, as though going through the mazes of a dance. Their most popular diversion seems to be the game of leap-frog, and their long legs being specially adapted to this sport, they achieve a wonderful success. One of the birds quietly assumes a squatting position upon the ground, when his sportive companions hop in turn over his expectant head. They then pirouette, turn somersaults, and go through various exercises with the skill of gymnasts. Their sportive proclivities seem to have no bounds; and being true humorists, they preserve through their gambols a ridiculously sedate appearance. Popular accounts of the nidification of these birds are frequently untrue. We are told that they build their cone-shaped nests of mud, sticks, and grass in shallow water, in colonies, and that their nests, BEING PLACED ON RAFTS of buoyant material, float about in the bayous, and are propelled and guided at the will of the sitting bird by the use of her long legs and feet as oars. The position of the bird upon the nest is also ludicrously depicted. It is described as sitting astride the nest, with the toes touching the ground; and to add still more comicality to the picture, it is asserted that the limbs are often thrust out horizontally behind the bird. The results of close observations prove that these accounts are in keeping with many others related by parlor naturalists. The cranes sit upon their nests like other birds, with their feet drawn up close to the body. The mound-shaped nests are built of sticks, grass, and mud, and usually placed in a shallow pond or partially submerged swamp, while at times a grassy hassock furnishes the foundation of the structure. In the saucer-shaped top of the nest two eggs are deposited, upon which the bird sits most

Popular Idea of the Nesting of Cranes.

assiduously, having no time at this season for aquatic amusements, such as paddling about with her nest.

The young birds are most hilarious babies, for they inherit the social qualities of their parents, and are ready to play or fight with each other before they are fairly out of the nest. A close observer of their habits writes from the prairies of Indiana: "When the young get a little strength they attack each other with great fury, and can only be made to desist by the parent bird separating them, and taking one under its fostering care, and holding them at a respectable distance until they reach *crane-hood*, when they seem to make up in joyous hilarity for the quarrelsome proclivities of youth."

Like geese and ducks, cranes winter in one locality so long as the ponds are open, but the first cold snap that freezes their swamp drives them two or three degrees further south. From this migration they soon return to their old haunts, the first thawing of the ice being the signal.

The mouths of the Tennessee and Cumberland rivers were passed, and the Ohio, widening in places until it seemed like a lake, assumed a new grandeur as it approached the Mississippi. Three miles below Wilkinsonville, but on the Kentucky side, I stole into a dark creek and rested until the next morning, Friday, December 31st, which was to be my last day on the Ohio River.

I entered a long reach in the river soon after nine o'clock on Friday morning, and could plainly see the town of Cairo, resting upon the flat prairies in the distance. The now yellow, muddy current of the Ohio rolled along the great railroad dike, which had cost one million dollars to erect, and formed a barrier strong enough to resist the rushing waters of the freshets. Across the southern apex of this prairie city could be seen the "Father of Waters," its wide surface bounded on the west by the wilderness. A few moments more, and my little craft was whirled into its rapid, eddying current; and with the boat's prow now pointed southward, I commenced, as it were, a life of new experiences as I descended the great river, where each day I was to feel the genial influences of a warmer climate.

The thought of entering warm and sunny regions was, indeed, welcome to a man who had forced his way through rafts of ice, under cloudy skies, through a smoky atmosphere, and had partaken of food of the same chilling temperature for so many days. This prospect of a genial clime, with the more comfortable camping and rowing it was sure to bring, gave new vigor to my arms, daily growing stronger with their task, and each long, steady pull TOLD as it swept me down the river.

The faithful sneak-box had carried me more

than a thousand miles since I entered her at Pittsburgh. This, of course, includes the various detours made in searching for camping-grounds, frequent crossings of the wide river to avoid drift stuff, &c. The descent of the Ohio had occupied about twenty-nine days, but many hours had been lost by storms keeping me in camp, and other unavoidable delays. As an offset to these stoppages, it must be remembered that the current, increased by freshets, was with me, and to it, as much as to the industrious arms of the rower, must be given the credit for the long route gone over in so short a time, by so small a boat.

Stern-wheel Western Tow-boat pushing Flatboats.

CHAPTER VI.

DESCENT OF THE MISSISSIPPI RIVER.

LEAVE CAIRO, ILLINOIS. — THE LONGEST RIVER IN THE WORLD. — BOOK GEOGRAPHY AND BOAT GEOGRAPHY. — CHICKASAW BLUFF. — MEETING WITH THE PARAKEETS. — FORT DONALDSON. — EARTHQUAKES AND LAKES. — WEIRD BEAUTY OF REELFOOT LAKE. — JOE ECKEL'S BAR. — SHANTY-BOAT COOKING. — FORT PILLOW. — MEMPHIS. — A NEGRO JUSTICE. — "DE COMMON LAW OB MISSISSIPPI."

MY floating home was now upon the broad Mississippi, which text-book geographers still insist upon calling "the Father of Waters — the largest river in North America." Its current was about one-third faster than that of its tributary, the Ohio. Its banks were covered with heavy forests, and for miles along its course the great wilderness was broken only by the half-tilled lands of the cotton-planter.

From Cairo southward the river is very tortuous, turning back upon itself as if imitating the convolutions of a crawling serpent, and following a channel of more than eleven hundred and fifty miles before its waters unite with those of the Gulf of Mexico. This country between the mouth of the Ohio and the Gulf of Mexico is

116   FOUR MONTHS IN A SNEAK-BOX.

truly the delta of the Mississippi, for the river north of Cairo cuts through table-lands, and is confined to its old bed; but below the mouth of the Ohio the great river persistently seeks for new channels, and, as we approach New Orleans, we discover branches which carry off a considerable portion of its water to the Gulf coast in southwestern Louisiana.

It is always with some degree of hesitation that I introduce geographical details into my books, as I well know that a taste for the study of physical geography has not been developed among my countrymen. Where among all our colleges is there a well-supported chair of physical geography occupied by an American? We sometimes hear of a "Professor of Geology and Physical Geography," but the last is only a sort of appendage — a tail — to the former. When a student of American geography begins the study in earnest, he discovers that our geographies are insufficient, are filled with errors, and that our maps possess a greater number of inaccuracies than truths. When he goes into the field to study the physical geography of his native land, he is forced to go through the disagreeable process of unlearning all he has been taught from the poor text-books of stay-at-home travellers and closet students, whose compilations have burdened his mind with errors. In despair he turns to the topographical charts and maps of the "United States Coast and Geodetic Survey," and of the "Engineer Corps of the United States Army," and in the truthful and interesting results of the practical labors of trained observers he takes courage as he enters anew his field of study. The cartographer of the shop economically constructs his unreliable maps to supply a cheap demand; and strange to say, though the results of the government surveys are freely at his disposal, he rarely makes use of them. It costs too much to alter the old map-plates, and but few persons will feel sufficiently interested to criticise the faults of his latest edition.

"How do you get the interior details?" I once asked the agent of one of the largest map establishments in the United States. "Oh," he answered, "when we cannot get township details from local surveys, we sling them in anyhow." An error once taught from our geographies and maps will remain an error for a generation, and our text-book geographers will continue to repeat it, for they do not travel over the countries they describe, and rarely adopt the results of scientific investigation. The most unpopular study in the schools of the United States is that of the geography of our country. It does not amount merely to a feeling of indifference, but in some colleges to a positive prejudice. The chief mountain-climbing club of America, counting among its members some of the best minds of our day, was confronted by this very prejudice. "If you introduce the study of physical geography in connection with the explorations of mountains, I will not join your association," said a gentleman living almost within the shadow of the buildings of our oldest university.

A committee of Chinese who called upon the school authorities of a Pacific-coast city, several years since, respectfully petitioned that "you will not waste the time of our children in teaching them geography. You say the world is ROUND; some of us say it is FLAT. What difference does it make to our business if it be round or flat? The study of geography will not help us to make money. It may do for Melican man, but it is not good for Chinese."

I once knew a chairman of the school trustees in a town in New Jersey to remove his daughters from the public school simply because the teacher insisted that it was his duty to instruct his pupils in the study of geography. "My boys may go to sea some day, and then geography may be of service to them," said this chairman to the teacher, "but if my daughters study it they will waste their time. Of what use can geography be to girls who will never command a vessel?"

While conscious that I may inflict an uninteresting chapter upon my reader who may have accompanied me with a commendable degree of patience so far upon my lonely voyage, I nevertheless feel it a duty to place on record a few facts that are well known to scientific men, if not to the writers of popular geographies, regarding the existence within the boundaries of our own country of the longest river in the world. It is time that the recognition of this fact should be established in every school in the United States. As this is a very important subject, let us examine it in detail.

THE MISSOURI IS THE LONGEST RIVER IN THE WORLD, AND THE MISSISSIPPI IS ONLY A BRANCH OF IT. The Mississippi River joins its current with that of the Missouri about two hundred miles above the mouth of the Ohio; consequently, as we are now to allow the largest stream (the Missouri) to bear its name from its source all the way to the Gulf of Mexico, it follows that the Ohio flows into the Missouri and not into the Mississippi River. The Missouri, and NOT the Mississippi, is the main stream of what has been called the Mississippi Basin. The Missouri, when taken from its fountain-heads of the Gallatin, Madison, and Red Rock lakes, or, if we take the Jefferson Fork as the principal tributary, has a length, from its source to its union with the Mississippi, of above three thousand miles. The United States Topographical Engineers have credited it with a length of two thousand nine hundred and eight miles, when divested of some of these tributary extensions. The same good authority gives the Mississippi a length of thirteen hundred and thirty miles from its source to its junction with the Missouri.

At this junction of the two rivers the Missouri has a mean discharge of one hundred and twenty thousand cubic feet of water per second, or one-seventh greater than that of the Mississippi, which has a mean discharge of one hundred and five thousand cubic feet per second. The Missouri drains five hundred and eighteen thousand square miles of territory, while the Mississippi drains only one hundred and sixty-nine thousand square miles. While the latter river has by far the greatest rainfall, the Missouri discharges the largest amount of water, and at the point of union of the two streams is from fifteen to seventeen hundred miles the longer of the two. Therefore, according to natural laws, the Missouri is the main stream, and the smaller and shorter Mississippi is only a branch of it. From the junction of the two rivers the current, increased by numerous tributaries, follows a crooked channel some thirteen hundred and fifty-five miles to the Gulf of Mexico. The Missouri, therefore, has a total length of four thousand three hundred and sixty-three miles, without counting some of its highest sources.

The learned Professor A. Guyot, in a treatise on physical geography, written for "A. J. Johnson's New Illustrated Family Atlas of the World," informs us that the Amazon River, the great drainer of the eastern Andes, is three thousand five hundred and fifty miles long, and is the LONGEST RIVER IN THE WORLD.

According to the figures used by me in reference to the Missouri and Mississippi, and which are the results of actual observations made by competent engineers, the reader will find, notwithstanding the statements made by our best geographers in regard to the length of the Amazon, that there is one river within the confines of our country which is eight hundred and thirteen miles longer than the Amazon, and is the longest though not the widest river in the world. The rivers of what is now called the Mississippi Basin drain one million two hundred and forty-four thousand square miles of territory, while the broader Amazon, with its many tributaries, drains the much larger area of two million two hundred and seventy-five thousand square miles.

A century after the Spaniard, De Soto, had discovered the lower Mississippi, and had been interred in its bed, a French interpreter, of

"Three Rivers," on the northern bank of the St. Lawrence River, named Jean Nicollet, explored one of the northern tributaries of the Mississippi. This was about the year 1639.

It was reserved for La Salle to make the first thorough exploration of the Mississippi. A few months after he had returned, alone, from his examination of the Ohio as far as the falls at Louisville, in 1669–70, this undaunted man followed the Great Lakes of the north to the western shore of Lake Michigan, and making a portage to a river, " evidently the Illinois," traversed it to its intersection with another river, " flowing from the north-west to the south-east," which river must have been the Mississippi, and which it is affirmed La Salle descended to the thirty-sixth degree of latitude, when he became convinced that this unexplored stream discharged itself, not into the Gulf of California, but into the Gulf of Mexico. So La Salle was the discoverer of the Illinois as well as of the Ohio; and during his subsequent visits to the Mississippi gave that river a thorough exploration.

My entrance to the Mississippi River was marked by the advent of severe squalls of wind and rain, which drove me about noon to the shelter of Island No. 1, where I dined, and where in half an hour the sun came out in all its glory. Many peculiar features of the Mississippi attracted my notice. Sand bars appeared above the water, and large flocks of ducks and geese rested upon them. Later, the high Chickasaw Bluff, the first and highest of a series which rise at intervals, like islands out of the low bottoms as far south as Natchez, came into view on the left side of the river. The mound-builders of past ages used these natural fortresses to hold at bay the fierce tribes of the north, and long afterward this Chickasaw Bluff played a conspicuous part in the civil war between the states. Columbus, a small village, and the terminus of a railroad, is at the foot of the heights.

A little lower down, and opposite Chalk Bluff, was a heavily wooded island, a part of the territory of the state of Illinois, and known as Wolf Island, or Island No. 5. At five o'clock in the afternoon I ran into a little thoroughfare on the eastern side of this island, and moored the duck-boat under its muddy banks. The wind increased to a gale before morning, and kept me through the entire day, and until the following morning, an unwilling captive. Reading and cooking helped to while away the heavy hours, but having burned up all the dry wood I could find, I was forced to seek other quarters, which were found in a romantic stream that flowed out of a swamp and joined the Mississippi just one mile above Hickman, on the Kentucky side. Having passed a comfortable night, and making an early start without breakfast, I rowed rapidly over a smooth current to the stream called Bayou du Chien Creek, in which I made a very attractive camp among the giant sycamores, sweet-gums, and cotton-woods. The warm sunshine penetrated into this sheltered spot, while the wind had fallen to a gentle zephyr, and came in refreshing puffs through the lofty trees. Here birds were numerous, and briskly hopped about my fire while I made an omelet and boiled some wheaten grits.

In this retired haunt of the birds I remained through the whole of that sunny Sunday, cooking my three meals, and reading my Bible, as became a civilized man. While enjoying this immunity from the disturbing elements of the great public thoroughfare, the river, curious cries were borne upon the wind above the tall tree-tops like the chattering calls of parrots, to which my ear had become accustomed in the tropical forests of Cuba. As the noise grew louder with the approach of a feathered flock of visitors, and the screams of the birds became more discordant, I peered through the branches of the forest to catch a glimpse of what I had searched for through many hundred miles of wilderness since my boyhood, but what had so far eluded my eager eyes. I felt certain these strange cries must come from the Carolina Parrot, or Parakeet (*Conurus Carolinensis*), which, though once numerous in all the country west of the Alleghanies as far north

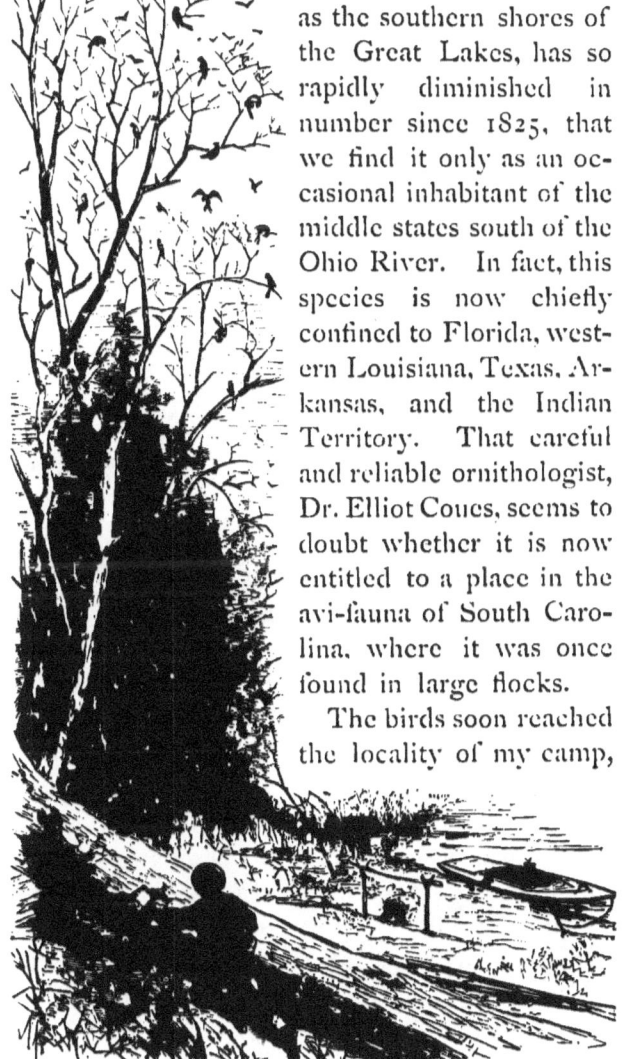

as the southern shores of the Great Lakes, has so rapidly diminished in number since 1825, that we find it only as an occasional inhabitant of the middle states south of the Ohio River. In fact, this species is now chiefly confined to Florida, western Louisiana, Texas, Arkansas, and the Indian Territory. That careful and reliable ornithologist, Dr. Elliot Coues, seems to doubt whether it is now entitled to a place in the avi-fauna of South Carolina, where it was once found in large flocks.

The birds soon reached the locality of my camp,

MEETING WITH THE PARAKEETS.

and circling through the clear, warm atmosphere above the tree-tops, they gradually settled lower and lower, suspiciously scanning my fire, screaming as though their little throats would burst, while the sunlight seemed to fill the air with the reflections of the green, gold, and carmine of their brilliant plumage. They dropped into the foliage of the grove, and for a moment were as quiet as though life had departed from them, while I kept close to my hiding-place behind an immense fallen tree, from beneath which I could watch my feathery guests.

The bodies of the adult birds were emerald green, with bright blue reflections. The heads were yellow, excepting the forehead and cheeks, which were scarlet. The large, thick, and hooked bill was white, as well as the bare orbital space around the eye. The feet were a light flesh-color. The length from tip of bill to end of tail was about fourteen inches. The young birds could be easily distinguished from the adults by their short tails and the uniform coat of green, while in some cases the frontlet of scarlet was just beginning to show itself. The adult males were longer than the females.

The Carolina Parrot does not put on its bright-yellow hues until the second season, and its most brilliant tints do not come to perfection until the bird is fully two years old. They feed upon the seeds of the cockle-burrs, which grow in abandoned fields of the planter, as well as upon fruits of all kinds, much of which they waste in their uneconomical method of eating. The low alluvial bottom-lands of the river, where pecan and beech nuts abound, are their favorite hunting-grounds.

It is singular that Alexander Wilson, and, in fact, all the naturalists, except Audubon, who have written about this interesting bird, have failed to examine its nest and eggs. By the unsatisfactory manner in which Audubon refers to the nidification of this parakeet, one is led to believe that even he did not become personally acquainted with its breeding habits.

The offer by Mr. Maynard of one dollar for every parrot's egg delivered to him, induced a Florida cracker to cut a path into a dense cypress swamp at Dunn's Lake, about the middle of the month of June. The hunter was occupied three days in the enterprise, and returned much disgusted with the job. He had found the nests of the parakeets in the hollow cypress-trees of the swamp, but he was too late to secure the eggs, as they were hatched, and the nests filled with young birds. The number of young in each nest seemed to leave no doubt of the fact of several adults nesting in one hole. Probably the eggs are laid about the last of May.

These birds are extremely gregarious, and

have been seen at sunset to cluster upon the trunk of a gigantic cypress like a swarm of bees. One after another slowly crawls through a hole into the cavity until it is filled up, while those who are not so fortunate as to obtain entrance, or reserved seats, cling to the outside of the trunk with their claws, and keep their position through the night chiefly by hooking the tip of the upper mandible of the beak into the bark of the tree. The backwoodsmen confidently assert that they have found as many as twenty eggs of a greenish white in a single hollow of a cypress-tree; and as it is generally supposed, judging from the known habits of other species of this genus, that the Carolina Parrot lays only two eggs, but few naturalists doubt that these birds nest in companies. It is a very difficult task to find the nests of parrots in the West Indies, some of them building in the hollowed top of the dead trunk of a royal palm which has been denuded of its branches; and there, upon the unprotected summit of a single column eighty feet in height, without any shelter from tropical storms, the Cuban Parrot rears its young.

The Carolina Parrot is the only one of this species which may truly be said to be a permanent resident of our country. The Mexican species are sometimes met with along the southwestern boundaries of the United States, but they emigrate only a few miles northward of their own regions. The salt-licks in the great button-wood bottoms along the Mississippi were once the favorite resorts of these birds, and they delighted to drink the saline water. It is to be regretted that so interesting a bird should have been so ruthlessly slaughtered where they were once so numerous. Only the young birds are fit to eat, but we read in the accounts of our pioneer naturalists that from eight to twenty birds were often killed by the single discharge of a gun, and that as the survivors would again and again return to the lurking-place of their destroyer, attracted by the distressing cries of their wounded comrades, the unfeeling sportsman would continue his work of destruction until more than half of a large flock would be exterminated. This interesting parakeet may, during the next century, pass out of existence, and be known to our descendants as the Great Auk (*Alca impennis*) is now known to us, as a very rare specimen in the museums of natural history.

On Monday, January 3, I rowed out of the Bayou du Chien, and soon reached the town of Hickman, Kentucky, where I invested in a basketful of mince-pies, that deleterious compound so dear to every American heart. A large flatboat, built upon the most primitive principles, and without cabin of any kind, was leaving the landing, evidently bound on a fishing-cruise, for her hold was filled with long nets and barrels of provisions. A large roll of canvas, to be used as a protection against rain, was stowed in one end of the odd craft, while at the other end was a large and very rusty cooking-stove, with a joint of pipe rising above it. The crew of fishermen labored at a pair of long sweeps until the flat reached the strong current, when they took in their oars, and, clustering about the stove, filled their pipes, and were soon reclining at their ease on the pile of nets, apparently as well satisfied with their tub as Diogenes was with his. As I rowed past them, they roused themselves into some semblance of interest, and gazed upon the little white boat, so like a pumpkin-seed in shape, which soon passed from their view as it disappeared down the wide Mississippi.

There was something in the appearance of that rough flatboat that made me wish I had hailed her quiet crew; for, strange to say, they did not send after me a shower of slang phrases and uncouth criticisms, the usual prelude to conversation among flatboat-men when they desire to cultivate the acquaintance of a fellow-voyager. In fact, it was rather startling not to have the usual greeting, and I wondered why I heard no friendly expressions, such as, "Here, you river thief, haul alongside and report yourself! Whar did you come from? Come and take a pull at the bottle! It's prime stuff, I tell ye; will kill a man at forty paces," &c. The rusty stove was as strong an attraction as the quiet crew, as I thought how convenient it would be to run alongside of the old boat and utilize it for my culinary purposes. The unwonted silence, however, proved conclusively that some refined instinct, unknown to the usual crews of such boats, governed these voyagers, and I feared to intrude upon so dignified a party.

Descending a long straight reach, after making a run of twenty-three miles, I crossed the limits of Kentucky, and, entering Tennessee, saw on its shore, in a deep bend of the river, the site of Fort Donaldson, while opposite to it lay the low Island No. 10. Both of these places were full of interest, being the scenes of conflict in our civil war. The little white sneak-box glided down another long bend, over the wrecks of seven steamboats, and passed New Madrid, on the Missouri shore. The mouth of Reelfoot Bayou then opened before me, a creek which conducts the waters from the weird recesses of one of the most interesting lakes in America, — a lake which was the immediate result of a disastrous series of disturbances generally referred to as the New Madrid ·earthquakes, and which took place in

1811-13. Much of the country in the vicinity of New Madrid and Fort Donaldson was involved in these serious shocks. Swamps were upheaved and converted into dry uplands, while cultivated uplands were depressed below the average water level, and became swamps or ponds of water. The inhabitants, deprived of their little farms, were reduced to such a stage of suffering as to call for aid from government, and new lands were granted them in place of their fields which had sunk out of sight. Hundreds of square miles of territory were lost during the two years of terrestrial convulsions.

The most interesting effect of the subsidence of the land was the creation of Reelfoot Lake, the fluvial entrance to which is from the tortuous Mississippi some forty-five miles below Hickman, Kentucky. The northern portion of the lake is west of and a short distance from Fort Donaldson, about twenty miles from Hickman, by the river route. As Reelfoot Lake possesses the peculiar flora and characteristics of a multitude of other swamp-lakes throughout the wilderness of the lower Mississippi valley, I cannot better describe them all than by giving to the reader a description of that lake, written by an intelligent observer who visited the locality in 1874.

"Nothing," he says, "could well exceed the singularity of the view that meets the eye as one comes out of the shadows of the forest on to the border of this sheet of water. From the marshy shore spreads out the vast extent of the seemingly level carpet of vegetation, — a mat of plants, studded over with a host of beautiful flowers; through this green prairie runs a maze of waterways, some just wide enough for a pirogue, some widening into pools of darkened water. All over this expanse rise the trunks of gigantic cypresses, shorn of all their limbs, and left like great obelisks, scattered so thickly that the distance is lost in the forest of spires. Some are whitened and some blackened by decay and fire; many rise to a hundred feet or more above the lake. The branches are all gone, save in a few more gigantic forms, whose fantastic remnants of the old forest arches add to the illusion of monumental ruin which forces itself on the mind. The singularity of the general effect is quite matched by the wonder of the detail.

"Taking the solitary dug-out canoe, or pirogue, as it is called in the vernacular, we paddled out into the tangle of water-paths. The green carpet, studded with yellow and white, that we saw from the shores, resolved itself into a marvellously beautiful and varied vegetation. From the tangle of curious forms the eye selects two noble flowers: our familiar northern waterlily, grown to a royal form, its flowers ten inches broad, and its floating pads near a foot across;

and another grander flower, the Wampapin lily, the queen of American flowers. It is worth a long journey to see this shy denizen of our swamps in its full beauty. From the midst of its great floating leaves, which are two feet or more in diameter, rise two large leaves borne upon stout foot-stalks that bring them a yard above the water; from between these elevated leaves rises to a still greater height the stem of the flower. The corolla itself is a gold-colored cup a foot in diameter, lily-like in a general way, but with a large pestle-shaped ovary rising in the centre of the flower, in which are planted a number of large seeds, the 'pins' of Wampapin. These huge golden cups are poised on their stems, and wave in the breeze above great wheel-like leaves, while the innumerable white lilies fill in the spaces between, and enrich the air with their perfume.

"Slowly we crept through the tangled paths until we were beyond the sight of shore, in the perfect silence of this vast ruined temple, on every side the endless obelisks of the decaying cypress, and as far as the eye could see were ranged the numberless nodding bells of the yellow lilies, and the still-eyed white stars below them. While we waited in the coming evening, the silence was so deep, the whir of a bald eagle's wings, as he swept through the air, was audible from afar. The lonely creature sat on the peak of one of the wooden towers over our boat, and looked curiously down upon us. The waters seemed full of fish, and, indeed, the lake has much celebrity as a place for such game. We could see them creeping through the mazes of the water-forest, in a slow, blind way, not a bit like the dance of the northern creatures of the active waters of our mountain streams.

"There is something of forgetfulness in such a scene, a sense of a world far away, with no path back to it. One might fall to eating our Wampapin lily, as did the Chickasaws of old, and find in it the all-forgetting lotus, for it is, indeed, the brother of the lotus of the Nile. We do not know how far these forgotten savages found the mystic influence of the Nilotic lotus in these queenly flowers of the swamps, but tradition says that they ate not only the seeds, but the bulbous roots, which the natives aver are quite edible. So we, too, can claim a lotus-eating race, and are even able to try the soul-subduing powers of the plant at our will.

"There is something in the weight of life and death in these swamps that subdues the mind, and makes the steps we take fall as in a dream. It was not easy to fix a basis for memory with the pencil, and recollection shapes a vast sensation of strangeness, a feeling as if one had trod for a moment beyond the brink of time, rather than any distinct images."

At sunset I came upon Joe Eckel's Bar, — not the fluvial establishment so much resorted to by people ashore, — but a genuine Mississippi sandbar, or shoal, which was covered with two feet of water, and afforded lodgment for a heavy raft of trees that had floated upon it. The island was also partly submerged, but I found a cove with a sandy beach on its lower end; and running into the little bay, I staked the boat in one foot of water, much to the annoyance of flocks of wildfowl which circled about me at intervals all night. The current had been turbid during the day, and to supply myself with drinking-water it was necessary to fill a can from the river and wait for the sediment to precipitate itself before it was fit for use. Fifty-six miles were logged for the day's row.

In the morning Joe Eckel's Bar was alive with geese and ducks, cackling a lusty farewell as I pushed through the drift stuff and resumed my voyage down the swelling river.

The reaches were usually five miles in length, though some of them were very much longer. Sometimes deposits of sand and vegetable matter will build up a small island adjacent to a large one, and then a dense thicket of cotton-wood brush takes possession of it, and assists materially in resisting the encroachments of the current. These little, low islands, covered with thickets, are called tow-heads, and the maps of the Engineer Corps of the United States distinguish them from the originally numbered islands in the following manner: "Island No. 18," and "Tow Head of Island No. 18."

In addition to the numbered islands, which commence with Island No. 1, below the mouth of the Ohio, and end with Island No. 125, above the inlet to Bayou La Fourche, in Louisiana, there are many which have been named after their owners. During one generation a planter may live upon a peninsula comprising many thousand acres, with his cotton-fields and houses fronting on the Mississippi. The treacherous current of this river may suddenly cut a new way across his estate inland at a distance of two miles from his home. As the gradual change goes on, he looks from the windows of his house upon a new scene. He no longer has the rapid flowing river, enlivened by the passage of steamboats and other craft; but before him is a sombre bayou, or crescent-shaped lake, whose muddy waters are almost motionless. He was the proprietor of Needham's Point, he is now the owner of Needham's *Island*, and lives in the quiet atmosphere of the backwoods of Tennessee.

This day's row carried me past heavily-wooded shores, cotton-fields with some of the cotton still unpicked; past the limits of Missouri on the left side, and into the wild state of Arkansas at Island No. 21. I finally camped on Island

No. 26, in a half submerged thicket, after a row of fifty-eight miles.

As there were many flat and shanty boats floating southward, I adopted a plan by means of which my dinners were frequently cooked with little trouble to myself or others. About an hour before noon I gazed about within the narrow horizon for one of those floating habitations, and rowing alongside, engaged in conversation with its occupants. The men would tell what success they had had in collecting the skins of wild animals (though silent upon the subject of pig-stealing), while the women would talk of the homes they had left, and sigh for the refinements and comforts of " city life," by which they meant their former existence in some small town on the upper river. While we were exchanging our budgets of information I would obtain the consent of the presiding goddess of the boat to stew my ambrosia upon her stove, the sneak-box floating the while alongside its tub-like companion. Many a half hour was spent in this way; and, besides the comfort of a hot dinner, there were advantages afforded for the study of characters not to be found elsewhere.

These peculiar boats, so often encountered, found refuge in the frequent cut-offs behind the many islands of the river; for besides those islands which have been numbered, new ones are forming every year. At times, when the water is very high, the current will cut a new route across the low isthmus, or neck, of a peninsula, around which sweeps a long reach of the main channel, leaving the tortuous bend which it has deserted to be gradually filled up with snags, deposits of alluvium, and finally to be carpeted with a vegetable growth. In some cases, as the stream works away to the eastward or westward, it remains an inland crescent-shaped lake, numbers of which are to be found in the wilderness many miles from the parent stream. I have known the channel of the Mississippi to be shortened twenty miles during a freshet, and a steamboat which had followed the great ox-bow bend in ascending the river, on its return trip shot through the new cut-off of a few hundred feet in length, upon fifteen feet of water where a fortnight before a forest had been growing.

The area of land on both sides of the Mississippi subjected to annual overflow, like the country surrounding the Nile, in Egypt, is very large. There are localities thirty or forty miles away from the river where the height of the overflow of the previous year is plainly registered upon the trunks of the trees by a coating of yellow mud, which sometimes reaches as high as a man's head. This great region possesses vast tracts of rich land, as well as millions of acres of low swamps and bayou bottoms.

The traveller, the hunter, the zoölogist, and

the botanist can all find here in these rich river bottoms a ready reward for any inconveniences experienced on the route. Strange types of half-civilized whites, game enough to satisfy the most rapacious, beast and bird of peculiar species, and over all the immense forests of cypress, sweet-gums, Spanish-oaks, tulip-trees, sycamores, cotton-woods, white-oaks, &c., while the most delicate wild-flowers " waste their sweetness on the desert air." Across all this natural beauty the whisper of desolation casts a cloud, for here during most of the year arises the health-destroying malaria.

Upon the high lands the squatter builds his log cabin, and makes his clearing where the rich soil and warm sun assist his rude agricultural labors, and he is rewarded with a large crop of maize and sweet potatoes. These, with bacon from his herd of wandering pigs, give sustenance to his family of children, who, hatless and bonnetless, roam through the woods until the sun bleaches their hair to the color of flax. With tobacco, whiskey, and ammunition for himself, and an ample supply of snuff for his wife, he drags out an indolent existence; but he is the pioneer of American civilization, and as he migrates every few years to a more western wilderness, his lands are frequently occupied by a more intelligent and industrious class, and his improvements are improved upon. The new-comer, with greater ambition and more ample means, raises cotton instead of corn, and depends upon the Ohio valley for a supply of that cereal.

Wednesday, January 5th, was a sunny and windy day. The Arkansas shores afforded me a protection from the wind as I rowed down towards Fort Pillow, which, according to the map of the United States Engineer Corps, is situated upon Chickasaw Bluff No. 1, though some writers and map-makers designate the Columbus Bluff, below the mouth of the Ohio, as the first Chickasaw Bluff. The site of Fort Pillow is about thirty feet above the water. It commands the low country opposite, and two reaches of the river for a long distance. A little below the fort, on the right bank of the river, was an extensive cotton-field, still white with the flossy cellulose. Here I landed under the shady trees, and gathered cotton, the result of peaceful labor. Truly had the sword been beaten into the ploughshare, and the spear into a pruning-hook, for above me frowned down Fort Pillow, the scene of the terrible negro massacre in our late war. Now the same sun shone so brightly upon the graves scattered here and there, and warmed into life the harvest sown in peace.

At intervals I caught glimpses of negro cabins, with their clearings, and their little crops of cotton glistening in the sun. The island tow-heads and sand-bars were numerous, and in places the

Mississippi broadened into lake-like areas, while the yellow current, now heavily charged with mud, arose in height every hour. The climate was growing delightful. It was like a June day in the northern states. Each soft breeze of the balmy atmosphere seemed to say, as I felt its strange, fascinating influence, "You are nearing the goal!" The shadows of the twilight found me safely ensconced behind the lower end of Island No. 33, where in the bayou between it and the Tennessee shore I lazily watched fair Luna softly emerging from the clouds, and lending to the grand old woods her tender light.

I proceeded southward the next day, rowing comfortably after having divested myself of all superfluous apparel. The negroes, on their one-horse plantations, gave a hearty hail as I passed, but I noted here a feature I had remarked when upon my "Voyage of the Paper Canoe," on the eastern coast. It was the silence in which these people worked. The merry song of the darky was no longer heard as in the "auld lang syne." Then he was the slave of a white master. Now he is the slave of responsibilities and cares which press heavily upon his heretofore unthinking nature. To-day he has a future IF he can make it.

During the day, a lone woman on a shanty-boat, which was securely fastened to an old stump, volunteered much information in regard to " her man," and the money he expected to receive for the skins he had been collecting during the winter. She said he would get in New Orleans thirty-five cents apiece for his coonskins, one dollar for minks, and one dollar and a half each for beaver and otter skins. She informed me that the sunken country below Memphis, on the Arkansas side, was full of deer and bears.

By rowing briskly I was able to pass Memphis, the principal river port of Tennessee, at five o'clock in the afternoon. This flourishing city is situated upon one of the Chickasaw bluffs, thirty feet above the river. At the base of the bluff a bed of sandstone projects into the water, it being the only known stratum of rock along the river between Cairo and the Gulf. From the Ohio River to Vicksburg, a distance of six hundred miles, it is asserted that there is no other site for a commercial city: so Memphis, though isolated, enjoys this advantage, which has, in fact, made her the busy cotton-shipping port she is to-day. Her population is about forty thousand. As Memphis is connected by railroads with the towns and villages of all the back country, in addition to her water advantages, she may be called the business centre of an immense area of cultivated land. The view of the city from the river is striking. Her esplanade,' several hundred feet in width, sweeps along the bluff, and is covered with large warehouses.

Pushing steadily southward, I looked out anxiously for a good camping-ground for the night, feeling that a rest had been well earned, for I had rowed sixty-one miles that day. Soon after passing Horn Lake Bend, the thickets of Crow Island attracted my attention, for along the muddy, crumbling bank the mast of a little sloop arose from the water, and a few feet inland the bright blaze of a camp-fire shone through the mists of evening. A cheery hail of, " I say, stranger, pull in, and tie up here," came from a group of three roughly-clad men, who were bending over the coals, busily engaged in frying salt pork and potatoes. The swift current forced me into an eddy close to the camp. One of the men caught my painter, and drew me close under the lee of their roughly constructed sloop of about two tons' burden. When seated by the bright fire, " the boys " told me their history. They were out of work; so, investing sixty dollars in an old sloop, putting on board a barrel of pork, a barrel of flour, some potatoes, coffee, salt, and molasses, (which cargo was to last three months,) they started to cut canes in the canebrakes of White River, Arkansas. These canes were to be utilized as fishing-poles, and being carefully assorted and fastened into bundles, were to be shipped to Cincinnati by steamer, and from there by rail to Cleveland, Ohio, where Mr. Farrar, their consignee, would dispose of them for the party.

They had come down the Mississippi from Keokuk, Iowa, having left that place December 13th, and had experienced various delays, having several times been frozen up in creeks. They would be able to cut, during the winter, twenty-five thousand fishing-rods, enough, one would think, to clear the streams of all the finny tribe. Mr. E. C. Stirling, of Painesville, Ohio, was the principal of the party, and I found him an unusually intelligent young man. He had passed the previous winter alone upon White River in an experimental sort of way, and had succeeded in obtaining the finest lot of fishing-rods that had ever been sent north.

There was so much to be talked about, and so many experiences in voyaging to be exchanged, that we decided to remain that night on Crow Island, as there was not much risk of my being deluged by the passing steamers, for it was evident that the steamboat channel hugged the bank of the opposite side of the river. I took ashore chocolate, canned milk, white sugar, and some of the Hickman mince-pies, while the boys rolled logs of wood on to the fire, and buried potatoes in the hot ashes. Stirling went to work at bread-making, and putting his dough in one of those flat-bottomed, three-legged, iron-covered vessels, which my reader will now recognize as the bake-pan, or Dutch oven, placed it on the coals, and loaded its cover with hot embers. The potatoes were soon baked, and possessed a mealiness not usually found in those served up by the family cook. Stirling's bread was a success, and my chocolate disappeared down the throats of the hearty western boys as fast as its scalding temperature would admit.

Stirling told me of his life during the previous winter in the swamps of White River. On one occasion, a steamer having lost her anchor near his locality, the captain of the boat offered to reward Stirling liberally if he would recover the lost property; so, while the captain was making his up-river trip, the Ohio boy worked industriously dredging for the cable. He found it; and under-running the heavy rope, raised it and the anchor. When the steamer returned to Beteley's Landing, Stirling delivered the anchor and coil of rope to the captain, who, intending to defraud the young man of the promised reward, ordered the mate to "cast off the lines." The gong had signalled the engineer to get under way, but not quick enough to escape the young salvage-owner, who grasped the coil of rope and dragged it ashore, shouting to the captain, "You may keep your anchor, but I will keep your cable as salvage, to which I am entitled for my trouble in saving your property."

A few days later, Stirling, wishing to know whether he could legally hold his salvage fees, paddled down to Bolivia, a small town in the state of Mississippi, to obtain legal advice in regard to the matter. The white people referred him to a negro justice of the peace, whom they assured him "had more law-larnin' than any white man in the diggings, and is the honestest nigger in these parts." Being ushered into the presence of a dignified negro, the cutter of fishing-poles informed the "justice" that he desired legal advice in a case of salvage.

"Dat's rite, dat's berry good, sah," said the negro; "now you jes' set rite down he'ar, and macadimize de case to me. I gibs ebery man justice — no turnin' to de rite or de left hand."

Stirling stated the facts, the colored justice puckering up his shiny brow, and his whole countenance expressing perplexity. "I want to know," said the possessor of the cable, "whether I can legally hold on to the coil of rope; use it or sell it for my own benefit, without being sued by the captain, who broke his agreement with me."

The colored man attempted to consult a volume containing a digest of laws; but being an indifferent reader, he handed it to Stirling, saying, "Now you, sah, jes look froo de book and find de larnin' on de case." Having carefully consulted the book, Stirling declared he found nothing that covered the salvage question in regard to cables and anchors. "Nuffin at all? nuffin at all?" asked the justice, seriously.

"Now let me rest de case a moment fur perspection." As he pondered on a case which could not be decided by precedent, an idea seemed to lighten his sable features, for he straightened himself up and exclaimed, "Den I will gib you an opinion. Dis court will apply de *common law* ob de state ob Mississippi; and dis is it: '*What you hab, dat you keep!*' Dis is de teachings ob de bar, de bench, and de code."

Having received this august opinion, Stirling paddled back in his dug-out canoe to the swamps of Arkansas, much amused, if not impressed, with the negro's simple method of successfully disposing of a case, so unlike the usual procrastinating customs which fetter the courts presided over by learned white men.

Early on the following day I left the camp of the Ohio boys, for their progress was assisted by a large sail, and it would have been impossible for me to have kept up with them. They also travelled by night as well as by day, keeping one man at the helm while the others slept. At the lower end of Crow Island I left the state of Tennessee and entered the confines of Mississippi, having Arkansas still on my right hand.

During part of the afternoon I accompanied a flatboat-man and his family as far as Island No. 60, where we ran into a little bayou for the night. There was a rowdy settlement here, and many rough fellows were in the streets, shouting and fighting; but as I entered the bayou after dark, and secreted myself in the half submerged swamp, no one knew of my being there: so I felt safe from insult. The owner of the flatboat with whom I had entered the bayou intended to fish for the settlement. He was an old trapper, and informed me that bears were still abundant in parts of Alabama. He said the Canada Goose bred in small numbers in the lakes of the back country. His experiences with human nature found expression in his advice to me when I parted from him the next morning. "Don't leave your boat alone for half an hour in these parts, stranger. Niggers is bad, and some white folks too." Promising my new friend to look out for number one, I waved an adieu to him and his, and went on my solitary way.

CHAPTER VII.

DESCENT OF THE MISSISSIPPI TO NEW ORLEANS.

A FLATBOAT BOUND FOR TEXAS. — A FLAT-MAN ON RIVER PHYSICS. — ADRIFT AND ASLEEP. — SEEING THE EARTH'S LITTLE MOON. — VICKSBURGH. — JEFFERSON DAVIS'S COTTON PLANTATION, AND ITS NEGRO OWNER. — DYING IN HIS BOAT. — HOW TO CIVILIZE CHINESE. — A SWIM OF ONE HUNDRED AND TWENTY MILES ON THE MISSISSIPPI. — TWENTY-FOUR HOURS IN THE WATER. — ARRIVAL IN THE CRESCENT CITY.

DURING the afternoon, while rowing out of the cut-off behind an island, I caught sight of a flatboat floating in the contour of a distant bend. There was something familiar in her appearance, and, as I drew nearer, I recognized the pile of nets, the rusty stove, and the civil but silent crew. She was the same flat which had left Hickman, Kentucky, the morning I had departed from that town with my basket of pies. This time the crew seemed like old friends. River life makes all men equal. A pleasant hail now greeted me, and the duck-boat was soon moored to the side of the flat. As we floated along with the current, sipping our coffee, the captain told me his history. The war had reduced him from affluence to poverty, and in order to support his family, he had built a scow and penetrated the weird waters of Reelfoot Lake, from which he was able, for several years, to supply the citizens of Hickman with excellent fish. The enterprise was a novelty at that time, and there being no competition, he made four thousand dollars the first year. After that others went into the business, and it became profitless. His mind was now bent upon a new field. Hearing that the people of northern Texas were destitute of a regular fish-market, he had provisioned his flat for a winter's campaign, and intended floating with his men down to the mouth of Red River, where he would be towed by a steamer through the state of Louisiana to the northeastern end of Texas. There entering Caddo Lake, which is from fifty to sixty miles long, and where game, ducks, and fish abound, he would camp upon the shores and set his nets. The railroads which penetrated that section would afford means for the rapid distribution of his fish.

The party, anxious to arrive at their scene of action, floated night and day. The society of an educated man was so delightful at the time that I remained beside the flat all night. A lantern was hung above the bow of the boat to show the pilots of steamers our position. Whenever one of these disturbers of our peace passed the flat, I was obliged to cast off and pull into the stream, as the swash would almost ingulf me if I remained tied to the side of the large boat. I could only sleep by snatches, for just as I would be dropping off into the land of Nod, the watch upon the flat would call out, "Here comes another steamer," which was the signal for me to take to my oars.

The next day was Sunday, but the flat kept on her way. I cooked my meals upon the rusty stove, and we floated side by side, conversing hour after hour. The low banks of the river showed the presence of levees, or artificial dikes, built to keep out the freshets. Upon these dikes the grass was putting forth its tender blades, and the willows were bursting into leaf. We passed White River and the Arkansas, both of which pour their waters out of the great wilderness of the state of Arkansas. Below the mouth of the last-named river was the town of Napoleon, with its deserted houses, the most forlorn aspect that had yet met my eye. The banks were caving into the river day by day. Houses had fallen into the current, which was undermining the town. Here and there chimneys were standing in solitude, the buildings having been torn down and removed to other localities to save them from the insatiable maw of the river. These pointed upward like so many warning cenotaphs of the river's treachery, and contrasted strongly in the mind's eye with the many happy family circles which had once gathered at their bases around the cheerful hearths.

About ten o'clock in the forenoon the proprietor of the flatboat decided, as it was Sunday, to run into a bend of the river and tie up for the day. That night the banks caved in so frequently that I was in danger of being entombed in my sneak-box; and I rejoiced when morning came and the dangerous quarters were left behind. My flatboat companions made known to me a curious feature of river physics well known to the great floating population of the western streams. If you start with a flatboat or raft of timber from any point on the Ohio or Mississippi rivers at the moment a rise in the water takes place, and continue floating night and day without interruption, you will in a few days *overrun* the effects of the rise, or freshet, and get below it. A little later you will discover, at some point a few hundred miles down-stream, that the river is just commencing to swell, as the result of the freshet upon which you originally started.

During Tuesday and Wednesday of January 11 and 12, I was at times with the flat, and at times miles away from it. Near Skipwith Landing, Mississippi, we passed large and well-cultivated cotton-plantations, but the river country in its vicinity was almost a wilderness.

My sleep had been much broken by night-travelling, and about nine o'clock on Wednesday evening I fastened my boat to the flat, and determined to have two or three hours of refreshing slumber. An hour's peaceful rest followed, and then a snorting, screeching stern-wheel steamer crossed the river with its tow of barges, and demoralized all my surroundings, driving me against the flat, and shooting water over the deck of my craft. Only half awake, I cast off from the flat, and thought that I was rowing down-river as usual; but I had dropped back into my nest just for *one* moment, and was in the land of Nod. I felt in my sleep that I was floating down the Mississippi. I was conscious that I had left the flatboat, and that steamers, snags, and eddies must be looked out for, or disaster would come quickly upon me.

I knew I *was* asleep, and tried to rouse myself. I seemed to be watching the moon, which shone with silver glory upon the glistening waters, and made the dark forests, rising wall-like on the banks, even darker by comparison. Then I seemed to enter the fields of astronomy, moving through the atmosphere still pulling at my oars. My mental vision stretched across the Atlantic, and enveloped the old astronomical observatory of the French city of Toulouse. It was the hour of sunset, and the learned Director Petit was at his post carefully adjusting his telescope, eager with the hope of identifying an undiscovered meteorite, the presence of which had been suggested by certain disturbances among the celestial bodies. The savant carefully pointed his instrument to the neighboring regions of the setting sun, when suddenly I saw him start, and heard him mutter, like a philosopher of old, "Eureka, I have found it!" Only a ray of light had flashed across the field of his telescope as an asteroid shot into the gloam of the sun. Its movements were so rapid, its disappearance so sudden, that it was impossible to obtain another glimpse of the unknown body. The god of day had enveloped the satellite in curtains of powerful light, so that no eye but that of its Creator could gaze again that night upon the little stranger which had been seen for the first time by man.

The astronomer moved away from his instrument and the wonderful machinery that had guided it in its search for the asteroid, slowly muttering: "The sun robbed me of a second sight of my discovery, yet only at this hour can I hope to get a glimpse of it. The difficulties attending this observation are the tremendous velocity with which it travels, its very small mass, and the rapidity with which, at the hour of sunset, it passes into the shadow of the earth. I will, however, calculate its orbit, and search for it again; for I have this evening seen what no human eye has ever beheld, I HAVE SEEN THE EARTH'S LITTLE MOON." While I watched, entranced, the astronomer, aided by his assistants, labored over multitudes of figures hour after hour, day after day; and from these computations an orbit was constructed for the Little Moon.

Their work was finished; and as they left the observatory, a shadow, which had thrown its dark outlines here and there about the professor during his investigations, assumed the proportions of a man; and I saw for an instant the brilliant French writer, Jules Verne, while a voice in the musical language of France fell upon my ear: "Ah, Monsieur, it IS true, then, and we have a second moon, which must revolve round our planet once in three hours and twenty minutes, at a distance of only four thousand six hundred and fifty miles from our terrestrial abiding-place!"

Then the professor and his figures faded out of my vision; and I seemed to be observing a little moon revolving with lightning rapidity round the earth, while I felt that I had, in some way, been sucked into its orbit, and was whirling around with it. Suddenly, with a keen sense of danger pervading my whole nervous system, I awoke. Yes, it was a dream! I was in my boat, gazing up into the serene heavens, where the larger moon was tranquilly following her orbit, while I was being whirled round in a strong eddy under a high bank of the river, with the giant trees frowning down upon me as though rebuking a careless boatman for being caught napping. And where was the flat? I gazed across the wide river into the quiet atmosphere now full of the bright light of the moon,—but no boat could be seen; and from the wild forest alone came back an echo to my shouts of "Flatboat, ahoy!" For hours I rowed in search of my *compagnon de voyage*.

As I hurried along the reaches of the river, every island cut-off, every tow-head, and every nigger-head, was inspected. I even peered into the mouths of dark bayous, thinking the party might have tied up to await my arrival, as the larger and deeper craft floated faster than my little boat. All search, however, proved fruitless. No flat could be seen. My endeavors to find my quondam friends had been so absorbing that things above my line of vision were not observed, when suddenly the bright moonlight revealed to my astonished eyes a lofty city apparently suspended in the heavens. By the aid of a candle and my map I discovered that the city and fortifications of Vicksburgh were close at hand, and that it was four o'clock in the morning.

My first view of Vicksburgh was over a long, low point of land, across the base of which was excavated, during the investment of the city by United States troops in the late war, "General Grant's Cut-off." By using this cut-off, light-draught gunboats could ascend or descend the river without passing near the batteries of the fortified city. This point, or peninsula, which the Union forces held, is on the Louisiana shore, opposite Vicksburgh. A year or two after I passed that interesting locality, a Natchez newspaper, in describing the change made in the channel of the Mississippi River, said that "St. Joseph and Rodney have been left inland; Vicksburgh is left on a lake; Delta will soon be washed away; a cut-off has been made at Grand Gulf, and by another season Port Gibson and Claiborne County will have no landing."

Floating quietly in my little boat, and gazing at the city upon the heights, I thought of the bloody scenes there enacted, and of the statement made that "three hundred tons of lead, mostly bullets, had been collected in and around the town since the close of the war." This lead, it has been asserted, would make nine million six hundred thousand ounce-balls. Of course, in this statement there is no mention of the lead buried deep in the earth, and that lost in the river.

Entering a great bend, the swift current swept me so rapidly past Vicksburgh that a few moments later I was among the islands and tow-heads of the river. At noon the plantation of Mr. Jefferson Davis was passed. It was situated twenty-five miles below Vicksburgh, and prior to February, 1867, was on a long peninsula with the estate of Colonel Joseph E. Davis and one belonging to Messrs. Quitman and Farrar. Then came the overwhelming river, sweeping across a narrow neck of land, and transforming the cotton-plantations into an island territory. In the old days of slavery, Colonel Joseph E. Davis, brother of the ex-president of the late Confederate States, had a body-servant named Ben Montgomery. He was the manager of his master's estates while a slave, and was so industrious and honest in all his dealings, and so successful in business, that after the war he was able to purchase his master's plantation for three hundred and fifty thousand dollars in gold.

While I lingered in the Davis cut-off to lunch, a boat-load of white men passed me on their way to the plantation of Jefferson Davis, which they said had also been purchased by Ben Montgomery of its former owner, who then resided in Memphis. One of the men said: " Mr. Davis will convey the property to Ben Montgomery as soon as he makes one more payment, and Ben told me he was about ready to close the transaction."

Montgomery was described as being fairly educated, and possessing the presence and address of a gentleman. His neighbors credited him with being "a right smart good nigger." It is a singular fact that these large landed estates should have become the property of the former slave so soon after the war. Ben Montgomery died recently, leaving an example to his colored brethren worthy of their imitation.

From Davis's Cut-off I followed Big Black Island Bend and Hard Times Bend, past the now silent batteries of Grand Gulf, down to the town of Rodney. I went ashore near the old plantation of an ex-president (General Taylor) of the United States, being attracted by a lot of dry drift-wood which promised a blazing fire. While cooking my rice and slowly developing an omelet, I calculated upon the chances of finding the lost flatboat. It was now evident that she was behind, not in advance of me. It was about four o'clock, and I determined to await her arrival. At half-past six o'clock clouds had obscured the sky, and it was impossible to see across the water, but I continued to watch and listen for the flat. The current was strongest on my side of the river, and I felt certain the boat would follow it and pass close to my camp. Her lantern and blazing stove-pipe would reveal her presence. Suddenly a man coughed within a few rods of the shore, and out of the gloom appeared the dark outlines of the fisherman's craft, but like a phantom ship, it instantly disappeared. It was but the work of a moment to embark and follow the vanishing flat. I soon overhauled it, and received a warm welcome from its occupants, who had supposed that after the steamer had driven me from them I had sought refuge in a creek to make up my lost hours of sleep. We floated side by side all night, disturbed but once, and then by the powerful steamer Robert Lee, which unceremoniously threw about a pail of water over me, gratuitously washing my blankets.

The next day, January 13, we passed Natchez, Mississippi, about four o'clock A. M. This city, founded by D'Iberville in 1700, is geographically divided into two parts. "Natchez on the Hill" is situated on a bluff two hundred feet above the river, while "Natchez under the Hill" is at the base of the cliff, and from its levee vessels sail for foreign as well as for American ports. Its inland and foreign trade is extensive, though it has a population of only ten or twelve thousand. The aspect of the country was changing as we approached New Orleans. Fine plantations, protected by levees, now lined the river-banks, while the forests of dense green, heavily draped with Spanish moss, threw dark shadows on the watery path.

We arrived at the mouth of the Red River about dark, and my companions were fortunate enough to find a steamer at the landing, the captain of which promised to take them in tow to their distant goal. We parted like old friends; and as I rowed in darkness down the Mississippi I heard the shrill whistle of the steamer which was dragging my companions up the current of Red River into the high lands of Louisiana.

Up Red River, three miles from its mouth, a stream branches off to the south, and empties into the Gulf of Mexico. This is the Atchafalaya Bayou. At Plaquemine, about one hundred and thirty miles below Red River, and on the west bank of the Mississippi, another bayou conducts a portion of the water from the main stream into Grand River, which, with other western Louisiana watercourses, empties into the Gulf of Mexico. There is a third western outlet from the parent stream at Donaldsonville, eighty-one miles above New Orleans, known as the Bayou La Fourche, which flows through one of the richest sugar-producing sections of the state. Dotted here and there along the shores of this bayou are the picturesque homes of the planters, made more attractive by the semi-tropical vegetation, the clustering vines, blooming roses, and bright green turf, than they could ever be from mere architectural beauty, while their continuous course along the shore gives the idea of a long and prosperous village.

The guide-books of the Mississippi describe

the Bayou Manchac as an outlet to the Mississippi on the left, or east bank, below Baton Rouge, and the statement is repeatedly made that steamboats can go through this bayou into the Amite River, and down that river to Lake Pontchartrain and the Gulf of Mexico, leaving, by this route, the city of New Orleans to the west. This is, however, far from the truth, as I shall presently show, for it had been my intention to descend the Bayou Manchac, and follow D'Iberville's ancient route to the sea. I soon found that the accomplishment of my plan was impossible, as the dry bottom of the bayou was FIFTEEN FEET ABOVE the water of the Mississippi.

Pursuing my solitary way, I rowed across the Mississippi, and skirted the shore in search of a camp where I could sleep until the moon arose, which would be soon after midnight. During the afternoon I had crossed the southern boundary of the state of Mississippi, and now the river ran through the state of Louisiana all the way to the sea.

About nine o'clock I found a little bayou in the dark woods, and moored my boat to a snag which protruded its head above the still waters of the tarn. The old trees that closely encircled my nocturnal quarters were fringed with the inevitable Spanish moss, and gave a most funereal aspect to the surroundings. The mournful hootings of the owls added to the doleful and weird character of the place. I was, however, too sleepy to waste much sentiment upon the gloomy walls of my apartment, and was soon lost to all sublunary things. These dark pockets of the swamps, these earthly Hades, are famous resting-places for those who know the untenable nature of ghosts, and who have become the possessors of healthy nerves by avoiding the poisonous influences of coal-gas in furnace-heated houses, the vitiated air of crowded rooms, and other detrimental effects of a city life. In such a camp the voyager need fear no intrusion upon his privacy, for the superstitions rife among men will prevent even Paul Pry from penetrating such recesses during the *wee sma' hours*. Of course such a camp would be safe only during the winter months, as at other seasons the invidious foe, *malaria*, would inevitably mark for its victim the man who slept beneath such deadly shades.

At midnight the light of the moon illuminated my dark quarters, and I stole noiselessly out of the bayou into the river, rowing until sunrise, when the small port of Bayou Sara was passed. It was soon left in the dim distance, and the little white boat floated ten miles down a nearly straight reach in the river to the frowning heights of Port Hudson, a place that figured prominently during the late war.

The country round Port Hudson is thickly

settled by descendants of the old Acadians, who came down the great rivers from Canada in the early days of Louisiana's history. Entering the mouth of the False River, on the west bank of the Mississippi, the traveller will penetrate the heart of an old and interesting Acadian settlement. If his mind be full of poetic fancies, and his eyes in search of Gabriels and Evangelines as he travels along this part of the Mississippi, his ears will be startled by the unmistakable *Yankee* names that are given him as representing the proprietors of the various estates he passes. Here and there the old French names appear; but in almost every such instance its possessor is a bachelor, and with him its musical accents will die away. Searching into the cause of this patent fact, I discovered that the creole women, descendants of the old Acadians, appreciated the sterling qualities of the Anglo-Saxon race, and found in them their ideals, leaving in a state of single blessedness the more indolent, and perhaps less persuasive, creole gentlemen. The results of these marriages are the gradual extinction of old family names; and in the not very far future the romance connected with these people will be a thing of the past, and the traveller, instead of thinking —

"This is the little village famed of yore,
  With meadows rich in flocks, and plenteous grain,
  Whose peasants knelt beside each vine-clad door,
    As the sweet Angelus rose over the plain,"

will be introduced to Mrs. Hezekiah Skinner, and partake of her baked beans.

My informant in these matters was an educated creole gentleman, and I must have the honesty to give his remarks in regard to these persistent " Yankees," who, he said, " were always successful with the fair maidens, but invariably selected those who owned fine plantations, having in love, as well as in war, an eye to the main chance."

About the middle of the afternoon I ran the sneak-box on to the sloping levee of Baton Rouge, the capital of Louisiana; and, locking the hatch, went to the post-office for letters, and to the stores for provisions. Returning to the levee, I found a good-natured crowd had taken possession of my boat, and at once availed myself of the local information in regard to the chances of a passage through Bayou Manchac, which was only fifteen miles below the town. Each told a different story. One gentleman said, " You will have to get four niggers to lift your boat over the levee of Mr. Walker's plantation, and put it into Bayou Manchac, which is about one hundred yards from the banks of the Mississippi. Its mouth was filled up a long time ago, but when once in the bayou you can float down to the Amite River, and so on to the Gulf." Another voice contradicted this statement, exclaiming, " Why, the bayou is dried up for a distance of at least eight miles from its head." At this point a well-dressed gentleman advanced, and quietly said: "I live on the Bayou Manchac, and can assure you that after you have hauled your boat through the Woodstock Plantation of the Walker family, you will find water enough in the bayou to float down upon to the Amite River."

The crowd now became fully alive to the discussion of the geography of their locality. Each man who favored me with an opinion on the Manchac question contradicted his neighbor; which was only a renewal of old experiences, for I always found LOCAL knowledge of geography and distances of little value. As the debate ran high, I thought of D'Iberville, who had thoroughly explored the short bayou several generations before, and who might now have enlightened these people in regard to a stream that ran through their own lands. D'Iberville was, however, born in Canada, and probably had more time to look into such matters, or he would not have travelled several thousand miles to explore Louisiana.

I thanked the company for their interest in the discussion, which, like the questions before a debating society, had ended only in opinions. I promised to let them know the truth of the matter if I visited Baton Rouge again, and pushing out into the current, pulled towards Woodstock Plantation, where I arrived soon after dark; but fearing to land on account of the dogs, whose reception of a stranger in the dark was, to say the least, unceremonious, I tied up to a high bank, and "turned in" for the night.

Having left the wilderness and its protecting creeks and islands, I was destined to feel all the annoyances attending a camper in a cultivated and settled region. The steamboats tossed me about all night, so that morning was indeed welcome, and having refreshed myself with a dip and a *déjeûner*, I climbed the bank, and was rewarded with the sight of a noble mansion, with its gardens of blooming roses, and lawns of bright green grass. This was the Woodstock Plantation, of which I had heard so much. I leisurely approached the large establishment, breathing an atmosphere laden with the fragrance of roses and orange-blossoms, which seemed to grow sweeter with every step. Finding an old negro, I sent my card to his master, with the request for information in regard to the Bayou Manchac. The young proprietor soon appeared with the "Report of the Secretary of War," 27th Congress, 3d session, page 21. December 30, 1842. This pamphlet informed me that the bayou was filled up at its mouth by order of the government, in answer to a petition from the planters of the lower country along the bayou and Amite River, to prevent the overflow of their cane-fields during freshets in the Mississippi River. We walked to a shallow depression near the house.

It was dry, and carpeted with short grass. "This," said Mr. Walker, " is the Bayou Manchac which D'Iberville descended in his boat after having explored the Mississippi probably as far as Red River. The bed of the bayou is *now* fifteen feet above the present stage of water in the Mississippi." A field-hand was then called, who was said to be the best geographer in those parts, white or black.

" Tell this gentleman what you know of the Bayou Manchac," said Mr. Walker, addressing the negro.

" Well, sah! " the darky replied, " I jus hab looked at yer boat. Four ob us can lif him ober de levee, an' put him on de cart. Den wees mus done cart him FOURTEEN miles 'long de Bayou Manchac to get to whar de warter is plenty fur him to float in. Dar is some places nearer dan dat, 'bout twelve miles off, whar dar is SOME warter, but de warter am in little spots, an' den you go on furder, an' dar is no warter fur de boat. Den all de way dar is trees dat falls across de bayou. Boss, you mus go all de fourteen miles to get to de warter, *sure* sartin."

Mr. Walker informed me that for fourteen miles down the bayou the fall was six feet to the mile. At that distance from the Mississippi, sloop navigation commenced at a point called Hampton's Landing, from which it was about six miles to the Amite River. The Amite River was navigated by light-draught vessels from Lake Pontchartrain. The region about the Amite River possesses rich bottom-lands, and many of the descendants of the original French settlers of Louisiana own plantations along its banks.

Mr. Walker then pointed to a long point of land some miles down the river, upon which the fertile fields of a plantation lay like patches of bright green velvet in the morning sun, and said: "Below that point a neighbor of mine found one of your northern boatmen dying in his boat. He rowed all the way from Philadelphia on a bet, and if he had reached New Orleans would have won his five thousand dollars, but he died when only ninety-five miles from the city, and was buried by Adonis Le Blanc on that plantation."

I had heard the story before. It had been told me by the river boatmen, and the newspapers of the country had also repeated it. The common version of it was, that a poor man, desirous of supporting his large family of children, had undertaken to row on a bet from Philadelphia to New Orleans. If successful, he was to receive five thousand dollars. The kind-hearted people along the river had shown much sympathy for Mr. John C. Cloud in his praiseworthy attempts to support his suffering family, and at any time during his voyage quite a liberal sum of money might have been collected from these generous men and women to aid him in his endeavor.

There was, however, something he preferred to money, and with which he was lavishly supplied, as we shall see hereafter.

So much for rumor. Now let us examine facts. A short time before Mr. Cloud's death, two reporters of a western paper attempted to row to New Orleans in a small boat, but met with an untimely end, being run down by a steamboat. Their fate and Mr. Cloud's were quoted as precedents to all canoeists and boatmen, and quite a feeling against this healthful exercise was growing among the people. Several editors of popular newspapers added to the excitement by warnings and forebodings. Believing that some imprudence had been the cause of Mr. Cloud's death, and forming my opinion of him from the fact of his undertaking such a voyage in August, — the season when the swamps are full of malaria, — I took the trouble to investigate the case, and made some discoveries which would have startled the sympathetic friends of this unfortunate man.

One of the first things that came to light was the fact that Mr. Cloud was *not* a married man. His family was a creation of his imagination, and a most successful means of securing the sympathy and ready aid of those he met during his voyage, though his daily progress shows that neither sympathy nor money were what he craved, but that WHISKEY alone would "fill the bill."

Mr. Cloud had once been a sailor in the United States navy, but having retired from the cruel sea, he became an actor in such plays as "Black-eyed Susan" in one of the variety theatres in Philadelphia. Mr. Charles D. Jones, of that city, who was connected with theatrical enterprises, and knew Mr. Cloud well, was one day surprised by the latter gentleman, who declared he had a "bright idea," and only wanted a friend to stand by him to make it a sure thing. He proposed to row from Philadelphia to New Orleans in a small boat. Mr. Jones was to act as his travelling agent, going on in advance, and informing the people of the coming of the great oarsman. When Mr. Cloud should arrive in any populous river-town, a theatrical performance was to be given, the boatman of course to be the "star." Mr. Jones was to furnish the capital for all this, while Mr. Cloud was to share with his manager the profits of the exhibitions.

A light Delaware River skiff, pointed at each end, was purchased, and Mr. Cloud left Philadelphia in the month of August, promising his friend to arrive in Pittsburgh, Pennsylvania, in twelve or fourteen days. After waiting a few days to enable Mr. Cloud to get fairly started upon his voyage, which was to be made principally by canals to the Alleghany River, the *manager* went to Pittsburgh with letters of introduction to the editors of that busy city. The representatives of the press kindly seconded Mr. Jones in advertising the coming of the great oarsman. Mr. Cloud was expected to appear in front of Pittsburgh on a certain day. A hall was engaged for his performance in the evening. An immense amount of enthusiasm was worked up among the people of the city and the neighboring towns. Having done his duty to his colleague, Mr. Jones anxiously awaited the expected telegram from Cloud, announcing his approach to the city. No word came from the oarsman; and in vain the manager telegraphed to the various towns along the route through which Mr. Cloud must have passed.

On the day that had been settled upon for the arrival of the boat before Pittsburgh, a large concourse of visitors gathered along the riverbanks. Even the mayor of the city was present in his carriage among the expectant crowd. The clock struck the hour of noon, but the little Delaware skiff was nowhere to be seen; and, as the sun declined from the zenith, the people gradually dispersed, muttering, "Another humbug!"

At midnight Mr. Jones retired in anything but an amiable mood. His professional honor had been wounded, and his industrious labors lost. Where was Cloud? Had the poor fellow been murdered? What was his fate, and why did he not come up to time? Revolving these questions in his mind, the manager fell asleep; but he was roused before five o'clock in the morning by a servant knocking at his door to inform him that his "*star*" was in Alleghany City, opposite Pittsburgh. Mr. Jones went to look up his man, and found him in a state of intoxication in a drinking-saloon. A hard-looking set of fellows were perambulating the streets, bawling at the top of their voices, "Arrival of John C. Cloud, the great oarsman! Photographs for sale! only twenty-five cents!"

When the intoxicated boatman had returned to a conversational state of mind, he explained that he had actually rowed as far as Harrisburgh, Pennsylvania, where he had been most generously entertained at the liquor saloons, and had been so fortunate as to make the acquaintance of some "good fellows" who had engaged to travel in advance of his boat, and sell his photographs, sharing with him in the profits of such sales. He had made his *voyage* from Harrisburgh to Alleghany City by rail, his boat being safely stowed in a car, and tenderly watched over by the red-shirted "good fellows" who had so generously taken him under their wing. The "great oarsman" had, in fact, rowed just about one-third of the distance between Philadelphia and Pittsburgh.

The disgusted manager left his man in charge of the new managers, and going at once to the editors, explained how he had been duped, and begged to be "let down gently" before the public. These gentlemen not only acceded to the request, but even offered to get up a "benefit" for Mr. Jones, who declined the honor, and waited only long enough in the city to see Mr. Cloud with his boat and whiskey fade out of sight down the Ohio, when he returned to Philadelphia considerably lighter in pocket, having provided funds for purchasing the boat and other necessaries, and full of righteous indignation against Mr. Cloud and his "*bright idea.*"

The little skiff went on its way down the Ohio, and was met with enthusiasm at each landing. The citizens of Hickman, Kentucky, described the voyage of Mr. Cloud as one continuous ovation. Five thousand people gathered along the banks below that town to welcome "the poor northern man who was rowing to New Orleans on a five-thousand-dollar bet, hoping to win his wager that he might have means to support his large family of children." One old gentleman seemed to have his doubts about the truth of this statement, "for," said he, "when the celebrated oarsman appeared, and landed, he repaired immediately to a low drinking-saloon, and announced that he was the greatest oarsman in America," &c.

The "boys" about the town subscribed a fund, and invested it in five gallons of whiskey, which Cloud took aboard his skiff when he departed. He plainly stated that the conditions of the bet prevented his sleeping under a roof while on his way; so he curled himself up in his blankets and slept on the veranda floors. The man must have had great powers of endurance, or he could not have rowed so long in the hot sun at that malarious season of the year. His chief sustenance was whiskey; and at one town, near Cairo, I was assured by the best authority, ten gallons of that fiery liquor were stowed away in his skiff. Such disregard of nature's laws soon told upon the plucky fellow, and his voyage came to an end when almost in sight of his goal. The malaria he was breathing and the whiskey he was drinking set fire to his blood, and the fatal congestive chills were the inevitable result.

The papers of New Orleans had announced the approach of the great oarsman, and the planters were ready to give him a cordial welcome, when one day a man who was walking near the shore of the Mississippi, in the parish of Iberville, and looking out upon the river, saw a boat of a peculiar model whirling around in the eddies. He at once launched his boat and pushed out to the object which had excited his curiosity. Stretched upon the bottom of the strange craft was a man dressed in the garb of a northern boatman. At first he appeared to be dead; but a careful examination showed that life was not yet extinct. The unknown man was carried to the nearest plantation, and there, among strangers whose hearts beat kindly for the unfortunate boatman, John C. Cloud expired without uttering one word. The coroner,

Dying in his Boat.

Mr. Adonis Le Blanc, found upon the person of the dead man a memorandum-book which told of the distances made each day upon the river, while the entries of the closing days showed how the keeper of the log had suffered from the "heavy shakes" occasioned by the malaria and his own imprudence. The story of the cruise was recorded on the boat. Men and women had written their names inside the frail shell, with the dates of her arrival at different localities along the route. I afterwards examined the boat at Biloxi, on the Gulf of Mexico, where it was kept as a curiosity in the boat-house of a citizen of New Orleans.

They buried the unfortunate man upon the plantation, and Mr. Clay Gourrier took charge of his effects. The most remarkable thing about this rowing match was the credulity of the people along the route. They accepted Cloud's statement without stopping to consider that if there were any truth in it, the other side, with their five thousand dollars at stake, would surely take some interest in the matter, and have men posted along the route to see that the bet was fairly won. The fact that no bet had been made never seemed to dawn upon them; but, like too many, they sympathized without reasoning.

Being forced to abandon all hopes of taking the Bayou Manchac and the interesting country of the Acadians in my route southward, I rowed down the river, past the curious old town of Plaquemine, and by four o'clock in the afternoon commenced to search for an island or creek where a good camping-ground for Sunday might be found. The buildings of White Castle Plantation soon arose on the right bank, and as I approached the little cooperage-shop of the large estate, which was near the water, a kindly hail came from the master-cooper and his assistant. Acceding to their desire "to look at the boat," I let the two men drag her ashore, and while they examined the craft, I studied the representatives of two very different types of laboring-men. One was from Madison, Indiana; the other belonged to the poor white class of the south. We built a fire near the boat, and passed half the night in conversation.

These men gave me much valuable information about Louisiana. The southern cooper had lived much among the bayous and swamps of that region of the state subjected to overflow. He was an original character, and never so happy as when living a Robinson Crusoe life in the woods. His favorite expression seemed to be, "Oh, shucks!" and his yarns were so interlarded with this exclamation, that in giving one of his stories I must ask the reader to imagine that expressive utterance about every other word. Affectionately hugging his knee, and generously expectorating as he made a transfer of his quid from one side of his mouth to the other, he said:

"A fellow don't always want company in the woods. If you have a pardner, he ort to be jes like yourself, or you'll be sartin to fall out. I was riving out shingles and coopers' stock once with a pardner, and times got mighty hard, so we turned fishermen. There was some piles standing in Plaquemine Bayou, and the drift stuff collected round them and made a sort of little island. Me and Bill Bates went to work and rived out some lengths of cypress, and built a snug shanty on top of the piles. As it wasn't real estate we was on, nobody couldn't drive us off; so we fished for the Plaquemine folks.

"By-and-by a king-snake swimmed over to our island, and tuck up his abode in a hole in a log. The cuss got kind of affectionate, and after a while crawled right into our hut to catch flies and other varmin. At last he got so tame he'd let me scratch his back. Then he tuck to our moss bed, and used up a considerable portion of his time there. Bill Bates hadn't the manners of a hog, and he kept a-droppin' hints to me, every few days, that he'd 'drap into that snake some night and squeeze the life out of him.' This made me mad, and I nat'rally tuck the snake's part, particularly as he would gobble up and crush the neck of every water-snake that cum ashore on our island. One thing led to another, till Bill Bates swore he'd kill my snake. Sez I to him, 'Billum,' (I always called him Billum when I MEANT BIZNESS,) 'ef you hurt a hair of the head of my snake, I'll hop on to you.' That settled our pardnership. Bill Bates knowed what I meant, and he gathered up his traps and skedaddled.

"Then I went to New Orleans, and out to Lake Pontchartrain, to fish for market. A lot of cussed Chinese was in the bizness, and when they found COARSE fish in their nets, they'd kill 'em and heave 'em overboard. Now, no man's got a rite to waste anything, so we fishermen begun to pay sum attention to the opium-smokers in good arnest."

Here I interrupted the speaker to ask him if it would be safe for me to travel alone through the fishing-grounds of these Chinese.

"Oh, shucks! safe enuf now," he answered. "Once they was a bad set; but a change has cum over 'em — they're CIVILIZED now."

A vision of schools and earnest missionary work was before me while I asked HOW their civilization had been accomplished.

"Oh, shucks! WE dun it — WE WHITE FISHERMEN civilized 'em," was the emphatic reply; "and not a bit too soon either, for the wasteful cusses got so bad they wasn't satisfied with chucking dead fish overboard, but would go on to the prairies, and after using the grass cabins we WHITE fishermen had built to go into in bad weather, the bloody furiners would burn them up to bother us. They thort they'd drive us teetotally out of the diggins; so we thort it was time to CIVILIZE 'em. We hid in the long grass fur a few nights and watched the cusses. One morning a Chinaman was found dead in a cabin. Pretty soon after, one or two others was found floatin' round loose, in the same way; and after that lesson or two the fellers got CIVILIZED; and you needn't fear goin' among 'em now, fur they're harmless as kittens. They don't kill coarse fish now fur the fun of it. Oh, shucks! there's nothin' like a little healthy CIVILIZATION fur Chinamen and Injuns. They both needs it, and, any way, this is a WHITE MAN'S country."

"And what of negroes?" I asked.

"Oh, the niggers is good enuf, ef you let 'em alone. The Carpet-baggers from up north has filled their heads with all kinds of stuff, so now they think, nat'rally enuf, that they ought to be office-holders, when they can't read or write no more than I can. I'd like to take a hand CIVILIZING some of them Carpet-baggers! They needs it more than the Chinamen or Injuns."

During part of the evening, Mr. Sewall, the nephew of the owner of the plantation, was with us round our camp-fire. We spoke of Longfellow's Evangeline, the bay-tree, and Atchafalaya River, which he assured me was slowly widening its current, and would in time, perhaps, become the main river of the basin, and finally deprive the Mississippi of a large portion of its waters. From his boyhood he had watched the falling in of the banks with the widening and increasing of the strength of the current of the Atchafalaya Bayou. Once it was impassable for steamers; but a little dredging opened the way, while the Mississippi and Red rivers had both contributed to its volume of water until it had deepened sufficiently for United States gunboats to ascend it during the late war. It follows the shortest course from the mouth of Red River to the Gulf of Mexico.

I left White Castle Plantation early on Monday morning, when I discovered a lot of fine sweet-potatoes stowed away in the hold of my boat. The northern cooper had purchased them during the night, and having too much delicacy to speak of his gift, secreted them in the boat. I fully appreciated this kind act, knowing it to be a mark of the poor man's sympathy for his northern countryman. The levee for miles was lined with negroes and white men gathering a harvest of firewood from the drift stuff. One old negro, catching sight of my boat, called out to his companion, "Randal, look at dat boat! De longer we libs, de mor you sees. What sort o' queer boat is she?"

Twenty miles below White Castle Plantation is the valuable sugar estate called Houmas, the property of General Wade Hampton and Colonel J. T. Preston. General Hampton does not reside upon his plantation, but makes Georgia his home. Beyond Houmas the parish of St. James skirts the river for twenty miles. Three miles back from the river, on the left side of the Mississippi, and fifty-five miles from New Orleans, is the little settlement of Grand Point, the place most famed in St. James for perique tobacco. The first settler who had the hardihood to enter these solitudes was named Maximilian Roussel. He purchased a small tract of land from the government, and in the year 1824 shouldered his axe and camping-utensils, and started for his new domain. He soon built a hut, and at once began the laborious task of clearing his land, which was located in a dense cypress swamp, alive with wild beasts and alligators. A rough house was completed at the end of a year, and into it Roussel moved his family, consisting of a wife and four children. Here "*he lived till he died*," as it has been expressively said.

Octave and Louis, two of his sons, and both now grandfathers, still live on the old place, and are highly respected. Only a few years ago the old homestead echoed to the voices of five of Roussel's sons, with their families; but death has taken two, one has removed, and two only now remain to relate the history of the almost unimaginable hardships encountered by the old and hardy pioneer.

There are at present nineteen families in the settlement, and they are all engaged in the cultivation of perique tobacco. An average farm on Grant Point consists of eight acres, and the average yield of manufactured tobacco is four hundred pounds to the acre. These simple-hearted people seem to be very happy and content. They have no saloons or stores of any kind, but their place is well filled with a neat Catholic church and a substantial school-house. Every man, woman, and child is a devout Roman Catholic, and in their daily intercourse with each other the stranger among them hears a patois something like the French language. The whole of the land cultivated by these people would not make more than an average farm in the north, while compared with the vast sugar estates on every side of it the dimensions are infinitesimal.

Villages were now picturesquely grouped along the shores, the most conspicuous feature in each being the large Catholic church, showing the religious belief of the people. Curious little stores were perched behind the now high banks of the levee. The signs over the doors bore such inscriptions as, "The Red Store," "The White Store," "St. John's Store," "Poor Family Store," &c. Busy life was seen on every side, but here, as elsewhere in the south, men seemed always to have time to give a civil answer to any necessary inquiries.

Only a month after I had descended this part of the river, Captain Boyton, clothed in his famous swimming-suit, paddled his way down the current from Bayou Goula to New Orleans, a distance of one hundred miles. The incidents of this curious voyage are now a part of the river's history, and this seems the place for the brave captain to tell his story. He says:

"I arrived at Bayou Goula on the 'Bismarck,' about six o'clock on Thursday morning; and, after considerable delay, succeeded in obtaining quarters at the Buena Vista Hotel in that village. At that point I engaged the services of a colored man named Brown, to pilot me down the river. At ten o'clock I took a breakfast, consisting of five eggs, bread, and a glass of beer, and ate nothing else during the day. At five o'clock precisely I took to the water and began my trip down to the city of New Orleans — a trip which proved to be a much more arduous one than I had anticipated, in consequence of the want of buoyancy in the water, the terrible counter-currents, and the large amount of drift-wood. It was some time before I could master the difficulty about the drift-wood, and at one time I was so annoyed and bruised by the floating debris, that I became somewhat apprehensive about the success of my enterprise. In some of the strong eddies particularly the logs played such fantastic tricks, rolling over and over with their jagged limbs and again standing upon their ends, that I feared I must either be carried under, or have my dress stripped completely off. By constant watching, however, I was enabled to steer out of harm's way and to keep steadily moving down the stream.

"Above Donaldsonville I was met by a fleet of boats filled with spectators, who accompanied me down to that point, which I reached about eight o'clock in the evening. The town was illuminated, and the citizens tendered me a polite invitation to land and take supper; but of course I was obliged to decline, accepting in lieu a drink and a sandwich. Of the sandwich I ate only the bread.

BOYTON DESCENDING THE MISSISSIPPI.

"Below Donaldsonville I was caught in the great eddy. It was about four o'clock in the morning when I got into it, and it was good daylight before I succeeded in getting out again into the down-stream current. It was a singular sensation, this going round and round over the same ground, so to speak, and for the life of me I could not understand how I seemed now and then to be passing the same plantation-houses and familiar landmarks. The skiff which accompanied me was also in the same predicament, sometimes pulling up and sometimes pulling down stream. I tried to guide myself by the north star, but before I was aware of it that luminary, which ought to have kept directly in my front, would pop up, as it were, behind me, and destroy all my calculations. When daylight came, however, and the fog lifted sufficiently, I was able to paddle out into the middle of the stream, and keep down it once again.

"Early in the morning, above Bonnet Carre, I asked several persons on shore for some coffee, but most of them seemed too much excited to attend to this pressing want of mine. At last a gentleman who spoke French got his wife to go and get me a cup of coffee, after drinking which I felt greatly refreshed. The sandwich and drink at Donaldsonville, and this cup of coffee next morning, were the only things in the shape of refreshments which I took during the twenty-four hours' voyage. At times I was almost certain I was being attacked by alligators, and thought I should have to use the knife with which I always go armed, but it only proved to be the annoying drift-wood in which I would become fearfully entangled. I only suffered from the cold in my feet. These I warmed, however, after the sun came out, by inflating the lower part of my dress, and holding them up out of the water.

"The banks all along the way were crowded with people to see me pass down. At one point, when I had allowed the air to escape from the lower part of my dress, and was going along rapidly, with nothing showing above water but my head and my paddle, I met a skiff, which contained a negro man and woman, who were crossing the river. The woman became fearfully alarmed, and her screams could have been heard for miles away. The man pulled for dear life, the woman in the stern acting the cockswain, and urging the boat forward in the funniest manner possible.

"While in the great eddy I drifted into an immense flock of ducks, and but for the noise made by those in the skiff I could easily have caught several of them, as they were not at all disturbed by my presence, but swam leisurely all about me.

"At the Red Church, the wind blowing up

against the current kicked up a nasty sea, which gave me a great deal of trouble. By sinking down very low, however, and allowing only my head above water, and taking the shower-bath as it came upon me continuously, I was enabled to keep up my headway down stream. When at my best speed I easily kept ahead of the boats, going sometimes at the rate of seven miles an hour without difficulty.

"This feat was a much more arduous one than my trip across the English Channel. Then I only slept two hours, and was up again, feeling all right; but when this thing was over I slept all night, had a refreshing bath, and still suffered from fatigue, to say nothing of my swollen wrists and neck-glands."

Having finished his remarkable voyage successfully, Captain Boyton concluded that his life-saving dress had been fully tested in America, and determined to rest on his laurels, and avoid Mississippi debris in future. In consequence of being caught in the eddy below Donaldsonville, this great swimmer estimated the distance he traversed from Bayou Goula to New Orleans as fully one hundred and twenty miles.*

About dusk I rowed into a grove of young

---

* Since this voyage ended, Captain Boyton has, in the same manner, successfully descended the Ohio and the Mississippi rivers from Cairo to New Orleans.

willows, on the left bank of the river, on the Shepard Plantation. My boat was soon securely fastened to a tree, and having partaken of my frugal meal I retired. A comfortable night's rest was, however, out of the question, for the passing steamers tossed me about in a most unceremonious manner, seeming to me in my dreams to be chanting for their lullaby, " Rock-a-by baby on the tree-top." Indeed, the baby on the tree-top was in an enviable position compared with my kaleidoscopic movements among the swashy seas. Many visions were before me that night, of the numerous little sufferers who are daily slung backwards and forwards in those pernicious instruments of torture called cradles.

Memory brought also another picture I hoped it had been my good fortune to forget. It was a scene on the veranda of a country house. Five sisters, all pretty girls, whose grace and vivacity I had often admired, were there, each in her rocking-chair, and each swinging to and fro, as though perpetual motion had been discovered. Why must an American woman have a rocking-chair? In no other country in the world, excepting among the creoles of South America, is this awkward piece of furniture so popular. Burn the cradles and taboo the graceless rocking-chair, and our children will have steadier heads and our women learn the attractive grace of quiet ease.

The following day I struggled against head

winds and swashy seas, until their combined forces proved too much for me, and succumbing as amiably as possible under the circumstances, the little white boat was run ashore on the Picou Plantation, where the coast was fortunately low. The rain and wind held me prisoner there until midnight, when, with a rising moon to cheer me, I forced a passage through the blockade of driftwood, and being once more on the river, waved an adieu to my last camp on the Mississippi.

I was now only thirty-seven miles from New Orleans. Rowing rapidly down the broad river, now shrouded in gloom, with the fleecy scuds flying overhead in the stormy firmament, I fully realized that I was soon to leave the noble stream which had borne me so long and so safely upon its bosom. A thunder-shower rose in the west, its massive blackness lighted by the vivid flashes which played over its surface. The houses of the planters along the river's bank were enveloped in foliage, and the air was so redolent with the fragrance of flowers that I seemed to be floating through an Eden. The wind and the clouds disappeared together, and a glorious sunrise gave promise of a perfect day. With the light came life. Where all had been silent and restful, man and beast now made known their presence. The rising sun seemed to be the signal for taking hold where they had let go the night before. The crowing of cocks, the cries of plantation hands, the hungry neigh of horses, the hundred and one sounds of this work-a-day world, greeted my ears, while my eyes, taking a rapid survey of the surrounding steamers, coal-arks, and barges of every description, carried quickly to my brain the intelligence that I was near the Crescent City of the Gulf. Soon forests of masts rose upon the horizon, for there were vessels of all nations ranged along the levee of this once prosperous city.

Anxious to escape the officious kindness always encountered about the docks of southern cities, I peered about, hoping to find some quiet corner in which to moor my floating home. Near the foot of Louisiana Avenue I saw the fine boat-house of the "Southern Boat Club," and being pleasantly hailed by one of its members, hove to, and told him of my perplexity. With the ever ready hospitality of a southerner, he assured me that the boat-house was at my disposal; and calling a friend to assist, we easily hauled the duck-boat out of the water, up the inclined plane, into her new quarters.

The row upon the Mississippi from its junction with the Ohio down to New Orleans, including many stoppages, had occupied nineteen days, and had been accelerated by considerable night voyaging. The flow of the Mississippi was about one third faster than that of the Ohio. Lloyd's River Map gives the distance from the mouth of the Ohio to the centre of New Orleans as ten hundred and fifty-five miles, but the surveys of the United States Engineer Corps make this crooked route ten hundred and twenty miles only.

My floating home being now in good hands, its captain turned his back on the water, and took a turn on land, leaving the river bounded by its narrow horizon, but teeming with a strange, nomadic life, the various types of which afforded a field where much gleaning would end in but a scanty harvest of good. Already my ears caught, in fancy, the sound of the restless waves of the briny waters of the Gulf of Mexico, and my spirits rose at the prospect of the broader experiences about to be encountered.

CHAPTER VIII.

NEW ORLEANS.

BIENVILLE AND THE CITY OF THE PAST. — FRENCH AND SPANISH RULE IN THE NEW WORLD. — LOUISIANA CEDED TO THE UNITED STATES. — CAPTAIN EADS AND HIS JETTIES. — TRANSPORTATIONS OF CEREALS TO EUROPE. — CHARLES MORGAN. — CREOLE TYPES OF CITIZENS. — LEVEES AND CRAWFISH. — DRAINAGE OF THE CITY INTO LAKE PONTCHARTRAIN.

THIS was my fifth visit to New Orleans, and walking through its quaint streets I observed many changes of an undesirable nature, the inevitable consequences of political misrule. As the past of the city loomed up before me, the various scenes of bloodshed, crime, and misery enacted, shifted like pictures in a panorama before my mind's eye. I saw far back in the distance an indomitable man, faint and discouraged, after the terrible sufferings of a winter at a bleak fort in the wilderness, drag his weary limbs to the spot where New Orleans now stands, and defiantly unfurling the flag of France, determined to establish the capital of Louisiana on the treacherous banks of the Mississippi. Such was Bienville, the hardy son of a Canadian father.

A little later we have the New Orleans of

1723. It is a low swamp, overgrown with ragged forests, and cut up into a thousand islands by ruts and pools of stagnant water. There is a small cleared space along the river's channel; but even this being only partly reclaimed from the surrounding marsh, is often inundated. It is cut up into square patches, round each of which runs a ditch of black mud and refuse, which, lying exposed to the rays of an almost tropical sun, sends forth unwholesome odors, and invites pestilence.

There is a palisade around the city, and a great moat; and here, with the tall, green grasses growing up to their humble doors, live graceful ladies and noble gentlemen, representatives of that nation so famed for finesse of manner and stately grace. It is an odd picture this rough doorway, surrounded with reeds and swamps, mud and misery, and crowned with the beauty of a fair French maiden, who steps daintily, with Parisian ease, upon the highway of the new world.

She is not, however, alone in her exile. Along the banks of the Mississippi, for miles beyond the city, stretch the fertile plantations of the representatives of aristocratic French families. The rich lands are worked by negro slaves, who, fresh from the African coast, walk erect before their masters, being strangers to the abject, crouching gait which a century of slavery afterwards imposes upon them. No worship save the Catholic is allowed, and to remind the people of their duty wooden crosses are erected on every side.

The next picture of New Orleans is in 1792. It has passed into other hands now, for the king of France has ceded it, with the territory of Louisiana, to his cousin of Spain, and has in fact, with a single stroke of the pen, stripped himself of possessions extending from the mouth of the Mississippi to the St. Lawrence. The type of civilization is now changed, and we see things moving in the iron groove of Spanish bigotry. The very architecture changes with the new rule, and the houses seem grim and fortress-like, while the cadaverous-cheeked Spaniard stands in the gloom with his hand upon his sword, one of the six thousand souls now within this ill-drained city. Successive Spanish governors hold their sway under the Spanish king; and then the Spaniard goes his way.

Spanish civilization cannot take so firm a hold in New Orleans as the French, and many privately pray for the old banner, until at last France herself determines to again possess her old territory. Spain, knowing opposition to be useless, and heartily sick of this distant colony, so hard to govern and so near the quarrelsome Americans, who seem ready to fulfil their threat of taking New Orleans by force if their commercial interests are interfered with, yields a ready assent. The city becomes the property of Napoleon the Great; but hardly have the papers been signed, when, in 1803, it is ceded to the United States. Half a generation later the conflicting national elements are settled into something like harmony, and the state of Louisiana has a population of fifty thousand souls.

In 1812 war is declared between Great Britain and the United States. Soon after, General Andrew Jackson wins a victory over the English on the lowlands near New Orleans, when, with the raw troops of the river states, he drives off, and sends home, fifteen thousand skilled British soldiers. Bowing his laurel-crowned head before the crowd assembled to do him honor, the brave American general receives the benediction of the venerable abbé, while his memory is kept ever fresh in the public mind by the grand equestrian statue which now stands a monument to his prowess.

But the New Orleans of to-day is not like any of these we have seen. The Crescent City has passed beyond the knowledge of even Jackson himself, and most startled would the old general be could he now walk its busy streets. Rising steadily, though slowly, from the effects of the civil war, her position as a port insures a glorious future. Much, of course, depends upon the success of Captain Eads in keeping open a deep channel from the mouth of the Mississippi River to the Gulf of Mexico. This great river deposits a large amount of alluvium at its North-east, South-east, South, and South-west Passes, which are the principal mouths of the Mississippi. When the light alluvium held in suspension in the fresh water of the river meets the denser briny water of the Gulf, it is precipitated to the bottom, and builds up a shoal, or bar, upon which vessels drawing sixteen feet of water, in the deepest channel, frequently stick fast for weeks at a time. In consequence of these bars, so frequently forming, deep sea-going vessels run the risk of most unprofitable delay in ascending the river to New Orleans.

Captain Eads, the projector of the great St. Louis bridge, which cost some seven or more millions of dollars, has succeeded, by narrowing and confining the river's current at the South Pass by means of artificial jetties, in scouring out the channel from a depth of about seven feet to one of more than twenty feet. Thus the most shoal pass has already become the deepest entrance to the Mississippi. If the results of Captain Eads's most wonderful success can be maintained, New Orleans will be able to support a fleet of European steamers, while the cereals and cotton of the river basins tributary to New Orleans will be exported from that city directly to Europe, instead of being subjected to a costly transportation by rail across the country to New York, Baltimore, and other Atlantic ports. Limited space forbids my presenting figures to support the theories of the people of New Orleans, but they are of the most interesting nature. A few words from an intelligent Kentuckian will express the views of many of the people of that state in regard to the system of transportation. He says:

"Nearly all the products of Kentucky have their prices determined by the cost of transportation to the great centres of population along the Atlantic seaboard, or beyond the sea. Its tobacco, pork, grain, and some of the costlier woods, with other products, find their principal markets in Europe, while cattle, and to a certain extent the other agricultural products of the state, have their values determined by the cost of transportation to the American Atlantic markets. Hitherto this access to the domestic and foreign markets of the Atlantic shores has been had by way of the railway systems which traverse the region north of Kentucky, and from which the state has been divided by opposing interests and the physical barrier of the Ohio River. All the development of the state has taken place under these disadvantages.

"A comparison of the tables of cost, given below, will show that the complete opening of the mouth of the Mississippi to ocean ships will result in the enfranchisement of the productions of Kentucky in an extraordinary way. They are taken from published freight rates, and give time and cost of transit from St. Paul, on the Mississippi, about two thousand miles from New Orleans, to Liverpool by the two routes: one being by rail, lake, canal, and ocean; the other by river and ocean:

	Cost per bushel. CENTS.	Time. DAYS.
From St. Paul to Chicago (by rail),	18	4
do. Chicago to Buffalo (by lake),	8	6
do. Buffalo to New York (by canal),	14	24
do. N. York to Liverpool (by ocean),	16	12
Elevator, or transshipment charges:		
Chicago,	2	2
Buffalo,	2	2
New York,	4	2
Total,	64	52

	Cost per bushel. CENTS.	Time. DAYS.
From St. Paul to New Orleans (via river), 1993 miles,	18	10
do. New Orleans to Liverpool,	20	20
Elevator charges, New Orleans,	2	1
Total,	40	31

"Here is a saving by direct trade of twenty-four cents per bushel, or eight shillings per quarter, and a saving of twenty-one days in time. To be fair, I have taken the extreme point; but the nearer the grain is to the Gulf, the cheaper the transportation. At the present time the freight rates from the lower Ohio to Liverpool would permit the profitable shipment of the canal coal, and native woods of different species, to Europe with one transshipment at New Orleans."

The gross receipts of cotton in New Orleans amount to thirty-three and one-third per cent. of the production of the entire country. In 1859–60 the receipts and exports of cotton from New Orleans exceeded two and a quarter millions of bales, the value of which was over one hundred millions of dollars. In the season of 1871–72 the cotton crop amounted to two million nine hundred and seventy-four thousand bales, one-third of which passed through New Orleans. A vast amount of other products, such as sugar, tobacco, flour, pork, &c., is received at New Orleans and sent abroad. Besides this export trade, New Orleans imports coffee, salt, sugar, iron, dry-goods, and liquors, to the average yearly value of seventeen millions of dollars.

In 1878 two hundred and forty-seven million four hundred and twenty-four thousand bushels of grain were received at the Atlantic ports of the United States from the interior. This great bulk of grain represented a portion only of the cereals actually raised in the whole country.

The largest portion of it was produced in the states tributary to the Mississippi River and its branches. This statement will give an idea of what might be saved to foreign consumers if a part of this great crop went down the natural water-way to New Orleans. In the same year, steamboats were freighting barrels of merchandise at fifty cents per barrel for fifteen hundred miles from New Orleans to up-river ports. This shows at what low rates freights can be transported on western rivers.

Each city has its representative men, and New Orleans has one who has done much to build up the great commercial and transportation interests of the Southwest. An unassuming man, destitute of means, went to the South many years ago. Uprightness in dealing with his fellow-man, industry in business, and large and comprehensive views, marked his career. Step by step he fought his way up from a humble station in life to one of the grandest positions that has ever been attained by a self-made man. More than one state feels the results of his tireless energy and successful commercial schemes. He is now the sole proprietor of two railroads, and the owner of a magnificent fleet of steamers which unite the ports of New York and New Orleans with the long seaboard of Texas.

So skilfully has this man conducted the details of the great enterprises he has created, that during a term of many years not one human life has been lost upon sea or land by the mismanagement of any of his numerous agents. He is now past eighty; but this remarkable man, with his tireless brain, goes persistently on, and within fourteen months past contracted for the building of two fine iron steamers, and nearly completed two more for ocean trade. A New Orleans paper asserts that within the same period "he has elevated his Louisiana Railroad bed, along its route for twenty miles, above the highest water-mark of overflows, and has converted a shallow bayou between Galveston and Houston, Texas, into a deep stream, navigable for his largest vessels. On these works he expended over two millions of dollars."

His shops for the construction of railroad stock, and for the repairing of his steamships, are in Louisiana, where he employs over one thousand workmen. In compliment to the virtues of this modest, energetic man, to whom the people of the Southwest owe so much, the citizens of Brashear, in the southwestern part of Louisiana, have changed the name of their town to Morgan City. May the last days of Charles Morgan be blessed with the happy consciousness that he deserves the reward of a well-spent life!

The winter climate of New Orleans is delightful, and many persons leave New England's cruel east winds to breathe its soft air and rejoice in its sunshine. These pale-faced invalids are strangely grouped in the quaint old streets with the peculiar people of the city, and add another to the many types already there. The New Orleans market furnishes, perhaps, the best opportunity for the ethnological student, for there strange motley groups are always to be found. Even the cries are in the quaint voices of a foreign city, and it seems almost impossible to imagine that one is in America.

We see the Sicilian fruit-seller with his native dialect; the brisk French madame with her dainty stall; the mild-eyed Louisiana Indian woman with her sack of gumbo spread out before her; the fish-dealer with his wooden bench and odd patois; the dark-haired creole lady with her servant gliding here and there; the old Spanish gentleman with the blood of Castile tingling in his veins; the graceful French dame in her becoming toilet; the Hebrew woman with her dark eyes and rich olive complexion; the pure Anglo-Saxon type, ever distinguishable from all others; and, swarming among them all, the irrepressible negro, — him you find in every size, shape, and shade, from the tiny yellow pickaninny to his rotund and inky grandmother, from the lazy wharf-darky, half clad in both mind and body, to the dignified colored policeman, who patrols with officious gravity the city streets,—in freedom or slavery, north or south, in sunshine or out of it, ever the same easy, improvident race; ever the same gleaming teeth and ready "Yes, sah! 'pon my word, sah!" and ever the same tardiness to DO.

Leaving the busy, surging mass of humanity, each so eager to buy or sell, the visitor to New Orleans will find a great contrast of scene in the quiet cemeteries with their high walls of shelves, where the dead are laid away in closely cemented tombs built one over the other, and all above the ground, to be safe from the encroachment of water, the ever-pervading foe of New Orleans. Not only must the dead be stowed away above-ground, but the living must wage a daily war against this insidious foe, and watch with vigilance their levees.

Notwithstanding all that has been said in regard to the enervating effects of a southern climate, the inhabitants of the state of Louisiana have shown a pertinacity in maintaining their levee system which is almost unexampled. They have always asserted their rights to the lowlands in which they live, and have under the most trying circumstances braved inundation. They have built more than one thousand five hundred miles of levees within the state limits. The state engineer corps is always at work along the banks of the Mississippi and its important bayous.

The work of levee-building has been pushed ahead when a thousand evils beset the community. Accurate and detailed surveys are a constant necessity to prevent inundation. The cost-value of the present system is seven millions of dollars, and as much more is needed to make it perfect. During the civil war millions of cubic feet of levees were destroyed; but the state in her impoverished condition has not only rebuilt the old levees, but added new ones in the intervening years, showing an industry and energy we must all appreciate.

The water has an assistant in its cruel inroads, and the peace of mind of the property-holders along the lower Mississippi is constantly disturbed by the presence of a burrowing pest which lives in the artificial dikes, and is always working for their destruction. This little animal is the crawfish (*Astacus Mississippiensis*) of the western states, and bores its way both vertically and laterally into the levees. This species of crawfish builds a habitation nearly a foot in height on the surface of the ground, to which it retreats, at times, during high water. The Mississippi crawfish is about four inches in length, and has all the appearance of a lobster; its breeding habits being also similar. The female crawfish, like the lobster, travels about with her eggs held in peculiar arm-like organs under her jointed tail, where they are protected from being devoured by other animals. There they remain until hatched; but the young crawfish does not experience the metamorphosis peculiar to most decapods.

These animals open permanent drains in the levees, through which the water finds its way, slowly at first, then rapidly, until it undermines the bank, when a crevasse occurs, and many square miles of arable and forest lands are submerged for weeks at a time. The extermination of these mischievous pests seems an impossibility, and they have cost the Mississippi property-owners immense sums of money since the levee system was first introduced upon the river.

The city of New Orleans is built upon land about four feet below the level of the Mississippi River at high-water mark, and, running along the great bend in the river, forms a semicircle; and it is from this peculiar site it has gained the appellation of "Crescent City." The buildings stretch back to the borders of Lake Pontchartrain, which empties its waters into the Gulf of Mexico. All the drainage of the city is carried by means of canals into the lake, while the two largest of these canals are navigable for steamers of considerable size. Large cargoes are transported through these artificial waterways to the lake, and from it into the Gulf of Mexico, and so on along the southern coast to Florida.

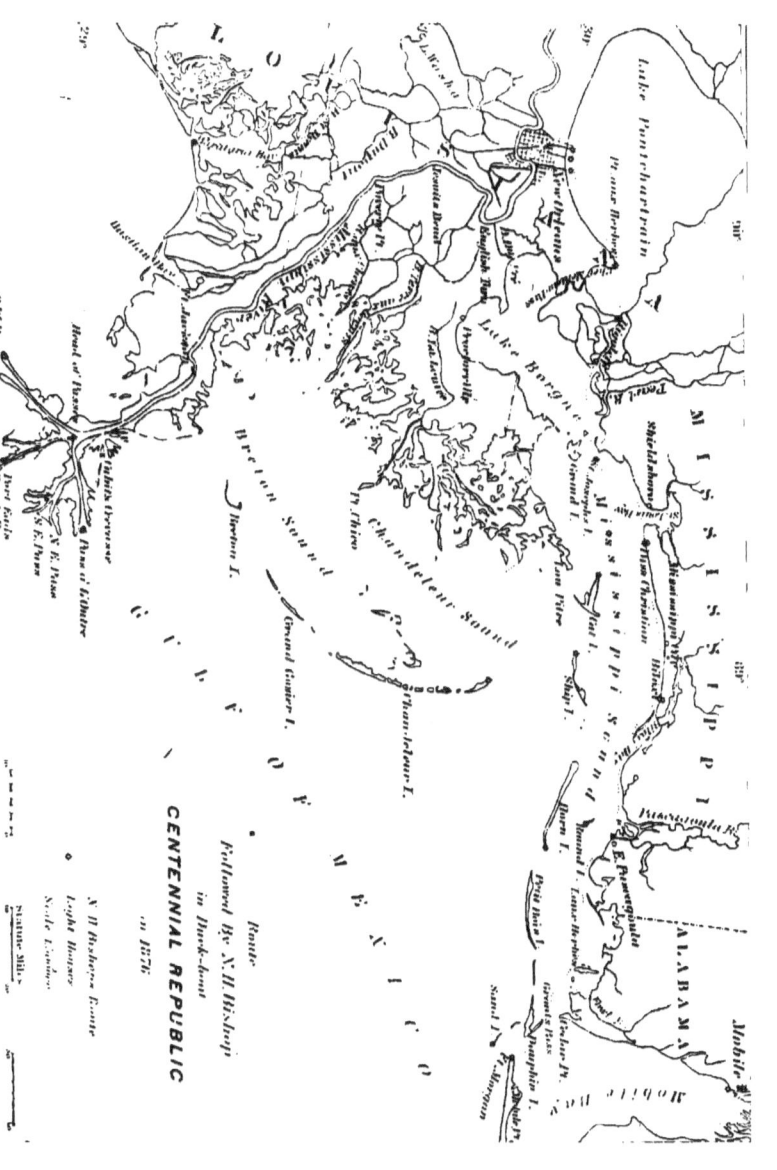

CHAPTER IX.

ON THE GULF OF MEXICO.

LEAVE NEW ORLEANS.—THE ROUGHS AT WORK.—DETAINED AT NEW BASIN.—SADDLES INTRODUCES HIMSELF.—CAMPING ON LAKE PONTCHARTRAIN.—THE LIGHT-HOUSE OF POINT AUX HERBES.—THE RIGOLETS.—MARSHES AND MOSQUITOES.—IMPORTANT USE OF THE MOSQUITO AND BLOW-FLY.—ST. JOSEPH'S LIGHT.—AN EXCITING PULL TO BAY ST. LOUIS.—A LIGHT-KEEPER LOST IN THE SEA.—BATTLE OF THE SHARKS.—BILOXI.—THE WATER-CRESS GARDEN.—LITTLE JENNIE.

ONE of the chief charms in a boatman's life is its freedom, and what that freedom is no one knows until he throws aside the chains of every-day life, steps out of the worn ruts, and, with his kit beside him, his oar in his hand, feels himself master of his time, and FREE. There is one duty incumbent on the voyager, however, and that is to keep his face set upon his goal. Remembering this, I turned my back upon the beguiling city of New Orleans, with its orange groves and sweet flowers, its old buildings and modern civilization, its French cafés and bewitching oddities of every nature, taking away with me among my most pleasant memories the recollection of the kind hospitality of the gentlemen of the "Southern Boat

Club," who presented me with a duplicate of the beautiful silk pendant of their club.

My shortest route to the Gulf of Mexico was through New Basin Canal, six miles in length, into Lake Pontchartrain, and from there to the Gulf. If I had disembarked upon the levee, at the foot of Julia Street, when I arrived in New Orleans, there would have been only a short portage of three-quarters of a mile, in a direct line, to the canal; but my little craft had been left in the keeping of the Southern Boat Club, and the position of their boat-house made a portage of two miles a necessity. An express-wagon was procured, and, accompanied by Mr. Charles Deckbar, a member of the club, the little boat was safely carried through the city streets, and once more shot into her native element in the waters of New Basin Canal. The first part of this canal runs through the city proper, and then through a low swampy region out into the shallow lake Pontchartrain. At the terminus of New Basin Canal I found a small light-house, two or three hotels, and a few houses, making a little village.

A small fleet of schooners, which had brought lumber and firewood from Shieldsboro and other Gulf ports, was lying idly along the sides of the canal, awaiting a fair wind to assist them in making the return trip.

I rowed out of the canal on to the lake; but

finding that the strong wind and rough waves were too much for my boat, I beat a hasty retreat into the port of refuge, and, securing my bow-line to a pile, and my stern-line to the bobstay of a wood-schooner, the "Felicité," I prepared to ride out the gale under her bow. The skippers of the little fleet were very civil men. Some of them were of French and some of Spanish origin, while one or two were Germans. My charts interested them greatly; for though they had navigated their vessels for years upon the Gulf of Mexico, they had never seen a chart; and their astonishment was unbounded when I described to them the bottom of the sea for five hundred miles to the eastward, over a route I had never travelled.

Night settled down upon us, and, as the wind lulled, the evening became lovely. Soon the quiet hamlet changed to a scene of merriment, as the gay people of the city drove out in their carriages to have a "*lark*," as the sailors expressed it; and which seemed to begin at the hotels with card-playing, dancing, drinking, and swearing, and to end in a general carousal. Men and women joined alike in the disreputable scene, though I was informed that this was a respectable circle of society, compared with some which at times enlivened the neighborhood of Lake Pontchartrain. Thinking of the wonderful grades of society, I tried to sleep in my boat, not imagining that my peace was soon to be invaded by the lowest layer of that social strata.

In spite of all my precautions an article had appeared that day in a New Orleans paper giving a somewhat incorrect account of my voyage from Pittsburgh. The betting circles hearing that there was no bet upon my rowing feat, — if such a modest and unadventurous voyage could be called a feat, — decided that there must be some mystery connected with it; and political strife being uppermost in all men's minds, strangers were looked upon with suspicion, while rumors of my being a national government spy found ready belief with the ignorant. Such a man would be an unwelcome visitor in the troubled districts where the "bull-dozing" system was compelling the enfranchised negro to vote the "right ticket." I had received an intimation of this feeling in the city, and had exerted myself to leave the neighborhood that day; but the treacherous east wind had left me in a most unprotected locality, floating in a narrow canal, at the mercy of a lot of strange sailors. The sailor, though, has a generous heart, and usually demands FAIR PLAY, while there is a natural antagonism between him and a landsman. I was, so to speak, one of them, and felt pretty sure that in case of any demonstration, honest "*Jack Tar*" would prove himself my friend.

It seemed at one time as though such an occasion was imminent.

First came the sound of voices in the distance; then, as they came nearer, I heard such questions as, "Where is the feller?" "Show us his boat, and we'll soon tell if he's a humbug!" "We'll put a head on him!" &c. All these expressions being interlarded with oaths and foul language, gave any but a pleasant prospect of what was to be looked for at the hands of these city roughs, who clambered nimbly on to the deck of the Felicité to inquire for my whereabouts.

The darkness seemed to shield me from their sight, and my good friend, the skipper of the wood-schooner, did not volunteer much information as they stood upon his forecastle only a few feet above my head. He told them they were on a fool's errand, if they came there to ask questions about a man who was minding his own business. The sailors all backed him, and the cook grew so bold as to consign the whole crowd, without mercy, to a place too hot for ears polite.

Swaggering and swearing, the roughs went ashore to refresh their thirsty throats at a low grog-shop. Having fired up, they soon returned to the bank of the canal, and, as ill luck would have it, in the darkness of the night caught a gleam of my little white boat resting so peacefully upon the foul water of the canal, made dark and heavy by the city's drainage. Then followed verbal shots, with various demonstrations, for half an hour.

The worst fellow in the crowd was a member of a fire-company, and being a city policeman was supposed to be a protector of the peace. He was very insulting; but I turned his questions and suspicions into ridicule, and, fortunately for me, he so often fell back upon the groggery for strength to fire away, that he was finally overpowered, and was given into the care of his bosom-friend, another blackguard, who dragged him tenderly from the scene. All this time the cook of the schooner had his hot water in readiness, threatening to scald the roughs if they succeeded in getting down to my boat.

At last, much to my relief, the whole party went off to "make a night of it," leaving me in the care of my protectors on the schooner, who had been busy deciding what they should do in case of any assault being made on me by the roughs, and showing their brawny arms in a menacing manner when the worst threats reached their ears.

I did not know this at the time, but as I looked cautiously around after the unwelcome guests had left, I saw a watchman standing on the forecastle of the Felicité, looking anxiously to the safety of the little white craft that by a

New Orleans Roughs amusing themselves.

slender cord held on to his vessel. All through the hours of that long night the kind-hearted master paced his deck; and then, as the sun arose, and the damp vapors settled to the earth, he hailed me with a pleasant "good morning;" and added, " if those devils had jumped on you last night I was to give ONE yell, and the whole fleet would have been on top o' 'em, and we would have backed every man's head down his own throat." This would have been, I thought, a singular but most effective way of settling the difficulty, and a novel mode of thinning out the city police and fire department.

During the day I was visited by a young northerner who had been for some time in New Orleans, but was very anxious to return to his home in Massachusetts. He had no money, but thought if I would allow him to accompany me as far as Florida he could ship as sailor from some port on a vessel bound for New York or Boston. Feeling sorry for the man who was homeless in a strange city, and finding he possessed some experience in salt-water navigation, I acceded to his request. Having purchased of the harbormaster, Captain M. H. Riddle, a light boat, which was sharp at both ends, and possessed the degree of sheer necessary for seaworthiness, the next thing in order was to make some important alterations in her, such as changing the thwarts, putting on half-decks, &c. As this labor would detain me in the unpleasant neighborhood, I determined to secrete my own boat from the public gaze. To accomplish this, while favored by the darkness of night, I ran it into a side canal, where the watchman of the New Lake End Protection Levee lived in a floating house. The duck-boat was drawn out of the water on to a low bank of the levee, and was then covered with reeds. So perfectly was my little craft secreted, that when a party of roughs came out to interview the "government spy," they actually stood beside the boat while inquiring of the watchman for its locality without discovering it.

I now slept in peace at night; but during the day, while working upon the new boat in another locality, was much annoyed by curious persons, who hovered around, hoping to discover the meaning of my movements. On Saturday evening, January 22, I completed the joining and provisioning of the new skiff, which was called, in honor of the harbor-master, the "Riddle." The small local population about the mouth of the canal was in a great state of excitement. The fitting out of the "Riddle" by the supposed "government spy" furnished much food for reflection, and new rumors were set afloat. I passed the first day of the week as quietly as possible amid the gala scenes of that section which knows no Sunday. All day long carriages rolled out from New Orleans, bringing rollicking men and women to the lake, where, free from all restraint, the daily robe of hypocrisy was thrown aside, and poor humanity appeared at its worst. Little squads of roughs came also at intervals, but their attempts to find me or my boat proved fruitless.

The next day my shipmate, whom, for convenience, I will call Saddles, was not prepared to leave, as previously agreed upon, so I turned over to him the " Riddle," her outfit, provisions, &c., and instructed him to follow the west shore of Lake Pontchartrain until he found me, preferring to trust myself to the tender mercies of the Chinese fishermen — whom the reader will remember had been " CIVILIZED " — rather than to linger longer in the neighborhood of the New Orleans firemen and police corps. Saddles had hunted and fished upon the lake, and therefore felt confident he could easily find me the next day at Irish Bayou, two miles beyond the low " Point aux Herbes " Light-house.

An hour before noon, on Monday, January 24, I rowed out of the canal, and most heartily congratulated myself upon escaping the trammels of too much civilization. A heavy fog covered the lake while I felt my way along the shore, passing the Pontchartrain railroad pier. The shoal bottom was covered with stumps of trees, and the coast was low and swampy, with occasional short, sandy beaches. My progress was slow on account of the fog; and at five P. M. I went into camp, having first hauled the boat on to the land by means of a small watch-tackle. The low country was covered in places with coarse grass, and, as I ate my supper by the camp-fire, swarms of mosquitoes attacked me with such impetuosity and bloodthirstiness that I was glad to seek refuge in my boat. This proved, however, only a temporary relief, for the tormentors soon entered at the ventilating space between the combing and hatch, and annoyed me so persistently that I was driven to believe there was something worse than New Orleans roughs. During this night of torture I heard in the distance the sound of oars moving in the oar-locks, and paused for an instant in the battle with the phlebotomists, thinking the "Riddle" might be coming, but all sound seemed hushed, and I returned to my dreary warfare.

Not waiting to prepare breakfast the next morning, I left the prairie shore, and rowed rapidly towards Point aux Herbes. At the light-house landing I found Saddles, with his boat drawn up on shore. He had followed me at four and a half P. M., and the evening being clear, he had easily reached the light-house at eleven P. M. on the same night. Mr. Belton, the light-keeper, kept bachelor's hall in his quarters, and at once went to work with hearty good-will to prepare a breakfast for us, to which we did full justice.

At eleven A. M., though a fog shut out all objects from our sight, I set a boat compass before me on the floor of my craft, and saying good-bye to our host, we struck across the lake in a course which took us to a point below the " Rigolets," a name given to the passages in the marshes through which a large portion of the water of Lake Pontchartrain flows into the Gulf of Mexico. The marshes, or low prairies, which confine the waters of Lake Pontchartrain, are extensive. The coarse grass grows to four or five feet in height, and in it coons, wildcats, minks, hogs, and even rabbits, find a home. In the bayous wild-fowl abound.

The region is a favorite one with hunters and fishermen; but during the summer months alligators and moccasin-snakes are abundant, when it behooves one to be wary. Upon some of the marshy islands of the Gulf, outside of Lake Pontchartrain, wild hogs are to be found. In 1853 it became known that an immense wild boar lived upon the Chandeleur Islands. He was frequently hunted, and though struck by the balls shot at him, escaped uninjured, his tough hide proving an impenetrable barrier to all assaults. There is always, however, some vulnerable point to be found, and in 1874 some Spanish fisherman, taking an undue advantage of his boarship, shot him in the eye, and then clubbed him to death.

The Rigolets are at the eastern end of Lake

Pontchartrain. Their northern side skirts the main land, while their south side is bounded by marshy islands. As we rowed through this outlet of the lake, Fort Pike, with its grassy banks, arose picturesquely on our right from its site on a knoll of high ground. Outside of the Rigolets we entered an arm of the Gulf of Mexico, called Lake Borgne, the shores of which were desolate, and formed extensive marshes cut up by creeks and bayous into many small islands.

As it was late in the day, we ran our two boats into a bayou near the mouth of the Rigolets, and prepared, under the most trying circumstances, to rest for the night. The atmosphere was soft and mild, the evening was perfect. The great sheet of water extended far to the east. On the south it was bounded by marshes. A long, low prairie coast stretched away on the north; it was the southern end of the state of Mississippi. The light-houses flashed their bright beacon-lights over the water. All was tranquil save the ever-pervading, persistent mosquito. Thousands of these insects, of the largest size and of the most pertinacious character, came out of the high grass and " made night hideous."

We had not provided ourselves with a tent, and no artifice on our part could protect us from these torments; so, vainly dealing blows right and left, we discussed the oft-mooted point of the mosquito's usefulness to mankind. We lords of creation believe that everything is made for the gratification of man, even thinking at one time, in our ignorance, that the beautiful colors of flowers served no other end, than to gratify the sense of sight. But this fancy, made beautiful by the songs of our poets, has been dealt with as the man of science must ever deal with stubborn facts, and the utility as well as the beauty of these exquisite hues have been discovered. The colors in the petals of the flowers attract certain insects, whose duty it is to fertilize the flowers by dusting the pistils with the pollen of the ripe anthers, some being attracted by one color, some by another.

Flowery thoughts were not, however, in keeping with the miserable state of mental and physical restlessness induced by the irritating mosquito, and its usefulness seemed to be a necessary thought to make me patient as I lay like a mummy, enveloped in my blankets. The coons were fighting and squealing around my boat, which lay snugly ensconced in a bayou among the reeds, for, once under my hatch-cover, the presence of man was unheeded by these animals, and they sportively turned my deck into a species of amphitheatre.

The vices and virtues of the mosquito may be summed up in a few words, always remembering that it is the FEMALE, and not the MALE, to whom humanity is indebted for lessons of patience. The female mosquito deposits about three hundred eggs, nearly the shape of a grain of wheat, arranging and gluing them perpendicularly side by side, until the whole resembles a solid, canoe-like body, which floats about on the surface of the water. Press this little boat of eggs deep into the water, and its buoyancy causes it to rise immediately to the surface, where it maintains its true position of a well-ballasted craft, right side up. The warmth of the sun, tempered with the moisture of the water, soon hatches the eggs, and the larva, as wigglers or wrigglers, descend to the bottom of the quiet pool, and feed upon the decaying vegetable matter. It moves actively through the stagnant water in its passage to the surface, acrifying it, and at the same time doing faithfully its work as scavenger by consuming vegetable germs and putrefying matter. Professor G. F. Sanborn, and other leading American entomologists, assert that the mosquito saves from twenty-five to forty per cent. in our death-list among those who are exposed to malarial influences.

With malaria, the curse of large districts in the United States, sowing its evil seeds broadcast in our land, and daily closing its iron grasp upon its victims, who could wish for the extermination of so useful an insect as the mosquito?

When the larva reaches the surface of the water, it inhales, through a delicate tube at the lower end of its body, all the air necessary for its respiration. Having lived three or four weeks in the water, during which time it has entered the pupa state, the original skin is cast off, and the insect is transformed into a different and more perfect state. A few days later the epidermis of the pupa falls off, and floats upon the water, and upon this light raft the insect dries its body in the warm rays of the sun; its damp and heavy form grows lighter and more ethereal; it slowly spreads its delicate wings to dry, and soon rises into the clear ether a perfected being.

The male mosquitoes retire to the woods, and lead an indolent, harmless life among the flowers and damp leaves. They are not provided with a lancet, and consequently do not feed upon blood, but suck up moisture through the little tubes nature has given them for that purpose. They are a quiet, well-behaved race, and do not even sing; both the music and the sting being reserved for the other sex. They rarely enter the abodes of man, and may be easily identified by their heavy, feathery antennæ and long maxillary palpi.

Unfortunately for mankind, the female mosquito possesses a most elaborate instrument of torture. She first warns us of her presence by the buzzing sound we know so well, and then settling upon her victim, thrusts into the quivering flesh five sharp organs, one of which is a delicate lancet. These organs, taken in one mass, are called the beak, or bill of the insect. A writer says: "The bill has a blunt fork at the end, and is apparently grooved. Working through the groove, and projecting from the centre of the angle of the fork, is a lance of perfect form, sharpened with a fine bevel. Beside it the most perfect lance looks like a handsaw. On either side of this lance two saws are arranged, with the points fine and sharp, and the teeth well-defined and keen. The backs of these saws play against the lance. When the mosquito alights, with its peculiar hum, it thrusts in its keen lance, and then enlarges the aperture with the two saws, which play beside the lance, until the forked bill, with its capillary arrangement for pumping blood, can be inserted. The sawing process is what grates upon the nerves of the victim, and causes him to strike wildly at the sawyer. The irritation of a mosquito's bite is undoubtedly owing to these saws. It is to be hoped that the mosquito keeps her surgical instruments clean, otherwise it might be a means of propagating blood diseases."

While the mosquito is a sort of parasite, Professor Sanborn, the "Consulting Naturalist" of Andover, Massachusetts, informs me that he has discovered as many as four or five parasitical worms preying upon the inside tissues of the minute beak of the insect.

When the young female mosquito emerges from the water, she lays her eggs in the way described, and her offspring following in time her example, several broods are raised in a single season. Many of the old ones die off, but a sufficient number hybernate under the bark of trees and in dwelling-houses, to perpetuate the species in the early spring months of the following year.

Another insect scavenger, found along the low shores of the Gulf, is the blow-fly, and one very useful to man. Of one species of this insect the distinguished naturalist Reaumur has asserted that the progeny of a single female will consume the carcass of a horse in the same time that it will require a lion to devour it. This singular statement may be explained in the following way. The female fly discovers the body of a dead horse, and deposits (as one species does) her six hundred eggs upon it. In twenty-four hours these eggs will hatch, producing about three hundred female larva, which feed upon the flesh of the horse for about three days, when they attain the perfected state of flies. The three hundred female flies will in their turn deposit some hundred and eighty thousand eggs, which become in four days an army of devourers, and thus in about twelve days, under favorable circumstances, the flesh is consumed by the progeny of one pair of flies in the same time that a lion would devour the carcass.

Our sleepless night coming at last to an end,

we rowed, at dawn, along the prairie shores of the northern coast towards the open Gulf of Mexico. Back of the prairies the forests rose like a green wall in the distance. A heavy fog settled down upon the water and drove us into camp upon the prairie, where we endured again the torture caused by the myriads of bloodthirsty mosquitoes, and were only too glad to make an early start the next morning. A steady pull at the oars brought us to the end of a long cape in the marshes. About a mile and a half east of the land's end we saw a marshy island, of three or four acres in extent, out of the grass of which arose a small wooden light-house, resting securely upon its bed of piles. There was a broad gallery around the low tower, and seeing the light-keeper seated under the shadow of its roof, we pulled out to sea, hoping to obtain information from him as to the "lay of the land." It was the Light of St. Joseph, and here, isolated from their fellow-men, lived Mr. H. G. Plunkett and his assistant light-keeper.

They were completely surrounded by water, which at high tide submerged their entire island. Mr. Butler, the assistant light-keeper, was absent at the village of Bay St. Louis, on the northern shore. The principal keeper begged us to wait until he could cook us a dinner, but the rising south-east wind threatened a rough sea, and warned us to hasten back to the land. The keeper, standing on his gallery, pointed out the village of Shieldsboro, nine miles distant, on the north coast, and we plainly saw its white cottages glimmering among the green trees.

Mr. Plunkett advised us not to return to the coast which we had just left, as it would necessitate following a long contour of the shore to reach Shieldsboro, but assured us that we could row nine miles in a straight course across the open Gulf to the north coast without difficulty. He argued that the rising wind was a fair one for our boats; and that a two hours' strong pull at the oars would enable us to reach a good camping-place on high ground, while if we took the safer but more roundabout route, it would be impossible to arrive at the desired port that night, and we would again be compelled to camp upon the low prairies. We knew what that meant; and to escape another sleepless night in the mosquito lowland, we were ready to take almost any risk.

Having critically examined our oar-locks, and carefully ballasted our boats, we pulled into the rough water. The light-keeper shouted encouragingly to us from his high porch, "You'll get across all right, and will have a good camp to-night!" For a long time we worked carefully at our oars, our little shells now rising on the high crest of a combing sea, now sinking deep into the trough, when one of us could catch only a glimpse of his companion's head. As the wind increased, and the sea became white with caps, it required the greatest care to keep our boats from filling. The light-keeper continued to watch us through his telescope, fearing his counsel had been ill-advised. At times we glanced over our shoulders at the white sand-banks and forest-crowned coasts of Shieldsboro and Bay St. Louis, which were gradually rising to our view, higher and higher above the tide. The piers of the summer watering-places, some of them one thousand feet in length, ran out into shoal water. Against these the waves beat in fury, enveloping the abutments in clouds of white spray. When within a mile of Shieldsboro the ominous thundering of the surf, pounding upon the shelving beach of hard sand, warned us of the difficulty to be experienced in passing through the breakers to the land.

It was a very shoal coast, and the sea broke in long swashy waves upon it. If we succeeded in getting through the deeper surf, we would stick fast in six inches of water on the bottom, and would not be able to get much nearer than a quarter of a mile to the dry land. Then, if we grounded only for a moment, the breaking waves would wash completely over our boats.

Having no idea of being wrecked upon the shoals, I put the duck-boat's bow, with apron set, towards the combing waves, and let her drift in shore stern foremost. The instant the heel of the boat touched the bottom, I pulled rapidly seaward, and in this way felt the approaches to land in various channels many times without shipping a sea.

Saddles kept in the offing, in readiness to come to my assistance if needed. It became evident that we could not land without filling our boats with water, so we hauled off to sea, and took the trough easterly, until we had passed the villages of Shieldsboro and Bay St. Louis, when, like a port of refuge, the bay of St. Louis opened its wide portals, which we entered with alacrity, and were soon snugly camped in a heavy grove of oaks and yellow pines. Here we found an ample supply of dry wood and fresh water, with wild ducks feeding within easy gunshot of our quarters. There were no mosquitoes, and that fact alone rewarded us for our exertions and anxieties.

It was after five o'clock in the afternoon, and, sitting over our cheerful camp-fire, we had little thought of the scene being enacted on the ground we had just gone over. The light-keeper was still at his post, not anxious now about our little craft; but, peering through the fast gathering gloom, he turned his telescope in the direction where he expected to find the boat of his assistant. He soon saw a tiny speck, which grew more and more distinct each moment as it rose and fell upon the waves, beating against a head wind, with sails set, and coming from Bay St. Louis to St. Joseph's Light. It was the boat he expected; and, adjusting his glass, he awaited her arrival.

The cheery light shot its pellucid rays over the dark water, inviting the little sail-boat to a safe harbor, while the mariner hopefully wrestled with the wind and sea, thinking it would soon be over, and his precious cargo (for his wife, her friend, and his three children were on board) safely landed upon the island, where they could look calmly back upon the perils of the deep.

Bravely the boat breasted the sea. It was within three miles of the light, though hardly visible in the gloom to the watchful eye of the light-keeper on his gallery, when Butler attempted to go upon another tack. Twice he tried, twice he failed, when, making a third attempt, the boom of the sail jibed, and instantly the boat capsized. The disappearance of the sail from his horizon told the man upon the gallery of the peril of his friends, and quickly launching a boat, he proceeded rapidly to the scene of disaster.

He found the two women clinging to the boat, and rescued them; but the man and his three children were drowned. A week later, the body of the assistant keeper with that of his oldest child were washed up upon the beach; the others were doubtless thrown up on some lonely coast and devoured by wild hogs or buzzards.

Four months later, some fishermen, while hauling their seine, found the boat imbedded in the sand, in about eight feet of water. Thus the treacherous sea is ever ready to swallow in its insatiable maw those who love it and trust to its ever varying moods.

The gale confined us to our camp for three days, during which time we roamed through the beautiful semi-tropical woods, cooked savory meals, and, lying idly near our fire, watched the fish leap from the water. While in our retreat, Dame Nature favored us with one sharp frost, but it was not sufficiently severe to injure vegetation.

On Monday, January 31, we left the beautiful bay, and rounding Henderson's Point, pulled an easterly course on the open Gulf, along the shores of the village of Pass Christian, which, like the other summer watering-places of this part of the Gulf coast, was made conspicuous from the water by the many long light piers, built of rough pine poles, which extended, in some cases, several hundred feet into the shoal water. Upon the end of almost every pier was the bath-house of the owner of some cottage. The bathers descended a ladder placed under the bath-house to the salt water below. The area beneath each house was enclosed by slats, or poles, nailed to the piling, to secure the bathers from the sharks, which are numerous in these waters.

Two of these ferocious creatures were having a fierce combat, in about four feet depth of water, as we rowed off Pass Christian. This coast is destitute of marshes, and has long sandy beaches, with heavy pine and oak forests in the background. The bathing is excellent, and is appreciated by the people of Louisiana and Mississippi, who resort here in large numbers during the summer months. All the hotels and cottages of these sea-girt villages are, however, closed during the winter, just the time of the year when the climate is delightful, and shooting and fishing at their best.

From Lake Pontchartrain to Mobile Bay, a distance of more than one hundred statute miles in a straight line, there extends a chain of islands, situated from seven to ten miles south of the main coast, and known respectively as Cat Island, Sloop Island, Horn Island, Petit Bois Island, and Dauphine Island. The vast watery area between the mainland and these islands is known as Mississippi Sound, because the southern end of the large state of Mississippi forms its principal northern boundary. The Chandeleur and many other low marshy islands lie to the south of the above-named chain.

Northern yachtmen can pass a pleasant winter in these waters. The fishing along the Gulf coast is excellent. Not having had an opportunity to identify their scientific nomenclature, I can give only the common names by which many species of these fish are known to the native fishermen. Among those found are red-fish, Spanish mackerel, speckled trout, black trout, blue-fish, mullet, sheep's-head, croakers, flounders, and the aristocratic pompano. Crabs and eels are taken round the piers in large numbers, while delicious shrimps are captured in nets by the bushel, and oysters are daily brought in from their natural beds. The fish are kept alive in floating wells until the cook is ready to receive them.

Venison is sold in the markets at a very low price, while the neighboring gardens supply all our summer vegetables during the winter months. I thought, while we rowed along this attractive coast in the balmy atmosphere, with everything brightened and beautified by the early moon, how many were suffering in our northern cities from various forms of pulmonary troubles induced by the severe winter weather, while here, in a delightful climate, with everything to make man comfortable, private houses and hotels were closed, and the life-giving air blowing upon the sandy coast, from the open Gulf of Mexico, dying softly away unheeded by those who so much needed its healing influences. This region, being entirely free from the dampness of the inland rivers of Florida, and having excellent communication by rail with the North and New Orleans, offers every advantage as a winter resort, and will doubtless become popular in that way as its merits are better known.

About nine o'clock in the evening we passed the Biloxi light-house, and decided, as the night was serene and the waters of the Gulf tranquil, to run under one of the bath-houses, and there enjoy our rest, not caring to enter a strange village at that hour. The piling of some of the piers was destitute of the usual shark barricade, and selecting two of these inviting retreats, we pushed in our boats, moored them to the piles, and were soon fast asleep.

About daybreak the weather changed, and the sea came rolling in, pitching us about in the narrow enclosure in a fearful manner. The water had risen so high that we could not get out of our pens; so, climbing into the bath-rooms above, we held on to the bow and stern lines of our boats, endeavoring to keep them from being dashed to pieces against the pilings of the pier. While in this mortifying predicament, expecting each moment to see our faithful little skiffs wrecked most ingloriously in a bath-house, sounds were heard and some men appeared, who, coming to our assistance, proved themselves friends in need. We fished the boats out of the pen with my watch-tackle, and hoisted each one at a time into the bath-house that had covered it.

Two gentlemen then approached, one claiming Saddles as his guest, while the other, Mr. J. P. Montross, conducted me to his attractive tree-embowered home; and with the soft and winning accent of an educated gentleman of Yucatan, the country of his birth, placed his house and belongings at my disposal. "I was in New Orleans when you went through that city," he said, "and learning that you would pass through Biloxi, I at once telegraphed to my agent here to detain you if possible as my guest until I should arrive."

We remained a week in Biloxi, where I became daily more and more impressed with the great natural advantages of these Gulf towns as winter watering-places for northern invalids or sportsmen. During one of my rambles about Biloxi, I stumbled upon a curious little plantation, the lessee of which was entirely absorbed in the occupation of raising water-cresses. In Mr. Scheffer's garden, which was about half an acre in extent, I found fifteen little springs flowing out of a substratum of chalk. The water was very warm and clear, while the springs varied in character. There was a chalk-spring, a sulphur-spring, and an iron-spring, all within a few feet of each other. The main spring flowed out of the ground near the head, or highest part of the garden, while ditches of about two feet in width, with boarded sides to prevent their caving in, carried the water of the various springs to where it was needed.

The depth of water in these ditches was not over eighteen inches. Their preparation is very simple, sand to the depth of an inch or two being placed at the bottom, and the roots, cuttings, &c., of the cresses dropped into them. This prolific plant begins at once to multiply, sending up thousands of hair-like shoots, with green leaves floating upon the surface of the running water. Mr. Scheffer informed me that he marketed his stock three times a week, cutting above water the matured plants, and putting them into bundles, or bunches, of about six inches in diameter, and then packing them with the tops downward in barrels and baskets. These bunches of cresses sell for fifteen cents apiece on the ground where they are grown. New Orleans consumes most of the stock; but invalids in various places are fast becoming customers, as the virtues of this plant are better understood. It is of great benefit in all diseases of the liver, in pulmonary complaints, and in dyspepsia with its thousand ills.

The ditches in this little half-acre garden, if placed in a continuous line, would reach six hundred feet, and the crop increases so fast that one hundred bunches a week can be cut throughout the year. The hot suns of summer injure the tender cresses; hence butter-beans are planted along the ditches to shade them. The bean soon covers the light trellis which is built for it to run upon, and forms an airy screen for the tender plants. During the autumn and winter months the light frame-work is removed, and sunlight freely admitted.

Cresses can be grown with little trouble in pure water of the proper temperature; and as each bed is replanted but once a year, in the month of October, the yield is large and profitable.

The intelligent cultivator of this water-cress garden frequently has boarders from a distance, who reside with him that they may receive the full benefit of a diet of tender cresses fresh from the running water. Few, indeed, know the benefit to be derived from such a diet, or the water-cress garden would not be such a novelty to Americans. We, as a nation, take fewer salads with our meals than the people of any of the older sister-lands, perhaps, because in the rush of every-day life we have not time to eat them. We are, at the same time, adding largely each year to the list of confirmed dyspeptics, many of whom might be saved from this worst of all ills by a persistent use of the fresh watercress, crisp lettuce, and other green and wholesome articles of food. Such advice is, however, of little use, since many would say, like a gentleman I once met, "Why, I would rather *die* than diet!" Three hundred feet from the garden the water of its springs flows into the Gulf of Mexico, the waves of which beat against the clean sandy shore.

Among other things in this interesting town, I discovered in the boat-house belonging to the summer residence of Mr. C. T. Howard, of New Orleans, John C. Cloud's little boat, the "*Jennie*." Strange emotions filled my mind as I gazed upon the light Delaware River skiff which had been the home for so many days of that unfortunate actor, whose disastrous end I have already related to my reader.

The boat had been brought from Plaquemine Plantation on the Mississippi River to this distant point. It was about fifteen feet in length, and four feet wide amidships. She was sharp at both bow and stern, and was almost destitute of sheer. There was a little deck at each end, and the usual galvanized-iron oar-locks, without out-riggers, while upon her quarters were painted very small national flags. She was built of white pine, and was very light.

Each summer, when guests are at Biloxi,

sympathizing groups crowd round this little skiff, and listen to the oft-repeated story of the poor northerner who sacrificed his own life while engaged in the attempt to win a bet to support his large and destitute family.

Here by the restless sea, which seems ever to be moaning a requiem for the dead, I left the little "Jennie," a monument of American pluck, but, at the same time, a mortifying instance of the fruitlessness of our national spirit of adventure when there is no principle to back it.

Arrival at the Gulf of Mexico. — Camp Mosquito.

CHAPTER X.

FROM BILOXI TO CAPE SAN BLAS.

POINTS ON THE GULF COAST. — MOBILE BAY. — THE HERMIT OF DAUPHINE ISLAND. — BON SECOURS BAY. — A CRACKER'S DAUGHTERS. — THE PORTAGE TO THE PERDIDO. — THE PORTAGE FROM THE PERDIDO TO BIG LAGOON. —PENSACOLA BAY. — SANTA ROSA SOUND. — A NEW LONDON FISHERMAN. — CATCHING THE POMPANO. — A NEGRO PREACHER AND WHITE SINNERS. — A DAY AND A NIGHT WITH A MURDERER. — ST. ANDREW'S SOUND. — ARRIVAL AT CAPE SAN BLAS.

ON the morning of February 8 we left Biloxi, and launching our boats, proceeded on our voyage to the eastward, skirting shores which were at times marshy, and again firm and sandy. At Oak Point, and Belle Fontaine Point, green magnolia trees, magnificent oaks, and large pines grew nearly to the water's edge. Beyond Belle Fontaine the waters of Graveline Bayou flow through a marshy flat to the sea, and offer an attractive territory to sportsmen in search of wild-fowl. Beyond the bayou, between West and East Pascagoula, we found a delta of marshy islands, and an area of mud flats, upon which had been erected enclosures of brush, within the cover of which the sportsman could secrete himself and boat while he watched for the wild ducks constantly attracted to his neighborhood by the submarine grasses upon which they fed.

At sunset we ran into the mouth of a creek near the village of East Pascagoula, and there slept in our boats, which were securely tied to stakes driven into the salt marsh. At eight o'clock the next morning, the tide being low, we waded out of the stream, towing our boats with lines into deeper water, and rowed past East Pascagoula, which, like the other watering-places of the Gulf, seemed deserted in the winter. The coast was now a wilderness, with few habitations in the dense forests, which formed a massive dark green background to the wide and inhospitable marshes. As we proceeded upon our voyage wildfowl and fish became more and more abundant, but few fishermen's boats or coasting vessels were seen upon the smooth waters of the Gulf. About dusk we ascended a creek, marked upon our chart as Bayou Caden, and passing through marshes, over which swarmed myriads of mosquitoes, we landed upon the pebbly beach of a little hammock, and there pitched our tent.

This portable shelter, which we had made at Biloxi, proved indeed a luxury. It was only six feet square at its base, weighing but a few pounds, and when compactly folded occupying little space; but after the first night's peaceful sleep under its sheltering care it occupied a large place in our hearts; for, having driven out the mosquitoes and closely fastened the entrance, we bade defiance to our tormentors, and realized by comparison, as we never did before, the misery of voyaging without a tent.

Moving out of the Bayou Caden the next day, a lot of fine oysters was collected in shoal water, and by a lucky shot, a fat duck was added to the *menu*.

We were now on the coast of Alabama, so named by an aboriginal chief when he arrived at the river, from which he thought no white man would ever drive him, and turning to his followers, exclaimed, *Alabama!* — " Here we rest." Alas for chief and followers, who to-day have no spot of ground where they can stand and cry, *Alabama!*

There were several bays to be crossed before we reached a point in the marshes which extended several miles to the south, and was called Berrin Point. To the east of this was a wide bay, bounded by Cedar Point, which formed one side of the entrance to Mobile Bay. Miles across the water to the south lay Dauphine Island, which it was necessary to reach before we could cross the inlet to Mobile Bay. The wind rose from the south, giving us a head sea, but we pulled across the shallow bay, through which ran a channel called " Grant's Pass," it having been dredged out to enable vessels to pass from Mississippi

Sound to Mobile Bay. This tedious pull ended by our safe arrival at Dauphine Island, upon the eastern point of which we found, close to the beach, a group of wooden government buildings, once occupied by some of the members of the United States Army Engineer Corps.

Here lived, as keeper of the property, a genial recluse, Mr. Robinson Cruse, who for eight years had led an almost solitary life, his nearest neighbor on the island being the sergeant in charge of Fort Gaines, which officer, I was informed, was seldom seen outside of his dismal enclosure. Solitude, however, did not seem to have had the usual effect upon Mr. Cruse, for he welcomed us most cordially, and cooked us a truly maritime supper of many things he had taken from the sea. When darkness came, and the winds were howling about us, he piled in his open fireplace pieces of the wrecks of unfortunate vessels which had foundered on the coast, and had cast up their frames and plankings on the beach near his door. Grouping ourselves round the crackling fire, our host opened his budget of adventures by sea and by land, entertaining us most delightfully until midnight, when we spread our blankets on the hard floor in front of the fire, and were soon travelling in the realms of dreamland.

The following day the wind stirred up the wide expanse of water about the island to such a degree of boisterousness that we could not launch our boats. Our position was somewhat peculiar. Between Dauphine Island and the beach of the mainland opposite was an open ocean inlet of three and a half miles in width, through which the tide flowed. Fort Gaines commanded the western side of this inlet, while Fort Morgan menaced the intruder on the opposite shore. North of this Gulf portal was the wide area of water of Mobile Bay, extending thirty miles to Mobile City, while to the south of it spread the Gulf of Mexico, bounded only by the dim horizon of the heavens. To the east, and inside the narrow beach territory of the eastern side of the inlet, was Bon Secours Bay, a sort of estuary of Mobile Bay, of sixteen miles in length. The passage of the exposed inlet could be made in a small boat only during calm weather, otherwise the voyager might be blown out to sea, or be forced, at random, into the great sound inside the inlet. In either case the rough waves would be likely to fill the craft and drown its occupant. In case of accident the best swimmer would have little chance of escape in these semi-tropical waters, as the man-eating shark is always cruising about, waiting, Micawber-like, for something "to turn up."

The windy weather kept us prisoners on Dauphine Island for two days, but early on the morning of February 13 a calm prevailed, taking advantage of which, we hurried across the open expanse of water, not daring to linger until our kind host could prepare breakfast. The shoal water of the approaches to the enterprising cotton port of Mobile make it necessary for large vessels to anchor thirty miles below the city, in a most exposed position. We passed through this fleet, which was discharging its cargo by lighters, and gained in safety the beach in Bon Secours Bay, near Fort Morgan.

While preparing our breakfast on the glittering white strand, we received a visit from Mr. B. F. Midyett, the light-keeper of Mobile Point. He was a North Carolinian, but told us that Indian blood flowed in his veins. He was from the neighborhood of the lost colony of Sir Walter Raleigh, a history of which I gave in my "Voyage of the Paper Canoe." Midyett (also spelled Midget) may have been a descendant of that feeble colony of white men which so mysteriously disappeared from history after it had abandoned Roanoke Island, North Carolina, being forced by starvation to take refuge among friendly Indians, when its members, through intermarriage with their protectors, lost their individuality as white men, and founded a race of blue-eyed savages afterwards seen by European explorers in the forests of Albemarle and Pamplico sounds.

The light-keeper begged us to make him a

visit; but it was necessary to hurry to the end of Bon Secours Bay before night, as a north wind would give us a heavy beam sea. Passing "Pilot Town," where the little cottages of oystermen, fishermen, and pilots were clustered along the beach, we pulled past a forest-clad strand until dusk, when we reached the end of Bon Secours Bay, where it was necessary to make a portage across the woods to the next inland watercourse.

The eastern end of Bon Secours Bay terminated at the mouth of Bon Secours River, which we ascended, finding on the low shores a well-stocked country store, and several small houses occupied by oystermen. We slept in our boats by the river's bank, and the next morning turned into a narrow creek, on our right hand, which led to a small tidal pond, called Bayou John, the bottom of which was covered in places with large and delicious oysters. Crossing the lagoon, we landed in a heavy forest of yellow pines. This desolate region was the home of John Childeers, a farmer; and we were informed that he alone, in the entire neighborhood, was the possessor of oxen, and was in fact the only man who could be hired to draw our boats seven miles to Portage Creek, which is a tributary of Perdido River.

Leaving Saddles to watch our boats, I entered the tall pine forest, and after walking a

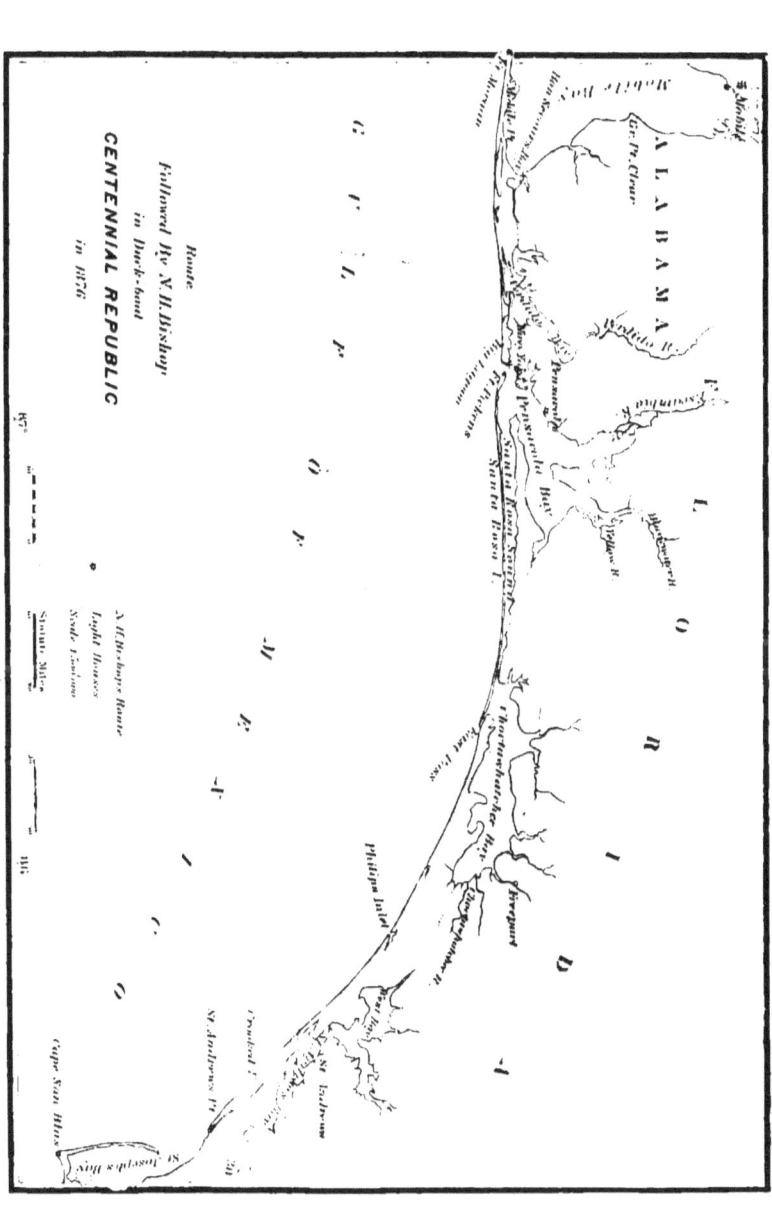

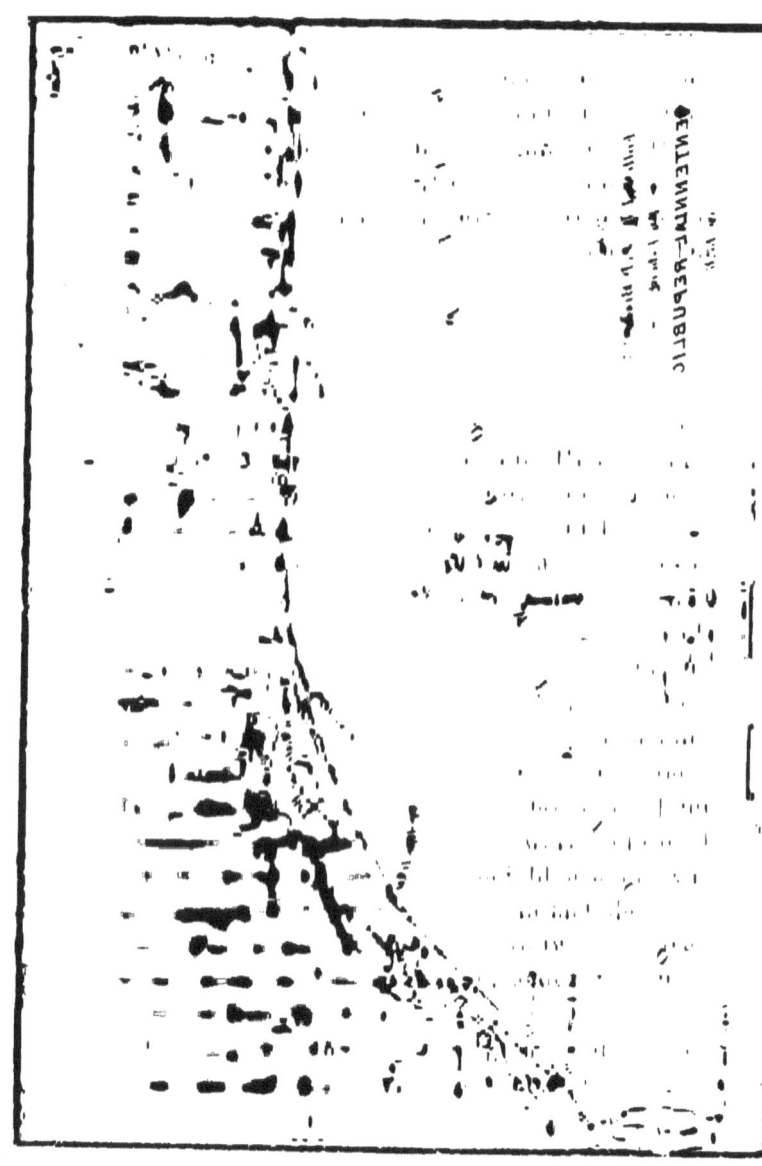

mile came upon the clearing of the backwoodsman. His two daughters, young women, were working in the field; but the sight of a stranger was so unusual to them, that, heedless of my remonstrances and gentle assurances of goodwill, they took to their heels and ran so fast that it was impossible to overtake them until they arrived at the log cabin of their father. The dogs then made a most unceremonious assault upon me, when the maidens, forgetting their fears, made a sally upon the fierce curs, and clubbed them with such hearty good-will that the discomfited canines hastily took refuge in the woods.

The family listened to my story, and insisted upon my joining them in their mid-day meal, which consisted of pork, sweet-potatoes, and corn-bread. My host agreed to haul the boats the next day to Portage Creek for five dollars, and I returned to Saddles to make preparations for the overland journey. That night we feasted sumptuously upon fat oysters six inches in length, rolled in beaten eggs and cracker-crumbs, and fried a delicate brown. These, with good hot coffee and fresh bread, furnished a supper highly appreciated by two hungry men.

With the morning came our farmer, when about an hour was spent in securely packing our boats in the long wagon. The duck-boat was placed upon the bottom, while the light skiff of my companion rested upon a scaffolding above, made by lashing cross-bars to the stanchions of the wagon. This peculiar two-storied vehicle swayed from side to side as we travelled over uneven ground, but the boats were securely lashed in their places, and the parts exposed to chafing carefully protected by bundles of coarse grass and our blankets.

We travelled slowly through the heavily grassed savannas and the dense forests of yellow pine towards the east, in a line parallel with, and only three miles from, the coast. The four oxen hauled this light load at a snail's pace, so it was almost noon when we struck Portage Creek near its source, where it was only two feet in width. Following along its bank for a mile, we arrived at the logging-camp of Mr. Childeers. There we found the creek four rods in width, and possessing a depth of fifteen feet of water. The lumbermen haul their pine logs to this point, and float them down the stream to the steam sawmills on Perdido River.

The boats were soon launched upon the dark cypress waters of the creek, the cargo carefully stowed, and the voyage resumed. Though the roundabout course through the woods was fully seven miles, a direct line for a canal to connect the Bon Secours and Portage Creek waters would not exceed four miles. About two miles from the logging-camp the stream entered "Bay

Lalanch," from the grassy banks of which alligators slid into the water as we rowed quietly along.

We now entered a wide expanse of bay and river, with shores clothed with solemn forests of dark green. The wide Perdido River, rising in this region of dismal pines, flows between Bear Point and Inerarity's Point, when, making a sharp turn to the eastward, it empties into the Gulf of Mexico. In crossing the river between the two points mentioned, we were only separated from the sea by a narrow strip of low land. The Perdido River is the boundary line between the states of Alabama and Florida. In a bend of the river, nearly three miles east of Inerarity's Point, we landed on a low shore, having passed the log cabins of several settlers scattered along in the woods.

It was now necessary to make a portage across the low country to the next interior watercourse, called "Big Lagoon." It was a shallow tidal sheet of water seven miles in length by one in width, and separated from the sea by a very narrow strip of beach. We camped in our boats for the night, starting off hopefully in the morning for the little settlement, to procure a team to haul our boats three-quarters of a mile to Big Lagoon. The settlers were all absent from their homes, hunting and fishing, so we returned to our camp depressed in spirits. There was nothing left for us but to attempt to haul our boats over the sandy neck of land; so we at once applied ourselves to the task. The boats were too heavy for us to carry, so we dragged the sneak-box on rollers, cut from a green pine-tree, half-way to the lagoon; and, making many journeys, the provisions, blankets, gun, oars, &c., were transported upon our shoulders to the half-way resting-place.

So laborious was this portage that when night came upon us we had hauled one boat only, with our provisions, tent, and outfit, to the beach of Big Lagoon. The Riddle still rested upon the banks of the Perdido River. The tent was pitched to shelter us from mosquitoes, and partaking of a hearty supper, we rolled ourselves in our blankets and slept. The camp was in a desolate place, our only neighbors being the coons, and they enlivened the solitude by their snarling and fighting, having come down to the beach to fish in apparently no amiable mood.

Before midnight, that unmistakable cry so human in its agonizing tone, warned us of the approach of a panther. Coming closer and closer, the animal prowled round our tent, sounding his childlike wail. It was too dark to get a glimpse of him, though we watched, weapons in hand, for his nearer approach. Saddles had hunted the beast in his Louisiana lairs, and was eager to make him feel the weight of his lead. We succeeded in driving him off once, but he returned and skulked in the bushes near our camp for half an hour, when his cries grew fainter as he beat a retreat into the forest.

We worked hard until noon the next day in the vain attempt to haul the Riddle from the Perdido, when I launched the duck-boat on Big Lagoon and rowed easterly in search of assistance, leaving Saddles behind to guard our stores. When six miles from camp, I discovered upon the high north shore of the lagoon the clearing and cabin of Rev. Charles Hart, an industrious negro preacher, who labored assiduously, cultivating the thin sandy soil of his little farm, that he might teach his fellow-freedmen spiritual truths on the Lord's day. This humble black promised to go with his scrawny horse to the assistance of Saddles, and at once departed on his mission, happy in the knowledge that he could serve two unfortunate boatmen, and honestly earn two dollars. Going into camp upon the shore, I kept up a bright fire to notify my absent companion of my whereabouts.

At seven o'clock the Rev. Mr. Hart returned and claimed his fee, reporting that he had hauled the Riddle to the lagoon, where he found Saddles pleasantly whiling away the hours of solitude in the useful occupation of washing his extra shirt and stockings. He assured me the Riddle would soon appear. A little later Saddles reached my camp, and we tented for the night on the beach. At daylight we took to our oars, and rowed out of the end of the lagoon into Pensacola Bay. Skirting the high shores on our left, we approached within a mile of the United States naval station Warrington, where we went into camp upon the white strand, in a small settlement of pilots and fishermen, who kindly welcomed us to Pensacola Bay. We slept in our boats on the sandy beach, beside a little stream of fresh water that flowed out of the bank.

The morning of the 19th of February was calm and beautiful, while the songs of mockingbirds filled the air. Across the inlet of Pensacola Bay was the western end of the low, sandy island of Santa Rosa, which stretches in an easterly direction for forty-eight miles to East Pass and Choctawhatchee Bay, and serves as a barrier to the sea. Behind this narrow beach island flow the waters of Santa Rosa Sound, the northern shores of which are covered with the same desolate forests of yellow pine that characterize the uplands of the Gulf coast. At the west end of Santa Rosa Island the walls of Fort Pickens rose gloomily out of the sands. It was the only structure inhabited by man on the long barren island, with the exception of one small cabin built on the site of Clapp's steam-mill, four miles beyond the fort, and occupied by a negro.

We crossed the bay to Fort Pickens, and followed the island shore of the sound until five o'clock P. M., when we sought a camp on the beach at the foot of some conspicuous sand hills, the thick "scrub" of which seemed to be the abode of numerous coons. From the top of the principal sand dune there was a fine view of the boundless sea. Our position, however, had its inconveniences, the principal one being a scarcity of water, so we were obliged to break camp at an early hour the next day.

The Santa Rosa Island shore was so desolate and unattractive that we left it, and crossed the narrow sound to the north shore of the mainland, where nature had been more prodigal in her drapery of foliage. Before noon a sail appeared on the horizon, and we gradually approached it. Close to the shore we saw a raft of sawed timbers being towed by a yacht. The captain hailed us, and we were soon alongside his vessel. The refined features of a gentleman beamed upon us from under an old straw hat, as its owner trod, barefooted, the deck of his craft. He had started, with the raft in tow, from his mill at the head of Choctawhatchee Bay, bound for the great lumber port of Pensacola, but being several times becalmed, was now out of provisions. We gave him and his men all we could spare from our store, and then inquired whether it would be possible for us to find a team and driver to haul our boats from the end of the watercourse we were then traversing, across the woods to the tributary waters of St. Andrew's Bay. The captain kindly urged us to go to his home, and report ourselves to his wife, remaining as his guests until he should return from Pensacola, — " when," he said, " I myself will take you across."

This plan would, however, have caused a delay of several days, so we could not take advantage of the kind offer of the ex-confederate general.

Having considered a moment, our new friend proposed another arrangement.

"There is," he said, "only one person living at the end of Choctawhatchee Bay, besides myself, who owns a yoke of oxen. He can serve you if he wishes, but remember he is a dangerous man. He came here from the state of Mississippi, after the war, and by exaction, brutality, and even worse means, has got hold of most of the cattle, and everything else of value, in his neighborhood. He can haul your boats to West Bay Creek in less than a day's time. The job is worth three or four dollars, but he will get all he can out of you."

Thanking the captain for the information, and the warning he had given us, we waved a farewell, and rowed along the almost uninhabited coast until dusk, when we crossed the sound to camp upon Santa Rosa Island, as an old fisherman at Warrington had advised us; "for," said he, "the woods on the mainland are filled with varmints, — cats and painters, — which may bother you at night."

On the morning of the 21st we rowed to the end of the sound, which narrowed as we approached the entrance to the next sheet of water, Choctawhatchee Bay. There were a few shanties along the narrow outlet on the main shore, where some settlers, beguiled to this desolate region by the sentimental idea of pioneer life in a fine climate, known as "FLORIDA FEVER," were starving on a fish diet, which, in the cracker dialect, was "powerful handy," and bravely resisting the attacks of insects, the bane of life in Florida.

Seven miles from the end of Santa Rosa Island the boats emerged from the passage between the sounds, and entered Choctawhatchee Bay. As the wind arose we struggled in rough water, shaping our course down to the inlet called East Pass, through which the tide ebbed and flowed into the bay.

Here we encountered an original character known as "Captain Len Destin." He was a fisherman, from New London, Connecticut, and had a comfortable house on the high bank of the inlet, surrounded by cultivated fields, where he had lived since 1852. Having married a native of the country, he settled down to the occupation of his fathers; and being a prince among fishermen, he was able to send good supplies of the best fish to the Pensacola markets. His *modus operandi* was rather peculiar. Having rowed along the beach on the open Gulf, a boat-load of fishermen, with their nets ready to cast, rested quietly upon their oars in the offing, while a sharp-eyed man walked along the coast, peering into the transparent water, searching for the schools of fish which feed near the strand. The fishermen cautiously follow him, until, suddenly catching sight of a lot of pompanos, sheep's-heads, and other fish, he signals to his companions, and they, quietly approaching the unsuspicious fish, drop their long net into the water, and enclose the whole school. Drawing the net upon the beach, the fish were taken out and carried to Captain Len's landing, inside of the inlet, where they were packed in the refrigerator of a fleet-sailing boat, which, upon receiving its cargo, started immediately for Pensacola. In this way the pompano, the most delicious of southern fishes, being repacked at Pensacola in hogsheads of ice, found its way quickly by rail to New York city, where they were justly appreciated.

Captain Len generously supplied our camp with fish; so making a good fire, we broiled them before it, baking bread in our Dutch oven;

and finishing our sumptuous repast with some hot coffee, we turned a deaf ear to the whistling wind that blew steadily from the north-east. A little schooner of four tons was riding out the gale near the landing. She was bound for Appalachicola and St. Marks, Florida. Her passengers were crowded into a cabin, the confined limits of which would have attracted the attention of any society for the prevention of cruelty to animals, had it contained a freight of quadrupeds instead of human beings. The heads of white and black men and women could be seen above the hatchway at times, as though seeking for a breath of pure air.

The Reverend Mr. B., a colored preacher, crawled out of the hold, and visited my camp. Finding that I sympathized strongly with his unfortunate race, he opened his heart to me, telling of his labors among them. He also gave me an account of his efforts to encourage some observance of the first day of the week among the white inhabitants of Key West; he and other colored Christians having petitioned the mayor of that city to enforce the laws which require a decent respect for the Lord's day. He grieved over the sinful condition of the inhabitants of that ungodly city, and gave me a sketch of his plans for improving the morality of his white brethren. He had been travelling, like St. Paul, upon the sea, to visit and encourage the weak negro churches in Florida. His address was that of a gentleman, and his heart beat with generous impulses.

I rowed out to the little craft in the offing, and found in the diminutive cabin eight FIRST-CLASS NEGRO passengers, while in the vessel's hold, reclining upon the cargo, were four white men who were voyaging SECOND class. The cordage of the little craft was rotten, and the sails nearly worn out, yet all these people were cheerful, and willing to put to sea as soon as the young skipper would dare to venture out upon the Gulf.

The gale finally exhausted itself. On the 24th we rowed along the southern wooded shore of Choctawhatchee Bay, towards its eastern end. The sound is put down on our charts as Santa Rosa Bay, though the people know it only by its Indian name. It is nearly thirty miles long, and has an average width of five miles. Its shores are covered by a wilderness, and the settlements are few and far between. As we had not left Captain Len's landing until afternoon, we made only ten miles that night, and camped, supperless, on "Twelve Mile Point," but making an early start the next morning, we reached at noon the eastern shore of the bay near the log cabin of the man of murderous deeds, to whom we were to look for assistance in the transportation of our boats across the wilderness to the next inland watercourse.

A tall man, with a most sinister countenance, but rather better dressed than the average backwoodsman, soon made his way to our boats. I plainly stated my object in calling upon him, and expressed a wish that he would not be severe in his charges, as in that case I should return to Captain Len's landing, put to sea, and follow the coast instead of the interior waters to the inlet of St. Andrew's Bay. He agreed to make the portage for ten dollars, stating that the distance was about fourteen miles; and we in our turn promised to be ready to attend to the loading of the boats the next morning.

As we walked about the plantation, its owner became quite communicative, even pointing out the spot where his wife's nephew had been shot dead, leaving him heir to five hundred head of cattle. He spoke of his differences with his neighbors, and assured us that nothing but lynch law would " go down " in their wild region, where, he said, no law existed. He had been a physician in his native state of Mississippi, but there were so many widows and orphans who could not pay his fees that he gave up his profession, and came to the Gulf coast of Florida, where he met a widow, who owned, with her nephew, one thousand head of cattle, which roamed through the savanna bottoms of the coast, requiring no care except an occasional salting. Having married the innocent woman, his first victim, he then, according to the testimony of his neighbors, hired a man to shoot his nephew, and had so become the sole owner of the whole herd of cattle, which roamed over thirty square miles of territory.

Here was, indeed, a cheerful guide for two lone voyagers through the uninhabited wilds! Saddles and I made up our minds, however, to accept the inevitable gracefully, and at nine o'clock the next morning the boats were lashed into the wagon, and the retired physician, with two of his men on horseback, accompanied by Saddles and myself on foot, slowly left the clearing, and defiled along an almost undefined trail through the forest. I noticed that the men were well armed, and all on the alert. Occasionally one of the men would be sent off to the right or left to search for cattle signs, but our guide himself hung close to the wagon, seeming to consider prudence the better part of valor.

Opening the conversation with this quondam physician, I asked his opinion in regard to several well-known remedies, and discovered that he used but three. The best medicine, he said, was CALOMEL, the next QUININE, and what they would not cure, GLAUBER'S SALTS would. In fact, he considered salts the specific for all diseases. Leading gently to the subject, I spoke of his nephew's death, when he assured me the cruel deed had been done by a settler named

Bridekirk, who had squatted upon some land belonging to the young man, and though the intruder never had it conveyed to him by government, he considered it his own. Anxious to protect his nephew's interest, the physician took up the claim, and moved his family to the disputed territory. "Bridekirk," he said, "swore my nephew should never live on what he called HIS claim, and a short time afterwards took his revenge. I had sent the boy for a spur I left at a neighbor's, and when just outside my fence a man who was concealed in a thicket shot the poor fellow. I KNOW it was the devil Bridekirk who did it."

"Did you find his trail?" I asked.

"No," he answered; "we could not pick it up. It was all stamped out. No one could recognize it, but I know Bridekirk was the assassin. He threatened my life too; *but he's dead now.*"

"Dead!" I exclaimed; "when did he die?"

"Oh, about a week ago. He lived a few miles from here, and one morning SOMEBODY shot him in his doorway."

"Who could have done that?" I inquired.

A savage gleam lit up the physician's eye, as he said, slowly:

"My wife's nephew had some relation in a distant state, and it was reported they would see that Bridekirk got his deserts."

"They came a long way to take their revenge," I remarked.

"Yes, a very long way," he answered; and then added: "This Bridekirk would have been arrested for stealing my cattle if he had lived a week or two longer. Me and a neighbor was out looking up our cattle round here, not long ago, and we saw there were a good many fresh burns in the woods, and as we knew that cattle would go to such places to nibble the fresh grass that starts up after a fire, we set out for a big burnt patch. While we were in the woods, towards sunset, we saw two men on horseback driving an old bell-steer and four or five young cattle, all of which we easily recognized in the distance as part of my herd. We followed the men cautiously, keeping so far in the woods that they could not see us, when they mounted a little hill, and the last rays of the setting sun striking upon them, we saw that it was Bridekirk and a neighbor who were stealing my stock. We hid in the swamp until nine o'clock at night, and then rode to Bridekirk's clearing. There was a stream in a hollow below his house, but his cattle-pen was on the rising ground a little way off. We tied our horses in the woods, and crawled up to the cow-pen. There we found all the cattle the thieves had stolen excepting the bell-steer. There was a fire down in the hollow by the stream, and we could see Bridekirk and the other fellow skinning my bell-steer, which they had just killed. Said I to my friend, ' Now we have 'em!' and I took aim at Bridekirk with my gun. My friend was a LAW man, so he said, 'No, don't shoot; there is *some* law left, and we have EVIDENCE now. Let's go and indict them. Then if the sheriff won't arrest them, we can find plenty of chances to pull the trigger on them. I go in for *law* first, and LYNCHING afterwards.' Well, it was a hard thing to lose such a chance when we were boiling over, but I put my gun on my shoulder, and my friend let the bars of the pen down, and we drove the other cattle out as quietly as possible into the woods.

"Next day, Bridekirk's neighbor, who had helped kill the beef, left for parts unknown. Why? because, when he found the bars let down, and the cattle gone, and measured our tracks, he knew WHO had been watching him, and he thought it safest to skedaddle. Bridekirk then kept close in his cabin. He knew who was on his trail THIS TIME. We got the men indicted, and the sheriff had the order of arrest; but he held it for a week, and probably sent word to Bridekirk to keep out of the way. So law, as usual in these parts, fizzled, and it became necessary to try something surer.

"Now I was told that one morning last week, before daybreak, Bridekirk and his hired man heard a noise in the yard that sounded as though some animal was worrying the hens. He suspected it was somebody trying to draw him out into the yard, so he would not go, but tried to get his man to see what was up. The man was afraid, too, for he had his suspicions. At last the noise outside stopped, and the sun began to rise. As nobody seemed to be about, Bridekirk stuck his head out of the door, and, not seeing anything, slowly stepped outside. Now there were two men hidden behind a fence, with their guns pointed at the door. As soon as that cow-thief got fairly out of his house, we — THESE FELLOWS, I MEAN — pulled trigger and shot him dead. The authorities held a sort of inquest on the case, but all that is known of the matter is that he came to his death by shots from unknown parties."

Little did this cold-blooded man suspect, while relating his story to me, that his own end would be like Bridekirk's, and that he would soon fall under an assassin's hand. I became thoroughly disgusted with my companion, who kept close to my side hour after hour as we trudged through the wilderness. One of his arms was held stiffly to his side, and seemed to be almost useless. He had attempted a piece of imposition on a man who lived near the creek we were approaching, and had received the contents of the settler's shot-gun in his side. Most of the charge had lodged in the shoulder and arm, and the cripple now inveighed against this man, and advised us to keep clear of him when we rowed down the creek. "I have nothing against Mr. B.," he said; "but he is no GENTLEMAN, and you better not camp near him."

Before sunset we entered a heavily grassed country, where deer were abundant. They sprung from their beds in the tall grass, and bounded away as we advanced. At twilight the oxen finished their long pull on the banks of a little watercourse known as West Bay Creek, so called because it flows into the West Bay of St. Andrew's Sound. Here we camped for the night.

The two hired men left us to visit a friend who lived several miles distant; but the doctor remained with his oxen in our camp all night. When the tent was pitched he was permitted to enjoy its shelter alone, for Saddles and I took to our boats, leaving the murderer to his own uneasy dreams. I settled his bill before retiring, so he decamped at an early hour the next morning, having first found out where I had hidden my cordage, and purloining therefrom my longest and best rope. This was a loss to me, for it was used to secure the boats when they were being hauled from place to place; but I would gladly have parted with any of my belongings to be free from the presence of my unwelcome guest; and how resigned his neighbors must have felt when, a few weeks later, they read in their newspapers that "W. D. Holly was shot last week in his house, in Washington County, Florida, by some unknown parties"!

We made a hasty Sunday breakfast of cornstarch, and pulled down the creek, anxious to put some distance between ourselves and the doctor. Four miles down the stream, where it debouched into West Bay, we found the homes of two settlers. The one living on the right bank was the man who had given Mr. Holly his stiff arm, the other had built himself a rude but comfortable cabin on the opposite shore. Though there was one delicate-looking woman only in this cabin, without any protector, she hospitably asked us to make our camp at her landing, adding, that when her husband returned from the woods she might be able to give us some meat.

Soon a dog came out of the dense forest, followed by a man who bore upon his shoulders the hind-quarters of a deer which he had killed. He bade us welcome, while he remarked that there were no Sundays in these parts, where one day was just like another; and then presenting us with half his venison, regretted that he had not been aware of our arrival, as he could have killed another deer, his dog having started fifteen during a short ramble in the woods. In the thickets of "ti-ti," which are almost as dense as cane-brakes, the deer, panthers, and bears take refuge; and in this great wilderness of St. Andrew's Bay expert hunters can find venison almost any day.

On Monday morning we rowed through West Bay, across the southern end of North Bay, and skirted the north coast of the East Bay of St. Andrew's, with its picturesque groves of cabbage-palms, for a few miles, when we turned southward into the inlet through which the tidal waters of the Gulf pass in and out of the sound.

We were now close to the sea, with a few narrow sandy islands only intervening between us and the Gulf of Mexico, and upon these ocean barriers we found breezy camping-grounds. Our course was by the open sea for six or eight miles, when we reached a narrow beach thoroughfare, called Crooked Island Bay, through which we rowed, with Crooked Island on our right hand, until we arrived at the head of the bay, where we expected to find an outlet to the sea. Being overtaken by darkness, we staked our boats on the quiet sheet of water, and at sunrise pushed on to find the opening through the beach. Not a sign of human life had been seen since we had left the western end of the East Bay of St. Andrew's Sound, and we now discovered that no outlet to the sea existed, and that Crooked Island was not an island, but a long strip of beach land which was joined to the main coast by a narrow neck of sandy territory, and that the interior watercourse ended in a creek.

Our portage to the sea now loomed up as a laborious task. We needed at least one man to assist us, and we were fully half a day's row from the nearest cabin to the west of us, while we might look in vain to the eastward, where the uninhabited coast line stretched away with its shining sands and shimmering waters for thirty miles to Cape San Blas. There, upon a low sand-bar, against which the waves lashed out their fury, rose a tall light-tower, the only friend of the mariner in all this desolate region. We could not look to that distant light for help, however, and were thrown entirely upon our own feeble resources.

Going systematically to work, we surveyed the best route across Crooked Island, which was over the bed of an old inlet; for a hurricane, many years before, washed out a passage through the sand-spit, and for years the tide flowed in and out of the interior bay. Another hurricane afterwards repaired the breach by filling up the new inlet with sand; so Crooked Island enjoyed but a short-lived notoriety, and again became an integral part of the continent.

Our survey of the portage gave encouraging results. The Gulf of Mexico was only four hundred feet from the bay, and the shortest route was the best one; so, starting energetically, we dragged the boats by main force across Crooked Island, and launched them in the surf without

FOUR MONTHS IN A SNEAK-BOX. 269

disaster. We then rowed as rapidly as the rough sea would permit along the coast towards the wide opening of St. Joseph's Bay, the wooded beaches of which rose like a cloud in the soft mists of a sunny day. The bay was entered at four o'clock in the afternoon, and, being out of

THE PORTAGE ACROSS CROOKED ISLAND.

water, we hauled our boats high on to the beach, and searched eagerly for signs of moisture in the soil.

Leaving Saddles to build a fire and prepare our evening meal, I proceeded to investigate our new domain, and soon discovered the remains of a cabin near a station, or signal-staff, of the United States Coast Survey. Men do not camp for a number of days at a time in places destitute of water; and the fact of the cabin having been built on this spot proved conclusively to me that water must be found in the vicinity. After a careful and patient search, I discovered a depression in the high sandy coast, and although the sand was perfectly dry, I thought it possible that a supply of water had been obtained here for the use of the United States Coast Survey party — the same party which had erected the cabin and planted the signal near it.

Going quickly to the beach, I found the shell of an immense clam, with which I returned, and using it as a scoop, or shovel, removed two or three bushels of sand, when a moist stratum was reached, and my clam-shovel struck the chime of a flour-barrel. In my joy I called to Saddles, for I knew our parched throats would soon be relieved. It did not take long to empty the barrel of its contents, which task being finished, we had the pleasure of seeing the water slowly rise and fill the cistern so lately occupied by the sand. In half an hour the water became limpid, and we sat beside our well, drinking, from time to time, like topers, of the sweet water. Our water-cans were filled, and no stint in the culinary department was allowed that evening.

The flames from our camp-fire shot into the soft atmosphere, while the fishes, attracted by its glare, leaped by scores, in a state of bewilderment, from the now quiet water. St. Joseph's Bay has an ample depth of water for sea-going vessels, while its many species of shells make it one of the best points on the northern Gulf coast for the conchologist.

Although sorry to leave our limpid spring, we launched the boats at seven o'clock the next morning, following the north side of the bay until we arrived at the deserted site of the city of St. Joseph. It seemed impossible to realize that on this desolate spot there had been, only thirty or forty years before, a prosperous city, with a large population and a busy cotton-port, accessible to the largest vessels, and threatening a steady rivalry with Appalachicola. Railroads were the enemies of these southern cities, as they diverted the cotton, grown in the interior, from its natural channels by river to the Gulf of Mexico.

The system of "time-freights," on railroads to the eastern Atlantic ports of Charleston and Savannah, had reduced the once promising city of St. Joseph to one shanty and a rotten pier. Appalachicola also felt the iron hand of competition, and her line of steamboats lost the carriage upon her noble river of the cotton from the distant interior. Railroads were rapidly constructed running east and west, and the rivers flowing to the south were robbed of their commerce.

Beyond St. Joseph city the scenery became almost tropical in its character, and palmettos grew in rank luxuriance on the low savannas. The long narrow coast on the south side of the bay trended suddenly to the south, and terminated in Cape San Blas, while the sound was ended abruptly by a strip of land which connected the long cape to the main. The system of interior watercourses here came to a natural end; and pulling our boats upon the strand, we landed by a large turtle-pen, near which was a deserted grass hut, evidently the home of the turtle-hunter during the "turtle season." Leaving the boats on the salt marsh, we entered the woods and ascended the sand-hills of the Gulf coast, when a boundless view of the sea broke upon us. The shining strand stretched in regular lines four miles to the south, where the light-tower on the point of the cape rose above the intervening forest. Greeting it as the face of a friend, we rejoiced to see it so near; and standing entranced with the beauty of the vision before us, — the boundless sea, the most ennobling sight in all nature, — we congratulated ourselves that we had arrived safely at Cape San Blas.

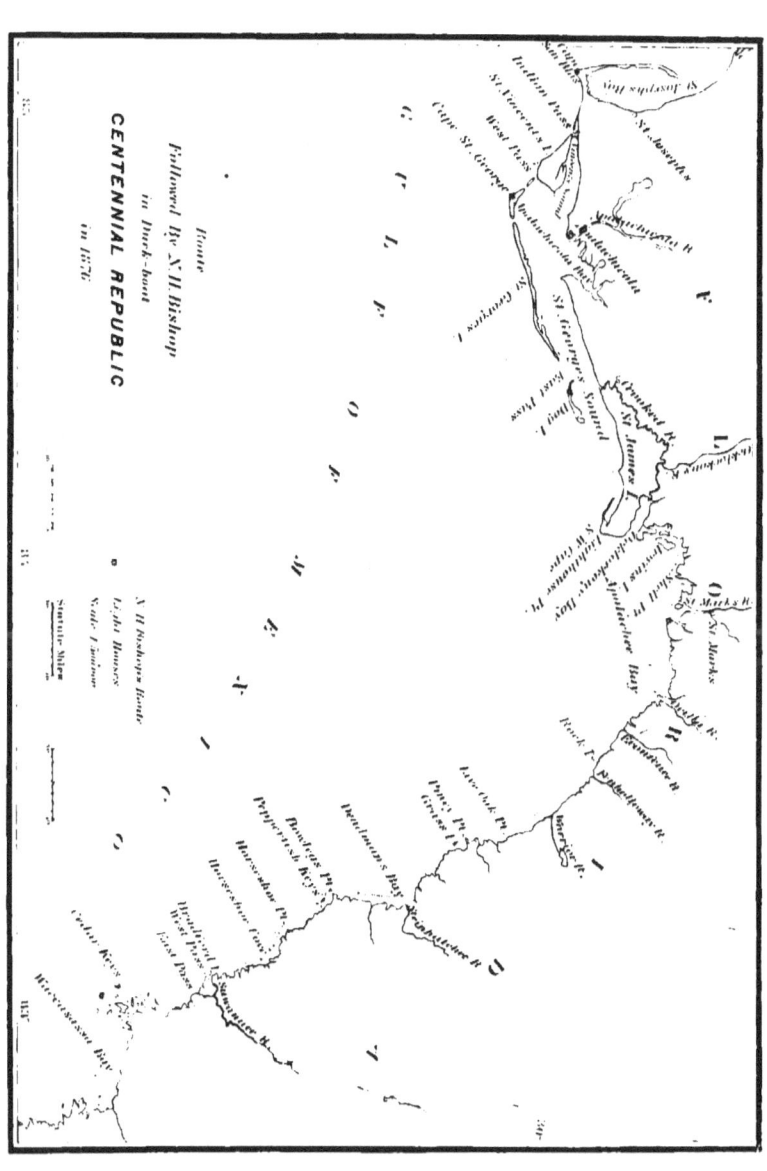

CHAPTER XI.

FROM CAPE SAN BLAS TO ST. MARKS.

A PORTAGE ACROSS CAPE SAN BLAS. — THE COW-HUNTERS. — A VISIT TO THE LIGHT-HOUSE. — ONCE MORE ON THE SEA. — PORTAGE INTO ST. VINCENT SOUND. — APALACHICOLA. — ST. GEORGE'S SOUND AND OCKLOCKONY RIVER. — ARRIVAL AT ST. MARKS. — THE NEGRO POSTMASTER. — A PHILANTHROPIST AND HIS NEIGHBORS. — A CONTINUOUS AND PROTECTED WATER-WAY FROM THE MISSISSIPPI RIVER TO THE ATLANTIC COAST.

A PORTAGE now loomed in our horizon. The distance across the neck of land was one-third of a mile only, but the ascent of the hills of the Gulf beach would prove a formidable task. I proposed to Saddles that he should return to the boats, while I hurried down the beach to the point of the cape to find a man to assist us in their transportation from the bay to the sea.

While discussing the plan, a noise in the thicket caught my ear, and turning our eyes to the spot, we saw two men hurrying from their ambush into the forest. We at once started in pursuit of them. When overtaken, they looked confused, and acknowledged that the presence of strangers was so unusual in that region that they had been watching our movements critically from the moment we landed until we discovered them. These men wore the rough garb of cow-hunters, and the older of the two informed me that his home was in Apalachicola. He was looking after his cattle, which had a very long range, and had been camping with his assistant along St. Joseph's Sound for many days, being now *en route* for his home. Two ponies were tied to a tree in a thicket, while a bed of palmetto leaves and dried grass showed where the hunters had slept the previous night.

These men assured us that the happiest life was that of the cow-hunter, who could range the forest for miles upon his pony, and sleep where he pleased. The idea was, that the nearer one's instincts and mode of life approached to that of a cow, the happier the man: only another version, after all, of living close to nature. One of these wood-philosophers, taking his creed from the animals in which all his hopes centred, said we should be as simple in our habits as an ox, as gentle as a cow, and do no more injury to our fellow-man than a yearling. He was certain there would be less sin in the world if men were turned into cattle; was sure cattle were happier than men, and generally more useful.

Upon learning our dilemma, the good-natured fellows set at once to work to help us. We cut two pine poles, and placing one boat across them, each man grasped an end of a pole, and thus, upon a species of litter, we lifted the burden from the ground and bore it slowly across the land to the sea. Returning to the bay, we transported the second boat in the same manner; and making a third trip, carried away our provisions, blankets, &c.

It was now evening, and viewing with satisfaction our little boats resting upon the beautiful beach, we thanked our new friends heartily for their kindness. The owner of a thousand cattle gave us a warm invitation to visit his orange grove in Apalachicola, and then retired with his man to their nest in the woods, while we slept in our boats, with porpoises and black-fish sounding their nasal calls all night in the sea which beat upon the strand at our feet.

In the morning the wind arose and sent the waves tumbling far in upon the beach. After breakfast I walked to the extremity of the cape, and dined with Mr. Robert Colman, the principal light-keeper. He was a most ingenious man, and an expert in the use of tools. The United States Light House Establishment selects its light-keepers from the retired army of wounded soldiers. In all my voyages along our coast, and on inland waters, I have found the good results of the perfect discipline exercised by the superintendents of this bureau. These keepers live along a coast of some thousands of miles in extent on the Atlantic and Pacific oceans and the Gulf of Mexico, many of them in isolated positions, but honesty, economy, and intelligent skill are everywhere apparent; and these men work like an army of veterans. I have intruded upon their privacy at all hours, but have never found one of them open to criticism. There is no shirking of the onerous duties of their position. Too much praise cannot be given to these light-keepers in their lonely towers, or to the intelligent heads which direct and govern their important work.

As I was leaving the light-house, a young woman approached me, and introducing herself as a visitor to the keeper's family, said she had a favor to ask. Would it be too much trouble for the stranger, after he reached New York, to inquire the price of a switch of human hair of just the shade of her own flaxen locks, and write her about it! Of course such an appeal could not be disregarded; but I confess that as I gazed upon the boundless sea, and along the uninhabited strand, and into the unsettled forests, I wondered where the men or women were to be found to appreciate the imported New York switch. Would it not "waste its sweetness on the desert air" in the unpeopled wilderness?

The boisterous weather kept us on the beach

until Friday, when we launched our boats and rowed along the coast three miles to a point opposite a lagoon which was separated from the sea by a narrow strip of land. While pulling along the beach, great black-fish, some of them weighing at least one thousand pounds, came up out of the sea and divided into four companies. The first ranged itself upon our right, the second upon our left, the third, forming a school, proceeded in advance, while the fourth brought up the rear. Unlike the frisky porpoises, these big fellows convoyed us in the most dignified manner, heaving their dark, shining, scaleless bodies half out of the water as they surged along within a few feet of our boats.

When we arrived at our point of disembarkation, and turned shoreward to run through the surf, our strange companions seemed loath to leave us, but rolled about in the offing, making their peculiar nasal sounds, and spouting, like whales, jets of spray into the air. A landing was accomplished without shipping much water, and we immediately hauled the boats across the beach, about three or four hundred feet, into a narrow lagoon, the western branch of St. Vincent's Sound.

Indian Pass was two miles east of our portage. It is an inlet of the sea, through which small vessels pass into St. Vincent's Sound, *en route* for the town of Apalachicola. Heavy seas were, however, breaking upon its bar at that time, and it would have been a dangerous experiment to have entered it in our small boats. Emerging from the lagoon, the broad areas of St. Vincent's Sound and Apalachicola Bay met our gaze, while beyond them were spread the waters of St. George's Sound.

Following the coast on our left, numerous reefs of large and very fat oysters continually obstructed our progress. We gathered a bushel with our hands in a very few minutes; but as the wind commenced to blow most spitefully, and the heavy forests of palms on the low shore offered a pleasant shelter, we disembarked about sunset in a magnificent grove of palmetto-trees, spending a pleasant evening in feasting upon the delicious bivalves, roasted and upon the half shell.

The tempest held us prisoners in this wild retreat for two days, and during that time, if we had been the possessor of a dog, we might have supped and dined upon venison and wild turkey. As it was, we were well content to subsist upon wild ducks and the fine oysters, with bread from fresh wheat-flour, baked in our Dutch oven, or bake-kettle, and coffee that never tastes elsewhere as it does in camp.

At last the gale went down with the sun, and we rowed in the evening thirteen miles up the bay to Apalachicola, and went into camp upon the sandy beach at the lower end of the town. While sleeping soundly in our boats, at an early hour the next morning some one came " gently tapping at my chamber-door," or, in sea phrase, pounding upon my hatch. I soon discovered that my visitor was Captain Daniel Fry, United States Inspector of Steamboats. His pretty cottage, environed with beds of blooming flowers, was perched upon the sandy bluff above us. The captain, in a nautical way, claimed us as salvage, and we were soon enjoying his generous hospitality. In this isolated town, once a busy cotton-shipping port, there was a population of about one thousand souls, among whom, conspicuous for his urbane manners and scientific ability, lived Dr. A. W. Chapman, the author of the " Flora of the Southern United States."

While at New Orleans I had addressed a letter to the postmaster at St. Marks, Florida, requesting him to forward my letters to Apalachicola, but the request had not been noticed. The mystery was, however, explained by Lieutenant N., of the Coast Survey schooner Silliman, who one day called upon me, and said that when he stopped at St. Marks for his mail, a few days previous to my arrival at Apalachicola, he saw about thirty letters addressed to me lying loosely upon the desk of the negro postmaster of that marshy settlement. My letter of instruction had been received, but as the postmaster could not read, no notice had been taken of it. The coast survey officer had kindly gathered my letters in one parcel, and had deposited them for safe-keeping with the postmaster's white clerk. The responsible position of postmaster was filled by an ignorant colored man, because his politics were those of the party then in power.

Nor was this an exceptional case, many such appointments having been made, as an inevitable result of a peculiar enfranchisement in which there is no restriction, and where *license* stands for *liberty*. While on my "Voyage of the Paper Canoe," I met in one county in Georgia, through which flows the beautiful Altamaha, the colored county treasurer, who lived in a little backwoods' settlement a few miles from Darien. He could neither read nor write, but his business was managed and the county funds handled by a white politician of the "reconstructing" element then in power, which was sapping the life-blood of the south, and bonding every state within its selfish grasp by dishonest legislative acts. The poor black man was simply a tool for the white charlatan, living in a miserable log cabin, and receiving a very small share of the peculations of his white clerk. When all the enfranchised are educated, and not until then, will the great source of evil be removed from our politics which to-day endangers our future liberty of self-government. We are floating in a sea of unlimited and unlettered enfranchisement, vainly tugging at the helm of our ship of state, while masterminds stoop to cater to the prejudices of hundreds of thousands of voters who cannot read the names upon the ticket they deposit in the ballot-box — the ballot-box which is the guardian of the constitutional liberties of a republic.

We left the kind people of Apalachicola, and crossed the bay to St. George's Sound, with a cargo of delicacies, for Captain Fry had filled our lockers with various comforts for the inner man, while our friend, the cattle-owner, whom we had met at Cape San Blas, and who had now returned to his home, stocked us with delicious oranges from his grove on the outskirts of the city.

Four miles to the east of Cat Point we saw the humble homes of Peter Sheepshead and Sam Pompano, two fishermen, whose uniform success in catching their favorite species of fish had won for them their euphonious titles. We camped at night near the mouth of Crooked River, which enters the sound opposite Dog Island, having rowed twenty-four miles. If we continued along the sound, after passing out of its eastern end, we would be upon the open sea, and might have difficulty in doubling the great South Cape; so we took the interior route, ascending Crooked River through a low pine savanna country, to the

Ocklockony River, which is, in fact, a continuation of Crooked River. The region about Crooked and Ocklockony rivers is destitute of the habitation of man.

About midway between St. George's Sound and the Gulf coast we traversed a vast swamp, where the ground was carpeted with the dwarf saw-palmettos. A fire had killed all the large trees, and their blasted, leafless forms were covered with the flaunting tresses of Spanish moss. The tops of many of these trees were crowned by the Osprey's nest, and the birds were sitting on their eggs, or feeding their young with fish, which they carried in their talons from the sea. So numerous were these fish-hawks that we named the blasted swamp the Home of the Osprey. We spent one night in this swamp serenaded by the deep calls of the male alligators, which closely resembled the low bellowing of a bull.

About noon the next day signs of cultivated life appeared, and we passed the houses of some settlers, and the saw-mill of a New Yorker. At dusk our boats entered a little sound, and by nine o'clock in the evening we arrived at the Gulf of Mexico, in a region of shoal water, much cut up by oyster reefs. The tide being very low, the boats were anchored inside of an oyster reef, which afforded protection from the inflowing swell of the sea. We shaped our course next day for St. Marks, along a low, marshy coast, where oyster reefs, in shoal water, frequently barred our progress. From South Cape to St. Marks the coast, broken by the mouths of several creeks and rivers, trends to the northeast, while for twenty miles to the east of the lighthouse, which rises conspicuously on the eastern shore of the entrance to St. Marks River, the coast bends to the southeast to the latitude of Cedar Keys, where it turns abruptly south, and forms one side of the peninsula of Florida.

The great contour of the Gulf of Mexico, into which St. Marks River empties, is known to geographers as Apalachee Bay. On that part of the coast between the St. Marks and Suwanee rivers, the bed of the Gulf of Mexico slopes so gradually that when seven miles away from the land a vessel will be in only eighteen feet of water. At this distance from the shore is found the continuous coral formation; but nearer to the coast it is found in spots only.

While traversing this coast from St. Marks to Cedar Keys, I observed the peculiar features of a long coast-line of salt marshes, against which the waves broke gently. With the exception of a few places, where the upland penetrated these savannas to the waters of the sea, the marshes were soft alluvium, covered with tall coarse grasses, the sameness of which was occasionally broken by a hammock, or low mound of firmer soil, which rose like an island out of the level sea of green. The hammocks were heavily wooded with the evergreen live-oaks, the yellow pine, and the palmetto. From half a mile to two miles back of the low savannas of the coast, rose, like a wall of green, the old forests, grand and solemn in their primeval character.

The marshes were much cut up by creeks, some of which came from the mainland, but most of them had their sources in the savannas, and served as drains to the territory which was frequently submerged by the sea. When the southerly winds send towards the land a boisterous sea, the long, natural, inclined plane of the Gulf bottom seems to act as a pacifier to the waves, for they break down as they roll over the continually shoaling area in approaching the marshes; and there is no undertow, or any of the peculiar features which make the surf on other parts of the coast very dangerous in rough weather. The submarine grass growing upon the sandy bottom as far as six or eight miles from shore, also helps to smooth down the waves.

When the strong wind blows off the coast on to the Gulf, it is known to seamen as a "norther," and so violent are these winds that their force, acting on the sea, rapidly diminishes its depth within twelve or fifteen miles of the marshes. A coasting-vessel drawing five feet of water will anchor off Apalachee Bay in

eight feet of water, at the commencement of a
"norther," and in four or five hours, unless the
crew put to sea, the vessel will be left upon the
dry bottom of the Gulf. After the wind falls,
the water will return, and the equilibrium will
be restored.

We ascended St. Marks River, and passed the
site of a town which had been washed out of
existence in the year 1843 by the effects of a
hurricane on the sea. These hurricanes are in
season during August and September. The
village of St. Marks consisted of about thirty
houses, the occupants of which, with two or
three exceptions, were negroes. The land is
very low, and at times subjected to inundation.
A railroad terminated here, but the business
of the place supported only two trains a week,
and they ran directly to the capital of Florida,
the beautiful city of Tallahassee, eighteen miles
distant.

The negro postmaster courteously presented
me with my package of letters, and I had an
opportunity to observe the way in which he fulfilled his duties. When the mail arrived, it was
thrown upon a desk in one corner of a small
grocery store, and any person desiring an epistle
went in, and, fumbling over the letters, took
what he claimed as his own.

The railroad agent, a young northerner, I
found sleeping soundly in his telegraph office,

though the noonday sun was pouring in his windows. He apologized for being caught napping, but declared it was his only amusement in that desolate region of damps, and assured me a man would deteriorate less rapidly by sleeping away his idle hours than by keeping awake to what was going on in the neighboring hamlet. Besides the United States Signal officer, his only intelligent neighbor was a brother of the Rev. Henry Ward Beecher, who had purchased a property, two or three years before, in the once flourishing town of Newport, a few miles up the river. He spoke feelingly of the efforts of the Rev. Charles Beecher to educate his enfranchised negro neighbors; of his inviting them to his house, and laboring for the welfare of their souls. All the patient and Christian efforts of the philanthropist had proved unavailing, and thieving and lying were still much in vogue.

It has been proposed by engineers to connect all the interior Gulf-coast watercourses from the Mississippi River at New Orleans to the Suwanee River in Florida. To achieve this end it will be necessary to excavate several canals at points now used as portages. From St. Marks to the Suwanee River there are some rivers which might be used in connecting and perfecting this great interior water-way.

I mentioned in my "Voyage of the Paper Canoe," that preliminary surveys, under General

Gilmore, had been made for a continuous waterway across northern Florida to the Atlantic coast, *via* the Suwanee and St. Mary's rivers. Detailed surveys are now in progress. Those interested in this enterprise hope to see the produce of the Mississippi valley towed in barges through this continuous water-way from New Orleans to the Atlantic ports of St. Mary's, Fernandina, Savannah, and Charleston. The northwestern as well as the southern states would derive advantage from this extension of the Mississippi system to the Atlantic seaboard, and its execution seems to be considered by many a duty of the national government.

There has been little written upon the watercourses of northwestern Florida, but several of the central, southern, and Atlantic coast rivers and lakes have been carefully explored by Mr. Frederick A. Ober, of Massachusetts, a young and enthusiastic naturalist, who, as correspondent of the "Forest and Stream," has published in the columns of that paper a mass of interesting and valuable geographical matter, throwing much light on regions heretofore unfamiliar to the public.

CHAPTER XII.

FROM ST. MARKS TO THE SUWANEE RIVER.

ALONG THE COAST. — SADDLES BREAKS DOWN. — A REFUGE WITH THE FISHERMEN. — CAMP IN THE PALM FOREST. — PARTING WITH SADDLES. — OUR NEIGHBOR THE ALLIGATOR. — DISCOVERY OF THE TRUE CROCODILE IN FLORIDA. — THE DEVIL'S WOOD-PILE. — DEADMAN'S BAY. — BOWLEGS POINT. — THE COAST SURVEY CAMP. — A DAY ABOARD THE "READY." — THE SUWANEE RIVER. — THE END.

LEAVING St. Marks, we rowed down the stream to the forks of the St. Marks and Wakulla rivers. The sources of the Wakulla were twelve miles above these forks, and consisted of a wonderful spring of crystal water, which could be entered by small boats. This curious river bursts forth as though by a single bound, from the subterranean caverns of limestone. Each of the several remarkable springs in Florida is supposed, by those living in its vicinity, to be the veritable "fountain of youth;" and this one shared the usual fate, for we were assured that this was the spring for which the cavalier Ponce de Leon vainly sought in the old times of Spanish exploration in the New World.

On Monday, March 13th, we left St. Marks River, and, as the north wind blew, were forced to keep from one to two miles off the land on the open Gulf to find even two feet of water. In many places we found rough pieces of coral rocks upon the bottom, and in several instances grounded upon them. As the wind went down, the tide, which on this coast frequently rises only from eighteen inches to two feet, favored us with more water, and by night we were able to get close to the marshes, and enter a little creek west of the Ocilla River, where, staking our boats alongside the soft marsh, we supped on chocolate and dry bread, and slept comfortably in our little craft until morning.

We were now in an almost uninhabited region, where only an occasional fisherman or sponger is met; but as we pulled along the coast the day after our camp in the marshes, we were struck with the absence of any sign of the presence of man. We had hoped to meet with the vessels of sponge-gatherers anchored in the vicinity of Rock Island, to which place they resort to clean their crop; but when we passed the island in the afternoon, so scantily clothed with herbage, and upon which a few palms grew out of the shallow soil, it was deserted, while not a single sail could be seen upon the horizon of the sea.

My companion had not been well for several

days, and he informed me at this late date that he was subject to malarial fever, or, as he called it, "swamp fever." It had been contracted by him while living on one of the bayous of southern Louisiana during a warm season. Swamp fever, when at its height, usually produces temporary insanity; and he alarmed me by stating that he had been deprived of his reason for days at a time during his attacks. The use of daily stimulants had kept up his constitutional vigor for several months; but as ours was a temperance diet, he gradually, after we left Biloxi and the regions where stimulants could be obtained, became nervous, lost his appetite, and was now suffering from chills and fever. He was much depressed after leaving St. Marks, and had long fits of sullenness, so that he would row for hours without speaking. I tried to cheer him, and on one occasion penetrated the forest a long distance to obtain some panacea with which to brace his unsettled nerves.

Saddles had deceived me as to the necessity of taking daily drams, which habit is, to say the least, a most inconvenient one for persons engaged in explorations of isolated parts of the coast, and voyaging in small boats; so we had both suffered much in consequence of his bad habit. To furnish one moderate drinker with the liquid stimulant necessary for a boat voyage from New Orleans to Cedar Keys, at least five gallons of whiskey, and a large and heavy demijohn in which to store it securely, must form a portion of the cargo. This bulk occupies important space in the confined quarters of a boat, every inch of which is needed for necessary articles, while the momentary and artificial strength given to the system is never, except as a remediable agent, productive of any real or lasting benefit. My unfortunate companion had become so accustomed to the daily use of liquor, and his shattered system had been so propped by it, that he had been like a man walking on stilts; and now that they were knocked away, his own feet failed to support him, and a reaction was the inevitable result.

After leaving Rock Island, and when about four miles beyond the Fenholloway River, while off a vast tract of marshes, poor Saddles broke down completely. He could not row another stroke. I towed his boat into a little cove, and was forced to leave him, with the fever raging in his blood, that I might search for a creek, and a hammock upon which to camp. Looking to the east, I saw a long, low point of marsh projecting its attenuated point southward, while upon it rose a signal-staff of the United States Coast Survey. A black object seemed heaped against the base of the signal; and while I gazed at what looked like a bear, or a heap of dark soil, it began to move, breaking up into three or four fragments, each of which seemed to roll off into the grass, where they disappeared.

I pulled for the point as rapidly as possible, for I hoped, while hardly daring to believe, that

SADDLES BREAKS DOWN

this singular apparition might be human beings. The high grass formed an impenetrable barrier for my curious vision; but nearing the spot, voices were plainly audible on the other side of the narrow point, as though a party of men were in lively discussion. Rowing close to the land, and resting on my oars to gain time to reconnoitre either friends or foes, the deep but cultivated voice of a man fell upon my ear. A patriot was evidently haranguing his fellow-fishermen, who, after lunching beside the Coast Survey signal, and not observing the proximity of a stranger, had repaired to their boats on the east side of the marsh.

"Yes," came the tones of the orator through the high grass, "yes, to this state have we Americans been reduced! Not satisfied with having ravaged our country, conquering BUT NOT SUBDUING our Confederate government, the enemy has put over us a CARPET-BAG government of northern adventurers and southern scalawags and NIGGERS. Fifty niggers sit as representatives of our state in the legislature of Florida, and vote in a solid body for whichever party pays them their price. They are giving away our state lands to monopolists, and we have tax-bills like THIS one imposed upon us." Here the orator paused, apparently taking a paper from his pocket. "Here it is," he resumed, "in black and white. On a wild piece of forest land, and a few acres of clearing, (which they appraise at twenty-five cents, when it cost me only six cents and a quarter per acre,) I was saddled with this outrageous bill. I will read to you the several items:

Mr. L. H. .... Dr.

To State Taxes proper, - - - .70	on	- - $100.00
General Sinking Fund, - - .30	"	- - - 100.00
Special Sinking Fund, - - .16	"	- - - 100.00
General School Tax, - - - .10	"	- - - 100.00
Total State Tax, - - 1.26	"	- - - 100.00
To County Tax proper, - - - .50	"	- - - 100.00
County School Tax, - - - .50	"	- - - 100.00
Special County Building Tax, .35	"	- - - 100.00
County Specific Tax, - - - 2.00	"	- - - 100.00
Total County Tax, - - 3.35	"	- - - 100.00
Total State and County Tax, $4.61	on	- - -. 100.00

"You will find by these figures that I am compelled to pay a state and county tax, on an over-appraised property, amounting to four dollars and sixty-one cents upon every one hundred dollars I possess. Under this kind of taxation we are growing poorer every day of our lives. Now, gentlemen, can you censure me for detesting the Carpet-bag government of my native state after you have heard this statement? Rome in days of tyranny did no such injustice to her citizens. To be a Roman was greater than to be a king; and here let me remark — Bob Squash! what's that you are squinting at through the grass?" "Lor' sakes,

Massa Hampton, I does b'lieve it's a man in a sort of a boat. I nebber see de like befo'!"

At this point the company struggled through the high grass and invited me to land. Being seriously alarmed for my companion, who was lying helpless in his boat half a mile away, I quickly explained my situation, and was at once advised to ascend Spring Creek, on the east side of the point of marsh, to the swamp, where the orator said I would find his camp, and his partner in the fishing-business, who would assist me to the best of his ability. The orator promised to follow us after making one more cast with his seine for red-fish. I returned as fast as possible to Saddles, and trying to infuse his failing heart with courage, fastened his boat's painter to the stern of the duck-boat, and followed the course indicated by the fishermen.

Upon entering Spring Creek, with my companion in tow, we were soon encompassed on all sides by the marshes; and as the boats slowly ascended the crooked stream, the fringes of the feathery-crested palms appeared close to the margins of the savanna. The land increased in height a few inches as I followed the reaches of the creek, and, when a mile from its mouth, entered the rank luxuriance of a swamp, where, in a thicket of red cedars, palmettos, and Spanish bayonets, I discovered two low huts, thatched with palm-leaves, which afforded temporary shelter to Captain F., a planter from the interior, his friend the orator, and their employees both white and black. The kind-hearted captain understood my companion's case at a glance, and when our tent was pitched, and a comfortable bed prepared, Saddles was put under his care.

He could not have fallen into better hands, for the planter had gone through many experiences in the treatment of fevers of all kinds. It was indeed a boon to find in the unpeopled wilds a shelter and a physician for the sick man; but the future loomed heavily before me, for though Saddles might improve, he would be pretty sure on the eighth day to have a return of his malady, and would probably again break down in a raving condition.

The camp was a restful and interesting retreat. To reach the spot, the fishing-party had been obliged to cut a road eight miles through a swampy district, in places building a rough crossway to make their progress possible. The creek had its sources in several springs, which burst from the earth just above the camp. The water was of a blue tint, and slightly impregnated with sulphur, lime, and iron. In this secluded place there was an abundance of deer and wild turkeys.

The early morning meal of these hunters and fishermen was a veritable *déjeuner a la four-*

chelle, for their *menu* included venison, turkey, sweet-potatoes, hoe-cakes made from fresh maize flour, and excellent coffee. Captain F. and an old negro woman remained in camp to clean and salt down the fish caught on the previous afternoon, while the orator and his party went down the creek in two long, narrow scows, loaded with two nets, their necessary fishing implements, and a hearty luncheon. Long poles were used to propel their craft. Upon meeting with a school of fish, they encompassed it with the two nets, each of which was three hundred feet long, and easily captured the whole lot, which was composed of several species.

When in luck, the fishing-party returned to the camp by noon; but when the wind interfered with their success, they did not reach their swampy retreat until night. After a rest, and a good warm supper, the orator and one of his white associates, each with his torch of resinous pine wood and well-loaded gun, would quietly traverse the silent forests and grassy savannas, luring to destruction the fascinated and unsuspecting deer. Thus stalking through the darkness, and peering eagerly on all sides, the appearance of the fire-like globes of the deer's eyes, from the reflected light of the hunters' torches, was the signal to fire, which meant, with their unerring aim, death to their prey and future feasts for themselves.

With their venison these men served a very palatable dish made from the terminal bud of the palmetto known as the "cabbage," and from which the tree derives its name of "cabbage-palm." A negro ascended the palm and cut the bud at its junction with the top of the tree. It was then thrown to the ground, and climbing other trees, more followed in quick succession. When a sufficient quantity had been gathered, the turnip part, from which the tender shoot starts, was cut off and thrown aside, as it was bitter to the taste. The shoot, divested of this part, resembled a solid roll, from four to six inches in diameter. From this was unrolled and thrown aside the outer coverings, leaving the tender white interior tissues about three inches in diameter and fourteen inches in length. Thus divested of all objectionable matter, the cabbage could be eaten raw, though it was much improved by cooking, the boiling process removing every trace of the acrid, or turnip, flavor. These men ate it dressed in the same way as ordinary cabbage, and it was an excellent substitute for that dish. The black bear is as fond of the palmetto-cabbage as his enemy the hunter. He ascends the tree, breaks down the palm-leaves, and devours the bud, evidently appreciating the feast. After the removal of the bud the tree dies; so this is after all an expensive dainty.

Captain F. had pre-empted a tract of one hundred and sixty acres of land, to cover the sources of Spring Creek, and it was his intention to resort to this camp every year during the mullet-fishing season, which is from September to January. The salted mullet is the popular market-fish with the back-country people, though the red-fish is by far the finer for table use.

While with these men, we were treated with the generous hospitality known only in the forest, but Saddles did not improve. He seemed to be suffering from a low form of intermittent fever, and looked like anything but a subject for a long row. Captain F. insisted upon sending the invalid in his wagon sixteen miles to his home, where he promised to nurse the unfortunate man until he was able to travel forty miles further to a railroad station. On the 15th of March, the party, having made their final arrangements, were ready to make the start for home. It was our last day together.

Circumstances over which I had no control forced me to part from Saddles. I furnished him with a liberal supply of funds to enable him to reach Fernandina, Florida, by rail, and afterwards sent him a draft for an amount sufficient to pay his expenses from Cedar Keys to New Orleans, as he abandoned all his previous intentions of returning to his old home in the north.

The Riddle with its outfit, and about sixty pounds of shot and a large supply of powder, I presented to the good captain who had so generously offered to care for my unfortunate companion. As I was to traverse the most desolate part of the coast between Spring Creek and Cedar Keys alone, I deemed it prudent to divest myself of every thing that could be spared from my boat's outfit, in order to lighten the hull. I had made an estimate of chances, and concluded that four or five days would carry me to the end of my voyage, if the weather continued favorable; so, on the evening of March 15, the little duck-boat was prepared for future duty.

The hunters and fishermen brought into camp the spoils of the forest and the treasures of the sea, while the grinning negress exerted herself to prepare the parting feast. Deep in the recesses of the wild swamp our camp-fire crackled and blazed, sending up its flaming tongues until they almost met the dense foliage above our heads, while seated upon the ground we feasted, and told tales of the past. Poor Saddles tried to be cheerful, but made a miserable failure of it; and his pale face was the skeleton at our banquet, for human nature is so constituted that a suffering man gains sympathy, even though he be only paying the penalty of his own past misdemeanors.

My boat was tied alongside the bank of the

creek, close to the palmetto huts. There were only two feet of water in the stream as I sat in the little sneak-box at midnight and went through the usual preparations for stowing myself away for the night. I touched the clear water with my hands as it laved the sides of my floating home, but my gaze could not penetrate the limpid current, for the heavy shades of the palms gave it a dark hue. I thought of the duties of the morrow, and also of poor Saddles, who was tossing uneasily upon the blankets in his tent near by, when there was a mysterious movement in the water under the boat. Something unusual was there, for its presence was betrayed by the large bubbles of air which came up from the bottom and floated upon the surface of the water. Being too sleepy to make an investigation, I coiled myself in my nest, and drew the hatch-cover over the hold.

The next morning my friends clustered on the bank, giving me a kind farewell as I pushed the duck-boat gently into the channel of the creek. Suddenly Saddles, who had been gazing abstractedly into the water under my boat, hurried into the tent, and in an instant reappeared with the gun I had given him in his hands. He slowly pointed it at the spot in the water where my boat had been moored during the night, and drawing the trigger, an explosion followed, while the water flew upward in fine jets into the air. Then, to the astonished gaze of the party on the bank, an alligator as long as my boat arose to view, and, roused by the shock, hurried into deeper water.

It was now evident what the lodger under my boat had been, and I confess the thought of being separated from this fierce saurian by only half an inch of cedar sheathing during a long night, was not a pleasant one; and I shuddered while my imagination pictured the consequences of a nocturnal bath in which I might have indulged.

Having observed in different countries the habits of some of the individuals which compose the order SAURIA, — the lizards, — I will present to the reader what I have gleaned from my observation upon two species, one of which is the true alligator (*A. Mississippiensis*), the other the well-known true crocodile (*C. acutus*). which recently has been declared an inhabitant of the United States. It is only a few years since it was found living on the North American continent, for previous to its discovery in southern Florida, its nearest known habitat to the United States was the island of Cuba.

The order of lizards is separated into families. The family to which the alligators, crocodiles, and gavials belong, is called by naturalists CROCODILO. The distinctions which govern the separation of the family CROCODILO into the

PARTING WITH SADDLES.

three genera of alligators, crocodiles, and gavials, consist of peculiarities in the shape of the head, in the peculiar arrangement of the teeth, webbing of the feet, and in some minor characteristics; for, outside of these not very important anatomical differences, the habits of the three kinds of reptiles are in most respects quite similar, some of the species being more ferocious, and consequently more dangerous, than others.

The alligator, also called *caiman* by the Spanish-American creoles, inhabits the rivers and bayous of the North and South American continents, while the crocodiles are natives of Africa, of the West Indies, and of South America. The fierce gavial genus is Asian, and abounds in the rivers of India. The alligator (*A. Mississippiensis*) and the crocodile (*C. acutus*) are the only species which particularly interest the people of the United States, for they both belong to our own fauna.

Our alligator inhabits the rivers and swampy districts of the southern states. I have never heard of their being found north of the Neuse River, though they probably ascend in small numbers some of the numerous rivers and creeks of the northern side of Albemarle Sound in North Carolina. The bayous and swamps of Louisiana and the low districts of Florida are particularly infested with these animals. The frequent visits of man to their haunts makes them timid of his presence; but where he is rarely or never seen, the larger alligators become more dangerous. During warm, sunny days this reptile delights in basking in the sunlight upon the bank of a stream for hours at a time. At the approach of man he crawls or slides from his slimy bed into the water, but if his retreat be cut off, or he become excited, a powerful odor of musk exudes from his body. During the winter months he hibernates in the mud of the bayous for days and weeks at a time. When the alligator enters the water, a pair of lips or valves close tightly, hermetically sealing his ears so that even moisture cannot penetrate them. His nostrils are protected in the same way.

As the season for incubation approaches, the female searches for a sandy spot, and digging a hole with her fore-feet, deposits there her eggs, which are somewhat smaller than those of a goose. They are usually placed in layers, carefully covered up in the sand, and if not disturbed by wild animals, are hatched by the heat of the sun. It frequently happens that the alligator cannot find a sand-bank in which to place her eggs, and on such occasions she scrapes together with her fore-feet grass, leaves, bark, and sticks, mixed with mud, and converting the whole into a low platform, deposits the eggs upon it in separate layers, each layer being sandwiched with the mixture of mud, sticks, &c., until more than one hundred white eggs, of a faint green tint, are carefully stowed away in the nest.

The exterior of the nest, which has a mound-like character, is daubed over with mud, the tail of the alligator being used as a trowel. The first duties of maternity being over, the female alligator acts as policeman until the eggs are hatched. Her office is not a sinecure, for the fowls of the air, and the creeping things upon earth, are attracted to the entombed delicacies secreted in this oven-like structure in the swamp. Many a luckless coon and cracker's pig searching for a breakfast, receive instead a blow from the strong tail of the female alligator, and are swept into the grasp of her terrible and relentless jaws.

Moisture and heat act their parts in assisting the process of incubation, and the little alligators, a few inches in length, issue from the shell, and are welcomed by their mail-clad mother into the new world.

Like young turtles just from the shell, the baby alligators make for the water, but unlike the young of the sea-turtles, the saurians have the assistance of their parent, who not unfrequently takes a load of them upon her back. From the first inception of nest-building until the young are able to take care of themselves, this reptile mother, like the female wild-turkey, resists the encroachments of her mate who would devour, not only the eggs, but his own crawling children.

In fact, if opportunity were offered by the absence of the mother from the nest and the young, his alligatorship would eat up all his progeny, and exterminate his species, without a particle of regret. He has no pride in the perpetuation of his family, and it is to the maternal instincts of his good wife that we owe the preservation of the alligator.

The young avoid the larger males until they are strong enough to protect themselves, feeding in the mean time upon fish and flesh of every description. In the water they move with agility, but on land their long bodies and short legs prevent rapid motion. They migrate during droughts from one slough or bayou to another, crossing the intervening upland. When discovered on these journeys by man, the alligator feigns death, or at least appears to be in an unconscious state; but if an antagonist approach within reach of that terrible tail, a blow, a sweep, and a snapping together of the jaws prove conclusively his dangerous character. He is a good fisherman, and can also catch ducks, drawing them by their feet under water. The dog is, however, the favorite diet of these saurians, and the negroes make use of a crying puppy to allure the creature from the bottom of a shoal bayou within reach of their guns.

Though clad in a coat of thick, bony scales, a well-directed charge of buckshot from a gun, or a lead ball from a musket, will penetrate the body, notwithstanding all that has been said to the contrary.

The negroes in the Gulf states say that "de 'gators swallows a pine knot afore dey goes into de mud-burrows for de winter;" and the fact that pine knots and pieces of wood are found in the stomachs of these animals at all seasons of the year, gives a shade of truth to this statement. Even the hardest substances, such as stones and broken bottles, are taken in considerable quantities from the bodies of dead alligators. Their digestive organs are certainly not sensitive, their nervous systems not delicate, and their intelligence not remarkable. It gives an alligator but little inconvenience to shoot off a portion of his head with a mass of the brain attached to it; and they have been known to fight for hours with the entire brain removed.

Though generally fleeing from man upon *terra firma*, the alligator will quickly attack him in the water. A friend of mine, mounted upon his horse, was crossing a Florida river in the wilderness, when entering the channel of the stream, the horse's feet did not touch the bottom, and he swam for a moment or two, struggling with the current. My friend suddenly felt a severe grip upon his leg, and the pressure of sharp teeth through his trousers, when, realizing in a flash that an alligator's jaws were fastened upon him, he clasped the neck of his horse with all his strength. For a few seconds he was in danger of being dragged from the back of his faithful animal; but his dog, following in the rear, gained quickly on the struggling horse, and the alligator, true to his well-known taste, loosed his hold upon the man, and catching the dog in his strong jaws, dragged the poor brute to the bottom of the river.

The alligator is fast disappearing from our principal southern rivers, and is also being captured in considerable numbers in isolated bayous by hunters, who kill the creature for his hide, as the alligator boots have a durability not possessed by any other leather.

There is much interest connected with the discovery of the existence of the true crocodile (*C. acutus*) in the Floridian peninsula. While the alligators have broader heads, shorter snouts, and more numerous teeth than the crocodiles, the unscientific hunter can at once identify the true crocodile (*C. acutus*) by two holes in the upper jaw, into which and through which the two principal teeth or tushes of the lower jaw protrude, and can be seen by looking down upon the head of the animal. The longest teeth of the alligator do not thus protrude through the head or snout, but fit into sockets in the upper jaw. I first studied the true crocodile in the island of Cuba, where there are two distinct species of the genus, one of which is our Florida species (*C. acutus*). At that time science was blind to the fact that the true crocodile was a member of the fauna of the United States. At a meeting of the " Boston Society of Natural History," held May 19, 1869, the late comparative anatomist, Dr. Jeffries Wyman, exhibited the head of a crocodile (*C. acutus*) which had been sent him by William H. Hunt, Esq., of Miami River, which stream flows out of the everglades and empties into Key Biscayene Bay, at the south-eastern end of the Floridian peninsula.

A second cranium of the Sharp-nosed Crocodile was afterwards obtained from the same locality, but the honor of killing and recognizing one of these huge monsters belongs to the young and enterprising author of the " Birds of Florida; " a work full of original information, the illustrations of which, as well as the setting up of the type, being the work of the author's own hands. I refer to Mr. C. J. Maynard, of Newtonville, Massachusetts, who has furnished me with a graphic description of his meeting with, and the capture of, the crocodile while engaged in his ornithological pursuits during the year 1867. Mr. Maynard says:

"This crocodile is particularly noticeable for its fierceness. I have met with it but once. Three of us were crossing the country which lies between Lake Harney and Indian River, on foot, when we came to a dense swamp. As we were passing through it we discovered a huge reptile, which resembled an alligator, lying in a stream just to the right of our path. He was apparently asleep. We approached cautiously within ten rods of him, and fired two rifle-shots in quick succession. The balls took effect in front of his fore-leg, and striking within two inches of each other, passed entirely through his body. As soon as he felt the wounds he struggled violently, twisting and writhing, but finally became quiet.

"We waded in, and approached him as he lay upon a bed of green aquatic plants with his head towards us. It was resting on the mud, and one of the party was about to place his foot upon it, when a lively look in the animal's eyes deterred him. Stooping down, he picked up a floating branch, and lightly threw it in the reptile's face. The result was somewhat surprising. The huge jaws opened instantly, and the formidable tail came round, sweeping the branch into his mouth, where it was crushed and ground to atoms by the rows of sharp teeth. His eyes flashed fire, and he rapidly glided forward. Never did magician of Arabian tale conjure a fiercer-looking demon by wave of his wand than had been raised to life by the motion of a branch. For a moment we were too astonished to move.

"The huge monster seemed bent on revenge, and in another instant would be upon us. We then saw our danger, and quicker than a flash of light, thought and action came. The next moment the gigantic saurian was made to struggle on his back with a bullet in his brain. It had entered his right eye, and had been aimed so nicely as not to cut the lids.

"To make sure of him this time, we severed his jugular vein. While performing this not very delicate operation, he thrust out two singular-looking glands from slits in his throat. They were round, resembling a sea-urchin, being covered with minute projections, and were about the size of a nutmeg, giving out a strong, musky odor. We then took his dimensions, and found he was over ten feet in length, while his body was larger round than a flour-barrel. The immense jaws were three feet long, and when stretched open would readily take in the body of a man. They were armed with rows of sharp, white teeth. The tusks of the lower one, when it was closed, projected out through two holes in the upper, which fact proved to us that it was not a common alligator, but a true crocodile (*C. acutus*)."

If Mr. Maynard had been at that time aware of the value of the prize he had captured, the market-price of which was some four or five hundred dollars, he would not have abandoned his crocodile. He afterwards sent for its head, but could not obtain it. This reptile will probably be found more numerous about the head-waters of the Miami River than further north. It sometimes attains a length of seventeen feet. Since Mr. Maynard shot his crocodile, others from the north have searched for the *C. acutus*, and one naturalist from Rochester, New York, captured a specimen, and attempted to make a new species of it by giving it the specific name of FLORIDANAS, in place of the older one of *C. acutus*.

The morning sun was shining brightly as I pulled steadily along the coast, passing Warrior Creek six miles from my starting-point off the shores of Spring Creek. About this locality the rocky bottom was exchanged for one of sand. Having rowed eleven miles, a small sandy island, one-third of a mile from shore, offered a resting-place at noon; and there I dined upon bread and cold canned beef. A mile further to the eastward a sandy point of the marsh extended into the Gulf. A dozen oaks, two palmettos, and a shanty in ruins, upon this bleak territory, were the distinctive features which marked it as Jug Island, though the firm ground is only an island rising out of the marshes. Sandy points jutting from the lowlands became more numerous as I progressed on my route. Four miles from Jug Island the wide debouchure of Blue Creek came into view, with an unoccupied fishing-shanty on each side of its mouth.

Crossing at dusk to the east shore of the creek, I landed in shoal water on a sandy strand, when the wind arose to a tempest, driving the water on to the land; and had it not been for my watch-tackle, the little duck-boat must have sought other quarters. As it was, she was soon high and dry on a beach; and once beneath her sheltering hatch, I slept soundly, regardless of the screeching winds and dashing seas around me.

Before the sun had gilded the waters the next morning, the wind subsided, my breakfast was cooked and eaten, and the boat's prow pointed towards the desolate, almost uninhabited, wilderness of Deadman's Bay. The low tide annoyed me somewhat, but when the wind arose it was fair, and assisted all day in my progress. The marine grasses, upon which the turtles feed, covered the bottom; and many curious forms were moving about it in the clear water. Six miles from Blue Creek I found a low grassy island of several acres in extent, and while in its vicinity frequently grounded; but as the water was shoal, it was an easy matter to jump overboard and push the lightened boat over the reefs.

About noon the wind freshened, and forced me nearer to the shore. As I crossed channel-ways, between shoals, the porpoises, which were pursuing their prey, frequently got aground, and presented a curious appearance working their way over a submarine ridge by turning on their sides and squirming like eels. By two o'clock P. M., the wind forced me into the bight of Deadman's Bay. The gusts were so furious that prudence demanded a camp, and it was eagerly sought for in the region of ominous name and gloomy associations. I had been told that there was but one living man in this bay, which is more than twenty miles wide. This settler lived two miles up the Steinhatchee River, which flows into the bight of Deadman's Bay.

In a certain part of the wilderness of this region a tract of savanna and pine lands approached near to the waters of the Gulf, and was known as the "Devil's Wood Pile." Superstition has made this much-dreaded forest the scene of wild and horrible tales. Fishermen had warned me of its dismal shades, and of the wild cattle which roamed unheeded through its dreary recesses. Hunters, they said, had entered it in strong force, but the wild bulls were so fierce that the bravest were driven back, and the dangerous task abandoned. Calves had been born in the fastnesses of the "Devil's Wood Pile," and had grown old without being branded by their owners, who feared the sharp horns of the paternal bulls, the courageous defenders of their native pastures.

Skirting the marshy savannas of His Satanic Majesty's earthly dominion, I ascended the Steinhatchee River, when a clearing with a rough house and store gave unmistakable signs of the proximity of the settler of whom I had heard. I was preparing to make my camp near the landing, when the proprietor made his appearance, courteously inviting me to his house, where he held me a willing prisoner for three days, giving me much information in regard to life in the woods. He had been a soldier in the Seminole war, and had passed through varied experiences, but had "settled down," as he expressed it, to the red-cedar business. Six long years had this man and his wife delved and toiled in the desolate region of Deadman's Bay, seeing no one except a few cedar-cutters from the interior, who stocked up at his store before going into the wilderness.

A great deal of red cedar is cut on the shores and in the back country of the Steinhatchee River. The squatters and small farmers, called *crackers*, engaged in this work, are not hampered by the eighth commandment, and Uncle Sam has to suffer in consequence, most of the timber being cut on United States government reserves. It finds its way to the cedar warehouses of merchants in the town of Cedar Keys. I have seen whole rafts of this valuable red cedar towed into Cedar Keys and sold there, when the parties purchasing knew it to be stolen from the government lands. My kind host, Mr. James H. Stephens, was the first honest purchaser of this government cedar I had met, for he cheerfully and promptly paid the requisite tax upon it, and seemed to be endeavoring to protect the property of the government.

From Mr. Stephens's hospitable home I proceeded along the Gulf, past Rocky Creek, to Frog Island, a treeless bit of territory where a little shanty had been erected by the Coast Survey officers to shelter a tide-gauge watcher. The island was now deserted. The coast was indeed desolate, and it was a cheering sight in the middle of the afternoon to catch a glimpse of signs of the past presence of man on Pepperfish Key, an island a little distance from land, rising out of the sparkling sea, and crowned with a rough but picturesque shanty,—another reminder of the untiring efforts of our Coast Survey Bureau.

A prominent point of land near this islet runs far into the Gulf, and is known as Bowlegs Point, supposed to be named after a chief of the Seminole Indians, whom I happened to meet many years before I saw the point which had the honor of bearing his name. Our meeting was in a southern city, but I had the misfortune to appear on the wrong day, and lost the honor of being received by that celebrity, as he had partaken too freely of the hospitality of his white friends, and could only utter, " Big Injuin don't receive! Big Injuin too much drunk!"

As night approached I crossed a large bay, and entered the very shoal water off Horse Shoe Point, close to Horse Shoe and Bird islands. These pretty islets were green with palmetto and other foliage, while upon the firm land of Horse Shoe Point appeared, in the last rays of the setting sun, a white sandy strand crowned with a palmetto hut and a little white tent. Two finely modelled boats rested upon the beach, and five miles out to sea was pictured upon the horizon, like a phantom ship, the weird and indistinct outlines of a United States Coast Survey schooner. The tide was on the last of the ebb, and finding it impossible to get within half a mile of the point, I anchored my little craft, built a fire in my bake-kettle, made coffee on board, and, quietly turning in for a doze, rested until the tide arose, when in the darkness I hauled my boat ashore and awaited the " break o' day."

As soon after breakfast as wood-etiquette admitted, I joined the party on the beach, and was welcomed to their breakfast-table under the shelter of their pretty white tent; learning, much to my satisfaction, that I was an expected guest, as my arrival had been looked for some days before. This party from the schooner "Ready" was engaged in establishing a base-line two miles in length at Horse Shoe Point, and was under the charge of Mr. F. Whalley Perkins, who was assisted by Messrs. John De Wolf, R. E. Duvall, Jr., and William S. Bond.

The readers of my "Voyage of the Paper Canoe" may recognize in Mr. Bond, a member of this party, a gentleman whom I had met on board the Coast Survey vessel "Casswell," in Bull's Bay, on the South Carolina coast, the previous winter. Only those who have gone through similar experiences can imagine what I felt at being thus brought into contact with men of intelligence. It was as though a man had been pulling through a heavy fog, and suddenly the sun burst forth in all its glory. Nature is grand and restful, and green savannas and tranquil waters leave fair pictures in our memories; but after all, man is eminently a social being, and needs companions of his kind.

My lonely voyage had been so monotonous that this return to the society of civilized man had a peculiar effect upon my mind, it being in so receptive a state that the most minute incident was noted; and the tent with its surroundings, the breakfast-table with its genial hosts, the very appearance of the water and the sky, were so indelibly impressed upon my memory that they never can be effaced. It is fortunate the pict-

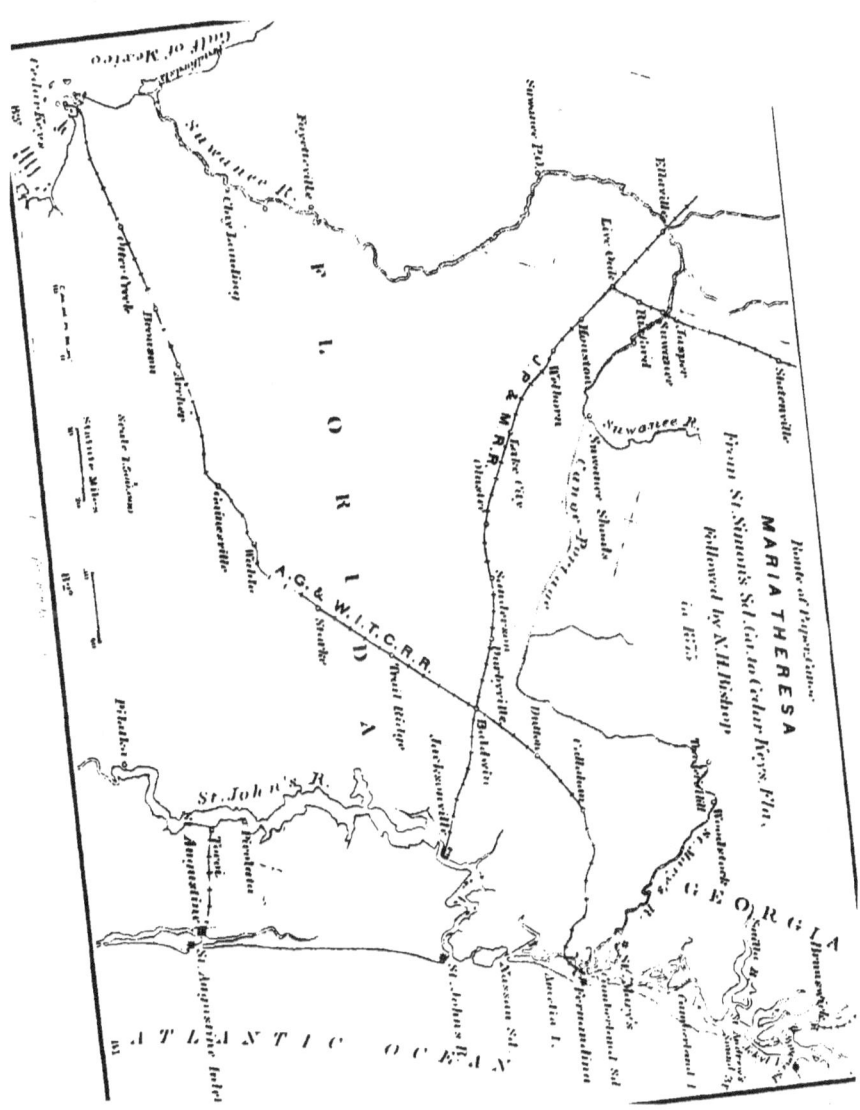

ure is a pleasant one, as in fact were all the hours passed with the gentlemen of the schooner Ready.

On Saturday evening the party prepared to go on board the Ready; and as I was to pass Sunday with them, it was deemed prudent to send my boat to a safe anchorage-ground on the east side of Horse Shoe Bay, where, moored among some islands, my floating home would be protected from boisterous seas and covetous fishermen.

Climbing the sides of the Ready, I was filled with admiration for the beautiful vessel, the last one built especially for the Coast Survey service. The entire craft, with its clean decks and well-arranged interior, was a model of order and skilful arrangement. The home-like cabin, with its books and various souvenirs of the officers, was in strange contrast with the close quarters of my own little boat. The day was most pleasantly passed; and as the morrow threatened to be windy, Mr. Perkins kindly offered to put me on board the sneak-box before sunset. The gig was manned by a stalwart crew of sailors, and the chief of the party took the tiller-ropes in his hands as we dashed away through the waves towards Horse Shoe Bay.

At four in the afternoon we entered the sheltered waters of a miniature archipelago close to the coast, and I beheld with a degree of affection and satisfaction, experienced only by a boatman, my own little craft floating safely at her moorings. The officers gave me a sailor's hearty farewell, the boat's crew bent to their oars and were soon far in the offing, growing each moment more indistinct while I gazed, until a white speck, like a gull resting upon the sea, was the only visible sign left me of Mr. Perkins and his party.

My voyage of twenty-six hundred miles was nearly ended. The beautiful Suwanee River, from which I had emerged in my paper canoe one year before, (when I had terminated a voyage of twenty-five hundred miles begun in the high latitude of Canada,) was only a few miles to the eastward. Upon reaching its debouchure on the Gulf coast, the termini of the two voyages would be united. It would be only a few hours' pull from the mouth of the Suwanee to the port of Cedar Keys, whose railroad facilities offered to the boat and her captain quick transportation across the peninsula of Florida to Fernandina, on the Atlantic coast, where kind friends had prepared for my arrival.

While I gazed upon the smooth sea, a longing to pass the night on the dark waters of the river of song took possession of me, and mechanically weighing anchor, I took up my oars and pulled along the coast to my goal. Before sunset, the old landmark of the mouth of the Suwanee (the iron boiler of a wrecked blockade-runner) appeared above the shoal water, and I began to search for the little hammock, called Bradford's Island, where one year before I had spent my last night on the Gulf of Mexico with the "Maria Theresa," my little paper canoe. Soon it rose like a green spot in the desert, the well-remembered grove coming into view, with the half-dead oak's scraggy branches peering out of the feathery tops of the palmettos.

Entering the swift current of the river, I gazed out upon the sea, which was bounded only by the distant horizon. The sun was slowly sinking into the green of the western wilderness. A huge saurian dragged his mail-clad body out of the water, and settled quietly in his oozy bed. The sea glimmered in the long, horizontal rays of light which clothed it in a sheen of silver and of gold. The wild sea-gulls winnowed the air with their wings, as they settled in little flocks upon the smooth water, as though to enjoy the bath of soft sunlight that came from the west. The great forests behind the marshes grew dark as the sun slowly disappeared, while palm-crowned hammocks on the savannas stood out in bold relief like islets in a sea of green. The sun disappeared, and the soft air became heavy with the mists of night as I sank upon my hard bed with a feeling of gratitude to Him, whose all-protecting arm had been with me in sunshine and in storm.

Lying there under the tender sky, lighted with myriads of glittering stars, a soft gleam of light stretched like a golden band along the water until it was lost in the line of the horizon. Beyond it all was darkness. It seemed to be the path I had taken, the course of my faithful boat. Back in the darkness were the ice-cakes of the Ohio, the various dangers I had encountered. All I could see was the band of shining light, the bright end of the voyage.

Last Night on the Gulf of Mexico.

VOYAGE OF THE PAPER CANOE:

A GEOGRAPHICAL JOURNEY OF 2500 MILES, FROM QUEBEC TO THE
GULF OF MEXICO, DURING THE YEARS 1874-5.

By NATHANIEL H. BISHOP.

With spirited Illustrations, and Ten Maps specially prepared for this work by the
U. S. Coast Survey Bureau. Crown 8vo. Cloth, $2.50.

Boston: LEE & SHEPARD, Publishers.

American Literary Notices.

"This is the most novel feat that has ever been performed by an American. The whole narrative is a living romance, whose perusal will occasion only delight to every reader. It is one of the fascinating books of the time, and has all the colors of a dream."
—*Banner of Light.*

"Mr. Bishop has given us a most interesting and instructive book, which we commend heartily to the perusal of all. It has the advantage of being true from beginning to end."
—*Catholic World.*

"The whole volume, though entertaining in the extreme, abounds with curious information, which raises it above the character of a mere work of amusement. Mr. Bishop is a natural and forcible writer."—*New York Tribune.*

"Jules Verne, our most startling romancist, has not written any fiction more deeply interesting than Mr. Bishop's realistic narrative of personal adventure."—*Philadelphia Press.*

"Mr. Bishop's is a capital book. He tells his story charmingly."—*Hartford Courant.*

"The most pleasing thing to us about this book is the liking it has begotten in us for its writer. Mr. Bishop's book abounds in humor as in other best characteristics ; but we should sum up our praise by saying, emphatically, that he knows how to make and to relate a manly and gentlemanly journey. It is a book to interest persons of all ages and pursuits."
—*Boston Book Bulletin.*

"Mr. Bishop's account of his lonely journey is capital reading. The aim of the book is not to support any political theory, but to state what the author saw."—*Atlantic Monthly.*

Notices from the Press of Great Britain.

"There are some capital stories in this book, with a racy American flavor; and Mr. Bishop especially shines in his delineation of the liberated and enfranchised negro."—*Pall Mall Gazette.*

"Cruises of 'ROB ROY,' or of 'NAUTILUS,' seem tame when compared with such enterprises as that recorded in Mr. Bishop's 'VOYAGE OF THE PAPER CANOE.' One thing is certain, Mr. Bishop did a very bold thing, and has described it with a happy mixture of spirit, keen observation, and *bonhommie.*"—*Graphic.*

"We may say that this voyage is most instructive and amusing, and the first few of the maps of the eastern coast of the States are, for their size, the most perfect in detail and execution which we have ever met. We cannot close the volume without paying a fitting tribute of its worth, by stating that we do not care how soon particulars of his last voyage are presented to us."—*Land and Water.*

"This well-known traveller, who, at the age of seventeen, walked one thousand miles across South America, and presented the world with a graphic account of his performance, now presents us with one of the most interesting works on modern travel and adventure that it is possible to conceive. Were we to be obliged to name volumes of travel equal in interest to Mr. Bishop's, we could only name one, and that is Captain Burnaby's 'RIDE TO KHIVA.'"—*Sporting and Dramatic News.*

THE PAMPAS AND ANDES:
A THOUSAND MILES' WALK ACROSS SOUTH AMERICA.
By NATHANIEL H. BISHOP.
12mo. Cloth. Illustrated. Price, $1.50.

Notices of the Work.

His Excellency Don Domingo F. Sarmiento, President of the Argentine Confederation, South America, in a letter written to the author during 1877, says: "Your book of travels possesses the merit of reality in the faithful descriptions of scenes and customs as they existed at that time.

"It has delighted me to follow you, step by step, by the side of the ancient and picturesque carts that cross the vast plains which stretch between the Parana River and the base of the Andes. As I have written about the same region, your book of travels becomes a valuable reminder of those scenes; and I shall have to consult your work in the future when I again write about those countries."

"Nathaniel H. Bishop, a mere lad of seventeen, who, prompted by a love of nature, starts off from his New England home, reaches the La Plata River, and coolly walks to Valparaiso, across Pampa and Cordillera, a distance of more than a thousand miles! It is not the mere fact of pedestrianism that will gain for Master Nathaniel Bishop a high place among travellers; nor yet the fact of its having been done in the face of dangers and difficulties, — but that, throughout the walk, he has gone with his eyes open, and gives us a book, written at seventeen, that wi'l make him renowned at seventy. It is teeming with information, both on social and natural subjects, and will take rank among books of scientific travel — the only ones worth inquiring for. One chapter from the book of an educated traveller (we don't mean the education of Oxford and Cambridge) is worth volumes of the stuff usually forming the staple of books of travels. And in this unpretending book of the Yankee boy — for its preface is signally of this sort — we have scores of such chapters. The title is not altogether appropriate. It is called 'A Thousand Miles' Walk across South America.' It is more than a mere walk. It is an exploration into the kingdom of Nature.

"Sir Francis Head has gone over the same ground on horseback, and given us a good account of it. But this quiet 'walk' of the American boy is worth infinitely more than the 'Rough Rides' of the British baronet. The one is common talk and superficial observation. The other is a study that extends beneath the surface." — *Captain Mayne Reid.*

"Regarded simply as a piece of adventure, this were interesting, especially when told of in a tone of delightful modesty. But the book has other recommendations. This boy has an admirable eye for manners, customs, costumes, &c., to say nothing of his attention to natural history. The reader seems to travel by his side, and concludes the book with a sense of having himself trodden the Pampas, and mingled with their barbarous inhabitants. So far as *writing* goes, this is the supreme merit of a book of travels. Let those explore who not only see for themselves, but have the rare ability to lend their eyes to others. Mr. Bishop is one of the few who can do this; the graphic simplicity of his narrative is above praise. Meanwhile, his personal impression is very charming. The quiet patience with which he accepted all the hardships of his position — without the slightest parade of patience, however — is beyond measure attractive. But the brave youth goes on quietly enduring what was to be borne, and not ever allowing his observation to be dulled by the infelicities of his situation." — *Boston Commonwealth.*

BOSTON: LEE & SHEPARD.
NEW YORK: CHARLES T. DILLINGHAM.

www.ingramcontent.com/pod-product-compliance
Lightning Source LLC
Chambersburg PA
CBHW030307240426
43673CB00040B/1090